Reckoning with Empire: Self-Determination in International Law

"The Algerian War In Algiers, Algeria", Sine Jensen, 2022 (original photo by Dominique Berretty/Gamma-Rapho via Getty Images)

# Reckoning with Empire: Self-Determination in International Law

*By*

Miriam Bak McKenna

BRILL
NIJHOFF

LEIDEN | BOSTON

Cover illustration: Hilma Af Klint, "The Ten Largest – No 2 Childhood". The Hilma af Klint Foundation, Stockholm.

The Library of Congress Cataloging-in-Publication Data is available online at https://catalog.loc.gov
LC record available at https://lccn.loc.gov/2022044470

Typeface for the Latin, Greek, and Cyrillic scripts: "Brill". See and download: brill.com/brill-typeface.

ISBN 978-90-04-47858-9 (hardback)
ISBN 978-90-04-47919-7 (e-book)



This book is printed on acid-free paper and produced in a sustainable manner.

# Contents


**Acknowledgements** VII
**Table of Cases** IX

**Introduction** 1
1 Recovering Self-Determination's History 5
2 An Aperture for Change 11
3 Organisation of the Book 17
4 Approach 21

1 **Self-Determination: Hierarchies of Empire** 26
1 Sovereignty and Empire 29
2 Popular Sovereignty and the Age of Revolution 32
3 National Self-Determination, Imperial Expansion and the Civilizing Mission 38

2 **Renegotiating Sovereignty in the Interwar Period** 47
1 Self-Determination as Political Strategy 50
2 Post WWI Resettlement and "The New International Law" 56
3 The Aaland Islands Dispute 62
4 Quasi-Sovereigns: The Mandate and Trusteeship System 67

3 **"One World" - Anticolonialism at the UN** 74
1 Self-Determination and the New World Order 77
2 Contesting Empire at the UN 82
3 Anti-Colonial Activism 91
4 The Colonial Declaration 95
5 The Boundaries of Independence 98

4 **Remaking the World after Empire** 108
1 A New International Law 111
2 Strengthening the Post-Colonial State 116
3 Economic Self-Determination and the New International Economic Order 126
4 The Human Rights Revolution and Self-Determination 131

5 **Sovereignty and Self-Determination at the End of History** 138
1 New and Old Claims 141
2 Adjudicating Secession 149
3 Human Rights, Democracy and the New Standards of Sovereignty 154
4 Re-working Sovereignty: Minority and Indigenous Rights 161

**Epilogue: Contesting Sovereignty** 169
**References** 179
**Index** 218

# Acknowledgements

Shepherding this project to completion has at times felt like a Sisyphean task. Luckily, I have had the support of colleagues, friends and family to help me navigate this process. Thanks first and foremost goes to my partner Morten, whose unwavering support and belief in me, has helped me stay the course. He has not only been a source of strength but a well of patience and practical support; picking up the bulk of childcare and housework in the past months, to enable me to finish this book. And to my mother Regina– my in-house editor – who with love, a sharp pen and a keen eye, vastly improved this text. This book is dedicated to them and to my children, Abigail, Elijah and Isobel.

Thank you to Maj Grasten and Matilda Arvidsson for their encouragement and support, for patiently listening to my complaints about the travails of academic life, reassuring my doubts and fears and for encouraging me to see this book through. Thank you to my former colleague at Lund University where I began the process of writing this book, including Britta Sjosted and Daria Davitti. And to my colleagues at Roskilde University – Kerstin Carlson, Lisbet Christoffersen, Klaas Dykmann and Laust Schouenborg, for their helpful comments on versions of the chapters. At the University of Copenhagen, where this book began life as a dissertation, I am grateful to my former supervisor and teachers whose mentorship and guidance inspired me to pursue this project. In particular I wish to thank Mikael Rask Madsen and Hanne Pedersen for mentoring me and guiding me through graduate school, and for planting the seeds of this project. It was their own unique and groundbreaking interdisciplinary work on law that gave me the inspiration to formulate my own research interests. I am also indebted to a number of scholars who took the time to help me with my research process. Many thanks must go to Karen Knop at the University of Toronto where I spent several happy months. Her incredible wisdom, warmth and guidance helped me to persevere when I couldn't see the forest for the trees. I am also grateful to my colleagues at the Lauterpacht Centre – in particular Evelyn Campos Sanchez and Inge Van Hulle – for their invaluable feedback and support. Thank you to Sine Jensen for creating the inside image and to my publisher, Lindy Melman at Brill.

Thank you to my parents – Regina, Dominic and Mary Ann - for instilling in me a love of learning and of justice, and for nurturing my ambition to write about a subject that has been a constant source of wonderment and frustration. And to my wider family – my sister Rachel and brother Lochlan, parents-in-law Pia and Kristian, Jakob and Priyanka and friends – Tim, Anders, Lucy,

Annegerd, Sigrid, Rikke, Lena, Freya, Liz, Jess, Ainslie - thank you for putting up my obscure rambling about this topic over the years and for being by my side through this process. My last words of dedication are to my Oma – Meika de Boer (1914–2013) – a woman of great strength, intelligence and perseverance, who will forever remain my inspiration.

# Table of Cases

*The Aaland Islands Question: Report Submitted to the Council of the League of Nations by the Commission of Rapporteurs*, League of Nations Doc. B7 [C] 21/68/106, (April 1921).

Aaland Islands, *Report of the International Commission of Jurists Entrusted by the Council of the League of Nations with the Task of Giving an Advisory Opinion upon the Legal Aspects of the Aaland Islands Question*, League of Nations Official Journal, Special Supplement No. 3, (October 1920).

*Accordance with international law of the unilateral declaration of independence in respect of Kosovo (Request for Advisory Opinion)* (2010).

*Case Concerning Military and Paramilitary Activities in and Against Nicaragua (Nicaragua v. United States of America), (Merits)*, ICJ Reports (1986).

*Case Concerning East Timor (Portugal v. Australia) (Judgment)*, ICJ Reports (1995).

*Conference on Yugoslavia, Arbitration Commission, Opinion No. 1*, 31 ILM (1992).

*Conference on Yugoslavia, Arbitration Commission, Opinion No. 2*, 31 ILM (1992).

*Conference on Yugoslavia, Arbitration Commission, Opinion No. 3*, 31 ILM (1992).

*Conference on Yugoslavia, Arbitration Commission, Opinion No. 4*, 31 ILM (1992).

*Conference on Yugoslavia, Arbitration Commission, Opinion No. 5*, 31 ILM (1992).

*Conference on Yugoslavia, Arbitration Commission, Opinion No. 6*, 31 ILM (1992).

*Interpretation of the Convention between Greece and Bulgaria Respecting Reciprocal Emigration, Signed at Neuilly-sur-Seine on November 27th (Advisory Opinion)*, PCIJ (1930).

*Island of Palmas Case* (Netherlands, USA), Max Huber, Award: April 1923, *(1928)*, 2 R. Int'l Arbitral Awards 829.

*Legal Consequences for States of the Continued Presence of South Africa in Namibia (South West Africa) Notwithstanding Security Council Resolution 276 (1970) (Advisory Opinion)*, ICJ Reports (1971).

*Legal Consequences of the Separation of the Chagos Archipelago from Mauritius in 1965*, Advisory Opinion (25 February 2019).

*Loizidou v. Turkey (Merits)*, Judgment of 18 December 1996, No. 40/1993/435/514, 18 Human Rights Law Journal (1997).

*Military and Paramilitay Activities in and Against Nicaragua (Nicaragua v. United Stales)*, Merits, [I986].

*Minority Schools in Albania (Advisory Opinion)*, PCIJ (1935).

*North Sea Continental Shelf (Federal Republic of Germany v. Denmark; Federal Republic of Germany v. Netherlands)*, [1969].

*Reference re Secession of Quebec*, No. 25506, 20 August 1998 (S.C.C.), [1998] S.C.J. No. 61 (QL).

*South West Africa* (*Ethiopia v. South Africa; Liberia v. South Africa*), *Preliminary Objections* (1962).

*South West Africa Cases* (*Ethiopia v. South Africa; Liberia v. South Africa*) (Second Phase), ICJ Reports (1966).

# Introduction

On a characteristically balmy morning in Jakarta on August 17, 1945, just two days after the Japanese surrender to Allied forces, a ceremony was held in front of a modest suburban house. Standing before the small, assembled crowd, the two nationalist leaders - Ahmed Sukarno and Mohammad Hatta - read a short proclamation declaring the independence of Indonesia "in the name of the people of Indonesia."[1] "As from this moment" they announced, "we build our state. A free state, the State of the Republic of Indonesia – evermore and eternally independent."[2] It would take it four more years of economic sanctions, military action, and UN mediation before the Netherlands agreed to officially transfer sovereignty in 1949, but as news of the proclamation spread throughout the world, and the tide of independence demands swelled, a transformation was underway that was to profoundly alter the shape of the international order. Over the next three decades, most colonies in Asia, Africa and the Caribbean were transformed into independent states, effectively ending the reign of European colonial rule which had spread across the globe over the preceding centuries.

Nearly 80 years after Indonesian independence, it would be easy to characterise this event, and the wave of decolonisation that followed, as a fated step in the progressive unfolding of colonial independence. Indeed, armed with the traditional retelling of self-determination's history as one that bends towards the arc of justice from empire to nation, the independence of colonial peoples was a predestined aspect of the post-war international order; guaranteed by the Mandate and Trusteeship systems under the League of Nations and the United Nations (UN) respectively, and consecrated in 1970 as an uncontested principle of international law.[3] For those present, however, the historical significance of the moment was clear, not least evidenced by the carefully worded proclamation couched in the language of self-determination. It was no coincidence that it was in the "people's name" that Indonesia was christened and that faced with Dutch intransigence in the aftermath of the proclamation of independence, Indonesia maintained that "the rights of self-determination of

1 Ministry of Foreign Affairs of Indonesia, 'Address of Insinjur Soekarno in Announcing the Proclamation of Indonesia's Independence on 17 August 1945,' (Official Translation of Indonesia's Proclamation of Independence) Yogyakarta, October 1948 in George McT Kahin, 'Sukarno's Proclamation of Indonesian Independence' [2000] 69 *Indonesia* 4 at 2.

2 *Ibid.*

3 1924 Covenant of the League of Nations, art. 22 and 1945 Charter of the United Nations, Chapters XII–XIII.

 | DOI:10.1163/9789004479197_002

the Indonesian people" was non-negotiable.[4] Later, Patrice Lumumba's assertion that Congolese independence could not "be considered by Belgium as a gift; on the contrary, it is a question of the enjoyment of a right that the Congolese people have lost" was only one of many that adopted a similar line.[5] For while the status of colonial peoples was recognised as a crucial factor in establishing a post-war international order, the full political independence of colonial peoples was anything but assured under international law. References to self-determination were conspicuously absent from the UN Charter chapters relating to both the non-self-governing territories and the trusteeships, which also deftly avoided any mention of independence. Instead, the rationale prevailed that many colonial territories were "either incapable or deficient in power of self-government"[6] and it was the duty of the "advanced" nations to guide them to attain the capacity to self-government. Commenting on the state of mind that prevailed during the drafting of the Trusteeship chapters, Huntington Gilchrist, a conference staff member, remarked that independence was not mentioned as a goal, for the simple reason that "no colonial power except the United States looks upon it as a normal and natural outcome of colonial status."[7]

As this book will argue, lacking the legal tools with which to complete independence, therefore, colonised people turned to innovative solutions to renegotiate the rules of international law to serve the purposes of the full decolonisation. Using the newly formed UN and its surrounding legal framework as an avenue to advance their goal for decolonisation, they challenged international law's relationship with colonialism from "within," using the language of the very international law that justified their subjugation.[8] Harnessing the rhetoric of self-determination, contained within articles 1 and 55 of the UN Charter, was one of a range of legal strategies pursued by actors in their attempt to challenge the international system of states that had excluded them

---

4 Idrus Nasir Djadjadiningrat, *The Beginnings of the Indonesian-Dutch Negotiations and the Hoge Veluwe Talks* (Ithaca: Southeast Asia Program Cornell University, 1958) 32.

5 Patrice Lumumba, *"Speech at Leopoldville", December 28, 1958, in Lumumba Speaks: The Speeches and Writings of Patrice Lumumba, 1958–1961* (Boston: Little, Brown, 1972) *66.*

6 Jan C Smuts, *The League of Nations: A Practical Suggestion* (London: Hodder and Stoughton, 1918) 11.

7 Huntington Gilchrist," Colonial Questions at the San Francisco Conference," 39 *The American Political Science Review*, 5 (1945) 987

8 This argument is also made by Luis Eslava, Michael Fakhri and Vasuki Nesiah, (eds), *Bandung, Global History, and International Law: Critical Pasts and Pending Futures* (Cambridge: CUP 2017) 9.

from sovereign independence.[9] Positing self-determination as the new standard of political legitimacy within international society, anti-colonialists were able to sever the legal ties that had protected foreign domination and imperial hierarchies. Integrating self-determination into the human rights regime, moreover, laid the foundations to the claim to democratic self-governance and citizenship in which colonial subjects as rights holders could demand sovereignty and independence as a prerequisite to the exercise of their individual rights, ultimately providing the legal foundation to crystalise decolonisation as a right.

This book studies this process, situating it in a longer history of self-determination as principally a story of transformation, and as such of conflict and struggle for authoritative meaning of the concept. As it will explore, the emergence of the right to self-determination and the independence of former colonies was far from inevitable or seamless, revealing itself to be deeply contested, beset by competing visions of the decolonisation process itself — that is, the means of attaining sovereignty—and the construction of the idea of self-determination and that of the post-colonial state. Far from being purely symbolic, self-determination emerged as a crucial legal instrument for renegotiating concepts of international law and State sovereignty, representing a break with existing legal frameworks of territorial control and legitimacy which excluded colonial peoples from the ambit of sovereign equality. This process sees the radical reconstruction of self-determination as a legal idea, its content and normative foundation redefined.

This book narrates a history of self-determination as a series of encounters in which various actors have sought to reinvent self-determination in different juridical and normative iterations to create the conditions for global transformation, not least the entry of groups of states into international society. Tracing the transformation and circulation of these diverse meanings of self-determination, reveals a fuller picture not only of the radical legal shift that occurred in the process of anti-imperial change, but of the multiple interpretive and normative visions of self-determination that were advanced by actors with alternative visions of international society. This exercise goes to the heart

9 For other accounts of the legal and political strategies employed by colonial peoples in their fight for independence see for instance Christian Reus-Smit, *Individual Rights and the Making of the International System*, (Cambridge: CUP 2013) 151–192. See also Roland Burke, *Decolonization and the Evolution of International Human Rights*, (Philladelphia: University of Pennsylvania Press, 2010); Jan Eckel, "Human Rights and Decolonization: New Perspectives and Open Questions', 1:1 *Humanity* (2010).

of the complexities of meaning and interpretation intrinsic to international law – where universalities are assumed but not always shared.

The value of the approach, it is hoped, lies not only in a more nuanced understanding of self-determination's international legal history, including its imperial entanglements, but in further excavating the multiple ways in which actors, particularly those from the Global South, challenged the existing normative and legal structures which rendered them unequal under the European system of international law, to create a transformation of the international order.[10] Rethinking this process touches on issues that are relevant not only to the enduring imperial legacies in our present, but also to contemporary discussions of the position self-determination has come to occupy in international law.[11] In doing so, the book seeks to join the expanding canon of international legal histories which challenge conventional renderings of the history of international law.[12]

---

10 Among the many works illuminating international law's imperial entanglement see Nehal Bhuta, 'Series Editor's Preface' in Jochen von Bernstorff and Philipp Dann (eds.), *The Battle for International Law: South-North Perspectives on the Decolonization Era* (Oxford: OUP 2019) at iii; Martti Koskenniemi, *The Gentle Civilizer of Nations: The Rise and Fall of International Law, 1870–1960* (Cambridge: CUP 2002); Antony Anghie, *Imperialism, Sovereignty, and the Making of International Law* (Cambridge: CUP 2005); Sundhya Pahuja, *Decolonising International Law: Development, Economic Growth, and the Politics of Universality* (Cambridge: CUP 2011); Martti Koskenniemi, 'Introduction: International Law and Empire—Aspects and Approaches,' in Martti Koskenniemi, Walter Rech, and Manuel Fonseca (eds.), *International Law and Empire—Historical Explorations* (Oxford: OUP, 2017).

11 This historical narrative, as the recent International Court of Justice case on the question concerning the legal consequences of the separation of the Chagos Archipelago from Mauritius demonstrates, is still very much the focus of dispute. Written Statement of the United Kingdom in the Advisory Proceedings before the International Court of Justice regarding the Legal Consequences of the Separation of the Chagos Archipelago from Mauritius (27 February 2018) 141. *See also* Counter-Memorial by the United Kingdom, Chagos Marine Protected Area Arbitration (*Mauritius* v. *United Kingdom*) (15 July 2013); *Mauritius* v. *United Kingdom*, Hearing on Jurisdiction and Merits in the Chagos Marine Protected Area Arbitration, vol 6 (1 May 2014) 706–708.

12 Relevant examples include: Christine Scwöbel (ed.) *Critical Approaches to International Criminal Law* (London: Routledge, 2015) Gerry Simpson, 'Linear Law: The History of International Criminal Law' 159; Emily Haslam, 'Silences in International Criminal Legal Histories and the Construction of the Victim Subject of International Criminal Law: The Nineteenth Century Slave Trading Trial of Joseph Peters' 180; Gretje Baars, 'From The Dutch East India Company to the Corporate Bill of Rights: Corporations and International Law', in Ugo Mattei and John Haskell (eds.), *Research Handbook on Political Economy and Law* (Cheltenham: Edward Elgar, 2016) Mathilde Cohen and Yoriko Otomo (eds.) *Making Milk: The Past, Present and Future of our Primary Food* (London: Bloomsbury, 2019) Michael Fakhri, *Sugar and the Making of International Trade Law* (Cambridge: CUP, 2014) G. Gordon, 'Railway clocks: Temporal bases of transnational law', in Jesse Hohmann and Daniel Joyce (eds.) *International*

## 1 Recovering Self-Determination's History

Within historical retellings of decolonisation, the radical nature of the anti-colonial mobilisation of self-determination has largely been obscured by the standard narrativisation of the shift from empire to nation as a mostly singular and inevitable event. Various interpretations have been posited as to why, and indeed how, the illegality of 'alien rule' under international law came about in the course of the twentieth century. Many interpretations posit the inevitability of this process given the wider diffusion of Western ideals of human rights during this period, and their incompatibility with continued European imperial rule.[13] Rupert Emerson, for example, argued that "through global conquest the dominant Western powers worked to reshape the world in their own image and thus roused against themselves the forces of nationalism which are both the bitterest enemies of imperialism, and perversely, its finest fruit."[14] In this account, the circulation of Western ideas of freedom brought about through imperialism thus becomes the sword upon which empire finally falls. Decolonisation is thus viewed as the 'natural' end of the civilizing mission, in which the democratic nation state is gradually globalized, culminating in the eventual inclusion of colonial peoples in the state system.[15] This progressive

---

*Law's Objects: Emergence, Encounter and Erasure* (Oxford: OUP, 2017) Kathryn Greenman, Anne Orford, Ntina Tzouvala and Anna Saunders (eds.), *Revolutions in International Law: The Legacies of 1917* (Cambridge: CUP, 2019); Immi Tallgren and Thomas Skouteris (eds.) *The New Histories of International Criminal Law: Retrials* (Oxford: OUP, 2019); Frederic Megret and Immi Tallgren (eds.) *The Dawn of a Discipline: International Criminal Justice and Its Early Exponents* (Oxford: OUP, 2019) Daniel Margolies, Umut Özsu, Maia Pal, and Ntina Tzouvala (eds.), *The Extraterritoriality of Law: History, Theory, Politics* (London: Routledge, 2019) Sundya Pahuja and Anna Saunders 'Rival Worlds and the place of the Corporation in International Law' in Phillip Dann and R. Jochen von Bernstoff (eds.), *Decolonialisation and the Battle for International Law* (Oxford: OUP, 2018); S. Pahuja and S. Chalmers (eds.) *International Law and the Humanities* (London: Routledge, 2020) James Parker, 'Judgwing the Rwandan Soundscape', in R.K. Sherwin and D. Selermajer (eds.), *A Cultural History of Law in the Modern Age* (London: Bloomsbury, 2019).

13 For earlier accounts of this process see John Plamenatz, *On Alien Rule and Self-Government* (London: Longman's, 1960) and Rupert Emerson, *From Nation to Empire: The Rise to Self-Assertion of Asian and African Peoples* (Cambridge, MA: Harvard University Press, 1960).

14 Emerson, (1960: 16–17).

15 As James Mayall wrote in 1990, over the course of the 20th century, "the naturalness of hierarchy was replaced by the naturalness of equality," James Mayall, Nationalism and International Society (Cambridge: CUP, 1990), 33.

expansion of the nation-state as the counterpoint to the imperial system forms the new normative core of the international order, replacing vertical logics of membership with horizontal ones.[16]

Accounts of self-determination's role in this process have been remarkably simple: it is an image of the inevitable post-war decline of the colonial order where self-determination largely played a symbolic, at best legally corrective, role in the independence of colonial peoples. Martti Koskenniemi, for example, argues that in terms of a right to self-determination "may not have been necessary to achieve what had already been decreed by politics – namely the entry into statehood of some hundred former colonial territories."[17] While Louis Henkin who conceived self-determination as only "an additional weapon against colonialism."[18] Standard legal historical accounts posit a largely progressive and then declensionist narrative, centred on self-determination's crystallisation in the 1960 Colonial Declaration and then its broader judicial development and application.[19] The wider political and legal battles, and

16 See Hedley Bull and Adam Watson. eds. *Expansion of International Society* (Oxford: Clarendon, 1984).

17 See M. Koskenniemi, "National Self-Determination Today: Problems of Legal Theory and Practice," *International and Comparative Law Quarterly*, XLIII (1994), 241.

18 Louis Henkin, "The United Nations and Human Rights," *International Organization* 19(3) (1965) at 513.

19 See Antonio Cassese, *Self- Determination of Peoples: A Legal Reappraisal* (Cambridge: CUP 1995); Donald Clark & Robert Williamson, eds., *Self-Determination: International Perspectives* (New York: St Martin's Press 1996); John Duursma, *Fragmentation and the International Relations of Micro-States: Self-Determination and Statehood* (Cambridge University Press, Cambridge 1996); Eyassu Gayim, *The Principle of Self-Determination: A Study of Its Historical and Contemporary Legal Evolution* (Norwegian Institute of Human Rights, Oslo, 1990); Hurst Hannum, *Autonomy. Sovereignty, and Self-Determination: The Accommodation of Conflicting Rights*, rev. ed., (Philadelphia: University of Pensylvania Press 1996); Thomas Musgrave, *Self-Determination and National Minorities* (Oxford: Clarendon Press 1997); James Crawford, *The Creation of States in International Law* (Oxford: Clarendon Press 1979); James Crawford, "The Right of Self-Determination in International Law: Its Development and Future" in Phillip Alston (ed.), *Peoples' Rights* (Oxford: OUP 2001) 7–67; Rupert Emerson, "Self-determination" 65 Am. J. Intl L. (1971) 459–475; Thomas Franck, *The Empowered Self Law and Society in the Age of Individualism* (New York: OUP 1999); Hurst Hannum, "Rethinking Self-Determination" 34 *Va. J. Int'l L.* (1993–1994) 1–69; Michla Pomerance, *Self-determination in Law and Practice: The New Doctrine in the United Nations* (The Hague: M. Nijhoff Publishers, 1982); A. Rigo Sureda, *The Evolution of the Right Of Self-Determination: A Study of United Nations Practice* (Leiden: Sijthoff 1973); Dov Ronen, *The Quest for Self-determination* (New Haven: Yale University Press 1979); Christian Tomuschat (ed.), *Modern Law of Self-determination* (Dordrecht: Martinus Nijhoff 1993); David Raic, *Statehood and the Law of Self-Determination* (The Hague: Kluwer 2002).

self-determination's strategic legal deployment by colonial peoples, is largely subsumed within these doctrinally focussed accounts – which largely seek to answer what self-determination 'is'. Indeed, as several scholars have remarked, whereas discussions on the nature and scope of self-determination are complex and provoke constant debate, it seems that the existing literature identifies the history of self-determination in a very linear way.[20]

In terms of its legal and normative content, moreover, self-determination has largely been understood as an extension and eventual juridification of an idea that largely emerges from Wilsonian thought, one linked to the universalization of Western ideals of liberal nationalism and its associated nation state form.[21] In these accounts, the liberal notion of self-determination is appropriated by anti-colonialist activists to operate as the symbolic banner for action to secure statehood and self-rule.[22] Underpinning this interpretation is the notion that self-determination, like many other ideas present in international legal and political thought, was generally a stable, universally accepted concept (most stemming from European legal and political thought) that was simply adopted, in an uncontested manner by anti-colonialists.

In contrast to these legalistic accounts, contributions from international relations scholars, have explored the manner in which self-determination has been understood and used over time.[23] Historians have also begun to explore

20 Arnulf Becker Lorca, "Petitioning the International: A 'Pre-History' of Self-Determination." *European Journal of International Law* 25, no. 2 (2014): 497–523 at 498. Nathaniel Berman similarly contends: "The striking disjunction between the sense of uncanny historical repetition and the concern for appalling current exigencies often leads to both the misrepresentation of history and the impoverishment of current doctrine and policy." Nathaniel Berman, "The International Law of Nationalism: Group Identity and Legal History" in David Wippman, ed., *International Law and Ethnic Conflict* (Ithaca: Cornell University Press 1998) pp. 25–57.

21 See Rupert Emerson, "The New Higher Law of Anti-Colonialism," in Karl W. Deutsch and Stanley Hoffmann (eds.), *The Relevance of International Law: Essays in Honor of Leo Gross* (Cambridge, MA: Schenkman Publishing, 1968), 157; For studies emphasizing the normative aspect of decolonisation see Robert Jackson, 'The Weight of Ideas in Decolonization: Normative Change in International Relations', in Judith Goldstein and Robert Keohane (eds.), *Ideas and Foreign Policy: Beliefs, Institutions and Political Change* (Ithaca: Cornell University Press, 1993).

22 Adom Getachew, *Worldmaking After Empire: The Rise and Fall of Self-Determination* (Princeton: Princeton University Press, 2019) 14.

23 See James Mayall, *Nationalism and International Society* (Cambridge CUP, 1990 Cambridge: CUP); Andrew Hurrell, *On Global Order*, (Oxford: OUP, 2007); Daniel Philpott, "*Revolutions in Sovereignty: How Ideas Shaped Modern International Relations* (Princeton: Princeton University Press, 2001); Neta Crawford, *Argument and Change in World Politics: Ethics, Decolonization, and Humanitarian Intervention.* (Cambridge: CUP, 2002).

the role political invocations of self-determination played in the demise of imperial orders.[24] Particularly within recent accounts of human rights, a number of scholars have explored the framing of self-determination in the language of human rights in order to posit anti-colonial demands for independence and equal rights.[25] Employed to ground the dismantling of imperial systems and their unequal regimes of rights' allocation, self-determination became attached to ideas of equal rights and non- discrimination, and in turn, came to delineate the model of the nation-state globally. While these works are foundational to the book's thesis of self-determination's wider circulation and change, they are also limited in their reflections on the transformation and mobilization of self-determination as an international legal idea. Firstly, they largely associate their accounts of self-determination with the realm of world politics, linking it predominantly to ideas of legitimacy, sovereignty and world order. This literature therefore largely overlooking its fundamental and yet contradictory role in the formation of the twentieth century legal order and the transformation of the imperial structures of international law. Moreover, few of the major works deal with the longer intellectual and political history of self-determination; most address it primarily as an issue of decolonization after 1945 or of the post–Cold War dissolution of states. In addition, whereas they acknowledge the critical role self-determination played in the constitution of new states, they largely treat self-determination and sovereignty as norms, which, though

24 See Erez Manela, *The Wilsonian Moment: Self-Determination and the International Origins of Anticolonial Nationalism* (Oxford: OUP 2007); Brad Simpson 'Self-Determination, Human Rights, and the End of Empire in the 1970s', 4:2 *Humanity* (2013) 239–260.

25 This argument is notably advanced by Christian Reus-Smit who argues that the right to self-determination was radically changed in the aftermath of World War II. As he notes: "The idea of the right to self-determination emerged from World War II morally and politically bankrupt. The notion that it was a right of ethnically defined nations had been discredited by the Nazi Holocaust and was ill-suited to the needs of anticolonial struggles in the non-Western world, which had been formally excluded from its purview, and where the colonial peoples seeking independence were ethnically heterogeneous. If it was to be any use in legitimating the dissolution of Europe's empires, therefore, the right to self-determination had to be rehabilitated, its content redefined and its normative foundations reconstructed." Christian Reus-Smit, *Individual Rights and the Making of the International System*, (Cambridge: CUP 2013) 151–192. See also Roland Burke, *Decolonization and the Evolution of International Human Rights*, (Philladelphia: University of Pennsylvania Press, 2010); Jan Eckel, "Human Rights and Decolonization: New Perspectives and Open Questions', 1:1 *Humanity* (2010); L. Walker, 'Decolonization in the 1960s: On Legitimate and Illegitimate Nationalist Claims-making', 242:1 *Past & Present* (2019) 227–264; Frederick Cooper, "Afterword: Social Rights and Human Rights in the Time of Decolonization," *Humanity* 3, no. 3 (2012): 473–492.

they are subject to change, are relatively stable ideas. Despite long running debates about the meaning of "the people," there is surprisingly little interrogation of self-determination as an idea and the multiple contexts in which it has emerged. Tracing broader shifts in the meaning of self-determination, while still treating self-determination as a coherent idea, is insufficient to detect the contestations and multivalent interpretations of self-determination that have accompanied its history.

As this book explores, self-determination's colonial entanglement, both legally and normatively, signalled a break with existing ideas of international law and sovereignty; ideas that were deeply complicit with sovereign hierarchies and colonial exclusion. Despite self-determination's political appeal to popular sovereignty and national independence, which accompanied its circulation in international legal circles at the beginning of the post-World War II period, these ideas went hand in hand with a system in which non-western states and colonial peoples were not entitled to the same rights to freedom from domination. As many scholars have underlined, the position in which colonial peoples were at best quasi-sovereign, at worst incapable international legal subjects, was embodied in the Mandate and Trusteeship systems that emerged after the two world wars.[26] Staking a claim to sovereignty required a dramatic reconfiguration of the normative underpinnings of the international system. Self-determination's inclusion in the Charter at the insistence of Western states provided an aperture in the international legal framework to lodge this challenge. From the vantage point of western universalism, self-determination was a stable, incontestable concept, and its presence in the Charter did not threaten the existing sovereign order. For colonial peoples, however, it opened a space (the Charter) and a forum (the United Nations) in which the rights and privileges related to sovereignty could be discussed and contested; which prior to this time were the exclusive domains of colonial powers.[27]

While self-determination emerged as core tenet of decolonisation, however, its content was not fixed, being highly variable and subject to constant re-interpretation. Indeed, it is precisely because of self-determination's unstable meaning that it could be mobilized in the pursuit of a number of different normative and political causes. As Adom Getachew has recently explored in her account of the history of black anti-imperialists who sought to secure

26 See Antony Anghie, *Imperialism, Sovereignty, and the Making of International Law* (Cambridge: CUP, 2005); Neta Crawford, *Argument and Change in World Politics: Ethics, Decolonization, and Humanitarian Intervention* (Cambridge: CUP, 2002).

27 See Siba N'Zatioula Grovogui, *Sovereigns, Quasi-Sovereigns and Africans*, (Minneapolis: University of Minnesota Press, 1996) 2.

the freedom of their postcolonial states, self-determination was remade in many instances as part of a project of 'worldmaking'. As she explores, theories of anti-colonial self-determination championed by W.E.B Du Bois, Nnamdi Azikiwe, George Padmore, Kwame Nkrumah and Julius Nyerere signified a symbolic break with earlier iterations of self-determination which had been implicated in global hierarchies that put people of colour on the bottom and whites on top. Normatively, the anti-colonial nationalist reconfigurations of self-determination went beyond nation building, but instead insisted upon "a reconstitution of the international order" to address deep-seated global inequalities.[28] For Nkrumah, decolonisation was a "hurricane of change....razing to the ground the many bastions of colonialism."[29] Independence, he argued, would only become a reality in a "revolutionary framework."

Similarly for anti-colonialist international lawyers, self-determination as a form of legal argumentation embodied a wholesale challenge to the international system and the body of international laws that supported it; a project "whose aim was to ensure that all peoples of the world benefited from what was claimed to be the twin building blocks of world order, sovereign statehood and international law."[30] This position is probably best embodied in the opinions of Judge Ammoun in two cases regarding self-determination which made their way to the International Court - the 1971 *Namibia* case[31] and the 1975 *Western Sahara*[32] case. For Ammoun, self-determination legal expression embodied a reconfiguration of ideas of non-Western sovereignty which existed prior to and in many cases during the colonial period, which had been suspended by the imposition of European ideas of international law. The 'bitter' struggle to consecrate self-determination within the UN system exhibited the tension between two different international laws – one a classic international law which protected "traditional interests," and a newer non-European tradition.

28 Getachew (2019: 17).

29 Cited in Getachew (2019: 17).

30 Luis Eslava, Michael Fakhri and Vasuki Nesiah (eds), *Bandung, Global History, and International Law: Critical Pasts and Pending Futures* (Cambridge: CUP 2017) at 4.

31 The Opinion, together with the separate judgement of Vice President of the Court Judge Faoud Ammoun, provide a clear illustration of the very expressions of self-determination's normative and judicial relevance in international law: one in which self-determination was the natural end to colonialism as a trust exercised by the colonizer for the benefit of the colonized as their 'beneficiaries;' the other formed upon the emancipatory and identity forming potential of self-determination as an ongoing struggle by peoples. *Legal Consequences for States of the Continued Presence of South Africa in Namibia (South West Africa) Notwithstanding Security Council Resolution 276 (1970) (Advisory Opinion)*, ICJ Reports (1971).

32 *Western Sahara* (Advisory Opinion), ICJ Reports (1975).

The latter, he notes "is a law discernible from the progress of humanity, not an obsolete law, a vestige of the inequalities between men, the domination and colonialism which were rife in international relationships up to the beginning of this century but are now disappearing, thanks to the struggle being waged by (the peoples and to the extension to the ends of the world of the universal community of mankind)."[33] The emergence of self-determination in this new international legal order is the result of a long struggle to dispense with these imported ideas and restore sovereignty or assist in the emergence of a new sovereign order, one not enmeshed in colonial hierarchies. As he notes, "jurists, statesmen, constitutions and declarations, and the United Nations Charter - have merely recognized and solemnly proclaimed" the right to self-determination whose sources lie in the struggles of the peoples concerned."[34]

## 2 An Aperture for Change

The argument that I develop throughout the chapters of this book by examining these moments of friction is the claim that self-determination is not and has never been a settled idea, but rather that its "in-built ambivalence,"[35] operates as a discursive means of engaging with the content and structure of law. In this sense the book situates itself in the work of earlier discussions of self-determination's history that focus on its broad interpretative variance outside the "logical and linear" manner in which self-determination's history has been depicted in international law.[36] Karen Knop has explored the discursive power of self-determination to "illuminate the deep structures, biases and stakes in the development of meaning in international law."[37] Using the challenge of diversity to frame her enquiry, Knop moves beyond strict doctrinal analysis to examine how marginalised groups in particular have impacted the shifting normative and legal valiance in the course of the twentieth century. Similarly,

33 *Namibia*, (sep. op. Ammoun). 1971 I.C.J. at 60.

34 *Western Sahara* (Advisory Opinion), ICJ Reports (1975) at 100.

35 Antonio Cassese, Self-*Determination of Peoples: A Legal Reappraisal* (Cambridge: CUP, 1995) 316.

36 I borrow the expression from Karen Knop, *Diversity and Self-Determination in International Law* (Cambridge: CUP 2002) 147.

37 Knop (2002: 5).

Catriona Drew[38] and Nathaniel Berman[39] have sought in various ways to move beyond traditional genealogies to detect the complexities in meaning and application that have accompanied self-determination's history.[40]

In framing my argument, I draw in particular on the framing of self-determination by Nathaniel Berman. As an idea, he argues, self-determination has assumed a unique role in the international legal order, due to its ability to challenge legal thought "by posing the problem of law's relationship to sources of normative authority lying outside the normal rules of a functioning legal order."[41] In this way self-determination bridges the divide between positive law and the realm of natural law, or indeed other political or moral ideas that may inform the content of the law. Self-determination's challenge to the normative foundations of international law, he explains, is a feature of its historical evolution; one marked by change, regress and exclusion.[42] It is through its unique relationship to the evolution of sovereignty as both a political and legal idea, in particular, that self-determination has come to occupy an extraordinary position "between the concepts of international law and sovereignty" – concepts which it may both challenge and affirm.[43] In this way, self-determination confronts international law with the latent conflict between these principles, and the largely uncontested idea notion that law and sovereignty are always complementary. If, as Berman explains, that "modern international law may be viewed as oscillating between these competing conceptions of the relationship

38 Catriona J. Drew, "Self-Determination, Population Transfer and the Middle East Peace Accords" in Stephen Bowen, ed., *Human Rights, Self-determination and Political Change in the Occupied Palestinian Territories* (The Hague: Martinus Nijhoff 1997) 119–168; Catriona J. Drew, "The East Timor Story: International Law on Trial" 12 *EJIL* (2001) 651 at 658.

39 Nathaniel Berman, "Sovereignty in Abeyance: Self-Determination and International Law" 7 *Wisconsin International Law Journal* (1988) 56.

40 See also Makua Mutua, "Putting Humpty Dumpty Back Together Again: The Dilemmas of the Post-Colonial African State" 21 *Brooklyn J. Int'l L.* (1995); Makua Mutua, "Why Redraw the Map of Africa: A Moral and Legal Inquiry" 16 *Mich. J. Int'lL.* (1995); Grovogui (1996); Christine Chinkin & Shelley Wright, "The Hunger Trap: Women, Food and Self-Determination" 14 *Mich. J. Int'l L.* (1993).

41 Berman (1988: 56).

42 *Ibid.*

43 In many respects the legitimacy of States is largely dependent upon their embodiment of self-determination, as they provide a setting in which groups of individuals may give expression to their values, their culture, and their sense of themselves. Andrew Hurrell, "The Making and Unmaking of Boundaries in International Law," in Allen Buchanan, Margaret Moore (eds.) *States, Nations and Borders: The Ethics of Making Boundaries* (Cambridge: CUP, 2003) 283.

between legal and political authority, the doctrine of self-determination may be understood as a hinge upon which this oscillation turns."[44]

This important aperture in the international legal order – which is sustained by self-determination's conceptual ambiguity and malleability – along with its broader cultural and political resonance as an idea – provides a rare space, I argue, in which to challenge the existing legal order and its foundations. Self-determination speaks to an idea that is inherent in all human cultures – that of human agency. While the linguistic sources of self-determination are largely traced to Immanuel Kant's usage of the term *Selbstbestimmung,* which was then taken up by German Enlightenment figures, as a conceptual idea it holds deep resonance across cultures.[45] Its adoption into the fabric of international political and legal rhetoric over the course of the past two centuries – particularly as a collectivist notion linked to the ideology of national unification and liberation - has provided a nexus between its broader conceptual limits and the structures and substance underpinning political organization, particularly at the international level. Self-determination simultaneously provides both a criterion and a normative platform for people to alter the ways in which they are governed, that should reflect their wishes.[46] For this reason, I argue that self-determination has provided a crucial battleground for struggles over the legal and political hierarchies of sovereignty, and indeed the system of international law and relations more generally.

This position is informed by the claim that sovereignty as a claim to authority in international law is grounded in a set of historical practices, influenced by tacit understandings of legitimate action in particular social contexts.[47]

44 Berman (1988: 60).

45 As Eric Weitz notes "No phrase has had greater political resonance in the last one hundred years than "self-determination." Eric D. Weitz, 'Self-Determination: How a German Enlightenment Idea Became the Slogan of National Liberation and a Human Right', *The American Historical Review*, 120 (2), (2015) 462–496. There is still disagreement as to its origins amongst scholars, with many viewing it as an age old concept extending to the Greeks, while others, notably Judge Ammoun in his dissenting opinions in Namibia and Western Sahara traces the concept to Zeno of Sidon. See, for example, Oskar Halecki, "The Problem of Self Determination," *Proceedings of the American Philosophical Society* 87, no. 2 (1943): 194–198.

46 Patrick Macklem explains, self-determination simultaneously provides a normative platform for people to alter the ways in which they are governed, thereby pitting the validity of current political arrangements against the validity of possible alternatives. Patrick Macklem, 'Militant Democracy, Legal Pluralism, and the Paradox of Self-Determination', *International Journal of Constitutional Law*, 4 (3) (2006) 488–516.

47 Rebecca Adler-Nissen, *Bourdieu in International Relations: Rethinking Key Concepts in IR*. (London: Routledge, 2012) 179. It is largely impossible to establish a clear-cut definition of state sovereignty under international law. Benn has identified at least six meanings

Self-determination has served as one particular articulation of political legitimacy and authority, structured around the notion of the 'people' as the legitimate bearer of the right.[48] It has served as an ethical standard setting principle for statehood, based upon the dialectical relationship between people and State.[49] Over the course of its history, the discursive power of self-determination has been employed to reinforce, but also to challenge existing ideas of sovereignty, and the entry or exclusion of certain groups into the framework of international law, underlining its destabilising, but also its emancipatory potential.[50] An analogous situation may be that of epochal change as described by Jacques Derrida:

> But is in law what suspends law. It interrupts the established droit to found another. This moment of suspense, this epokhē, the founding or revolutionary moment of law is, in law, and instance of non-law. But it is also the whole history of law.[51]

The suspension in the ordinary functioning of law becomes the point of friction between legal orders, symbolically giving rise to the creation and reproduction of the 'self'. Inclusion and exclusion of groups from claiming the status of 'a people' and thus the right to claim international legal personality as states will constitute one, if not the, principle explanatory 'red thread' running through

---

given to the word 'sovereignty', while others have argued that due to the ambiguities in the term any attempt at a general definition would be useless. See S.I. Benn, 'The Uses of Sovereignty' (1955) 3(2) *Political Studies* 122.

48 In its broadest legal and political sense self-determination denotes – "the freedom for all peoples to decide their political, economic and social regime" This description of the right can be found in article 1(1) of the *International Covenant on Economic, Social and Cultural Rights and the International Covenant on Civil and Political Rights* 1966, 6 ILM (1967) at pp. 360, 368; the *Colonial Independence Declaration*, GA Res. 1514(XV), 15 GAOR (1960) Supplement No. 16, (A/4684) at pp. 667; the *Friendly Relations Declaration*, GA Res. 2625(XXV), 25 GAOR (1970) Supplement No. 28, (A/8028) at pp. 1214; the *Helsinki Final Act*, 14 ILM (1975) pp. 12921324 at p. 1295; Vienna Declaration and Programme of Action, 32 ILM (1993) pp. 166387 at p. 1665; *Declaration on the Occasion of the Fiftieth Anniversary of the United Nations*, GA Res. 50/6, 50 GAOR (1995) Supplement No. 49, (A/50/49) at 13.

49 The State is the "central bank for symbolic credit" in Bourdieu's terminology, which renders valid social and political origination within a given territory and for a given population. Pierre Bourdieu, *'La Nobless L'Etat',* (Miniut, Paris, 1989).

50 As Martti Koskenniemi notes due to, or perhaps in spite of, its relationship to freedom, there lies a paradoxical tension at its core: self-determination both *legitimates* and *challenges* sovereign authority. See Koskenniemi (1994: 245).

51 Jacques Derrida, 'Force of Law: The "Mystical Foundation of Authority" 11 *Cardozo Law Review* (1990) 991. *Epokhē* is derived from the Greek meaning suspension.

the historical narrative of this study. As Antonio Cassese notes in his seminal study on the role self-determination has played in the international system:

> In the hands of would-be-States, self-determination is the key to opening the door and entering into that coveted club of statehood. For existing States, self-determination is the key for locking the door against the undesirable from within and outside the realm[52]

While retellings of self-determination are often framed through a logic of emancipation, as we will see, self-determination has been a legal tool used to not only to establish who could be part of international society, but also, who could not. While redefinitions of self-determination have often been used to open the door to sovereignty, more often than not they have also been used to justify sovereign hierarchies and exclusion within international law. As I will explore, these 'moments of encounter' have primarily been fought along the lines of identity (ethnic or civic), level of advancement (civilised or non-civilised) and most crucially the practical effects of recognising a claim (stabilising or destabilising). The impact of this process on both legal and normative conceptions of sovereignty is most visible in self-determination's mobilization during the decolonisation era, when the widening of sovereignty was simultaneously met with its contraction with the imposition of the principle *uti possedetis juris* to retain existing colonial boundaries, as well at the insistence on territorial integrity to counter the inevitable secessionist demands emanating from the "Janus face of the modern nation," in the words of Jürgen Habermas.[53] The net result, as Karen Knop points out, is that "some states in international law represent the exercise of self-determination by a people, others do not; some peoples have their own state, others do not."[54] However, it is also evident in the struggles to define self-determination beyond the colonial context. Self-determination is increasingly being adapted to promote changing ideas of sovereign statehood, particularly in matters of governance, human and minority

---

52 Cassese's analysis argues that, overall, self-determination "was advanced in at least five different versions:" as a criterion for territorial change (populations should be able to choose via elections or plebiscite which state they belong to); as a democratic principle calling for the consent of the governed in any sovereign state; as an anti-colonialist principle; as a right for minorities within sovereign states; and as a principle of non-intervention. Cassese (1993).

53 Jurgen Habermas, "A Genealogical Analysis of the Cognitive Content of Morality" in *The Inclusion of the Other: Studies in Political Theory.* (Cambridge, Mass: The MIT Press, 1998).

54 Karen Knop, 'Statehood: Territory, People, Government' in J. Crawford and M. Koskenniemi (eds), *The Cambridge Companion to International Law* (Cambridge: CUP, 2012), 107.

rights. These new expectations of sovereignty, linked to a discourse of equality of individuals and human rights as constitutive of the nation-state, are framed in the language of 'internal self-determination.' The conditions of state formation in the post-imperial period have often made sovereign equality contingent upon respect for this new discourse of self-determination.

These transformations are also driven at a more academic level by normative ideas of the quality and role of international law. This study also contends that the polysemy and indeterminacy of the concept of self-determination is generated not only by its multi-layered history and its circulation amongst and appropriation by various actors, but by the struggle to define not only its content but also its very nature as a legal idea. The history of self-determination in international law also records the struggles within the academic discipline of law over the normative stakes of international law by sceptics and idealists alike. The former, to varying degrees, seeks largely to empty self-determination of any continuing relevance to international law, highlighting its volatile potential for undermining the state system.[55] The latter having identified its malleable potential seeks to harness its ring of universal applicability to propose a range of both national and international legal implications.[56] Of course academic discourse on self-determination is not as neatly polarised as this assessment. Views on the definition, scope and legal implications of self-determination by leading authors are dotted across the spectrum. And yet the discourse on self-determination contains little that is apparent, or on which everyone can agree. The dynamism of self-determination as will be seen, is largely incompatible with the standard function of international law, which never the less seeks to stabilise and solidify its inherently shifting nature. The difficulties inherent in the interpretation and application of self-determination have meant that international society and international law navigate constantly between the fundamental and universal nature of the concept and its disruptive potential. The resulting tension that emerges from attempts to integrate and then either promote or mitigate its transformative potential is the untold story of self-determination that is generally lacking from traditional accounts.

---

55 The more conservative approach is embodied in the following: Malcolm Shaw, "Peoples, Territorialism and Boundaries" (1997) 8 *EJIL* 478, Malcolm Shaw, "The Heritage of States: The Principle of Uti Possidetis Today" (1996) 67 *BYIL* 75; James Crawford, *The Creation of States in International Law* (Oxford: OUP 2006).

56 To varying degrees this approach is embodied in the following: Hurst Hannum (ed.), Documents on Autonomy and Minority Rights, (Dordrecht: Martinus Nijhoff 1993); Thomas Franck, "Legitimacy and the Democratic Entitlement" in Gregory Fox and Brad Roth (eds.), *Democratic Governance and International Law* (Cambridge: CUP 2001).

## 3 Organisation of the Book

In developing this argument, I am concerned with examining three particular facets of the relationship between self-determination and international law, which are explored through a number of historical cases. The first is to explore the unique position self-determination has come to occupy between international law and sovereignty, which has provided a space in which to challenge the normative and legal order of international law. Chapter 1 sketches the contours of this relationship. Its focal point is the relationship between empire and sovereignty as an international legal and political idea, charting how self-determination, as a normative contention concerning the function and identity of territorial distribution and authority, came to play a central role in this relationship. The tensions that emerged from the formulations of self-determination in political thought during this time demonstrate that the egalitarian aspirations of self-determination were tightly bound with strategies of sovereign conditioning and hierarchies. I build on the (widely made) argument that international law has been a pivotal part of a power-complex that has, since the period of European colonialism, enabled Western countries to define the nature and characteristics of sovereignty and the law of nations as an idea.[57] These developments provide the first unique points of conflict over normative ideas of self-determination namely (1) the symbiotic but uneasy relationship to sovereignty and statehood it maintains, and (2) the nature of the entities, the "selves" which may be entitled to exercise self-determination.

The second phenomenon I seek to elicit in this book relates to the manner in which the self-determination's normative malleability has been deployed to challenge the juridical and normative contours of the state and ideas of sovereignty in the international order. While recent literature has drawn attention to the manner in which the meaning associated with self-determination

57 Among the many works illuminating the subordinate position into which non-European peoples have been placed in the law of nations see Ram Prakash Anand (ed.), *Asian States and the Development of Universal International Law* (Mumbai: Vikas Publications 1972); Okon Udokang, *Succession of New States to International Treaties* (New York: Oceana 1972); Ram Prakash Anand, *International Law and Developing Countries: Confrontation or Cooperation*? (Dordrecht: Nijhoff 1987); Arnulf Becker Lorca, *Mestizo International Law: A Global Intellectual History 1842–1933* (Cambridge: CUP 2016); Charles Henry Alexandrowicz, *An Introduction to the History of the Law of Nations in the East Indies (16th, 17th and 18th Centuries)* (Oxford: Clarendon Press 1967); Jennifer Pitts, *A Turn to Empire: The Rise of Imperial Liberalism in Britain and France* (Princeton NJ: Princeton University Press 2006); Georg Schwarzenberger, *Power Politics: An Introduction to the Study of International Relations and Post-War Planning* (The Camelot Press Ltd, 1941).

has changed over the twentieth century, particularly the manner in which it was mobilized for political purposes in the inter-war period, less attention has been paid to self-determination's impact on conceptions of juridical sovereignty during this time. Chapter 2 turns to the interwar period, which as Gertrude Stein asserted, marked the beginning of the twentieth century.[58] Against the backdrop of the institutionalization of international law and processes and the popularization of democratic practices and ideas, self-determination was to assume a central role in attempts by various actors to articulate a new vision of world relations,[59] in which the normative foundation of the state would be based on self-determination for ethnically defined 'peoples' or 'nations.' These early mobilizations of self-determination, as several scholars have explored, was to provide the political and normative impetus for the anti-colonial lobby to reframe their own claims to self-determination.[60] Absent from most accounts of this period, however, is that the impact of the circulation of self-determination during this time on the nexus between internal and external sovereignty. While the construction of the minority protection and Mandate regimes are primarily seen as a redeployment of the standards of civilization under new guises, their creation also opened a crucial legal space in which domestic political structures and state action were subject to international oversight (at least in theory), tempered by new internal expectations of the juridical state, thereby creating a crucial legal space for marginalised groups who had largely been kept apart from international law.

Chapter 3 continues this line of enquiry by following the anti-colonial reinvention of self-determination through the decolonisation process, which was catalysed through the United Nations. Contrary to the claim made by Martti Koskenniemi and others that "decolonisation was not accompanied by a

58 Quoted in Joan Hoff, "From Sarajevo to Sarajevo" in Michael Hogan (ed), *The Ambiguous Legacy: US Foreign Relations in the America Century* (Cambridge: CUP 1999) p. 204.

59 See, e.g, Frederick C. Hicks, *The New World Order: International Organization, International Law, International Cooperation* (London: Doubleday 1920).

60 Both Daniel Philpott and Neta Crawford advance this position, suggesting that self-determination was used to foster change in colonial ideas and practices. See Daniel Philpott, "*Revolutions in Sovereignty: How Ideas Shaped Modern International Relations* (Princeton: Princeton University Press, 2001) and Neta Crawford, *Argument and Change in World Politics Ethics, Decolonization, and Humanitarian Intervention.* Cambridge; CUP 2002). Erez Manela contends that ideas on self-determination shaped thoughts on independence within the colonised world between what the author terms "the 1919 Wilsonian movement" and the 1950s. See Erez Manela, *The Wilsonian Moment: Self-Determination and the International Origins of Anticolonial Nationalism* (Oxford: OUP 2007).

challenge to statehood,"[61] I argue that the mobilization of self-determination by anti-colonialists was directed towards existing modes of sovereign authority, and their underlying normative and legal bases which were structured around the exclusion of non-European peoples deemed 'unfit' for sovereign rule. Self-determination's emergence in international law is often depicted as grounded in the expansion of already existing ideas of sovereignty linked to the liberal national Westphalian state. In contrast to this, I argue that anti-colonial self-determination was marked by a struggle to dispense with these ideas in order to pave the way for a new sovereign order, one not enmeshed in colonial hierarchies. This was evident from concurrent demands to not only independence based on non-domination but to non-intervention and economic self-determination, which sought to recalibrate sovereign expectations and rebalance an unequal international system marked by imperial interventionism. While these debates played out in the Third Committee and other human rights fora, which emerged as a critical forum for newly independent states who had been excluded from the San Francisco conference to debate the fundamentals of the international order, this was not because decolonisation was solely a human rights movement – although I disagree with Samuel Moyn's characterization that the politics of self-determination and human rights were distinct projects.[62] Rather self-determination, through its reanimation in the human rights movement posed a fundamental challenge to existing ideas of sovereign legitimacy. That these efforts towards a reconstituted sovereignty as non-domination continued into the postimperial period with the creation of the New International Economic Order, attests to this radical position of self-determination by anti-colonialists. By invoking self-determination as the legal and normative basis for decolonisation, however, the anti-colonial lobby faced questions about the limits of its application. The process of decolonisation posed the question whether self-determination was a right only relevant in the context of European decolonisation, or whether it could be extended to other cases.[63] Ultimately the rupture in sovereignty that had been deployed to remove sovereign control, resumed its normal functioning, as the primacy of existing sovereign arrangements was stressed despite the deep divisions that characterized many post-colonial states.

The subsequent chapters examine this aspect, namely the relationship between self-determination and the oscillation between law and sovereignty

---

61 Koskenniemi (1993: 256).

62 Samuel Moyn, *The Last Utopia* (Cambridge, MA: Harvard University Press, 2010) 88.

63 Roger Normand and Sarah Zaidi, *Human Rights at the UN: The Political History of Universal Justice* (Bloomington: Indiana University Press, 2008), 212–20; Burke (2010: 35–59).

in the international system. The debate regarding legitimacy of authority as one of the fatal arguments against colonial rule continued to raise fundamental questions regarding the dynamic between the 'internal' and 'external' dimensions of statehood. While anti-colonialist self-determination came to define a standard of political legitimacy with which colonialism was at odds, it posed the question of what this would mean for ongoing normative standards of legitimate authority.[64] With its universalization the contestations over self-determination's meaning and limitations only intensified as a host of international actors vied to harness or contain its emancipatory potential in line with their competing visions of a new international order. During the period immediately following decolonisation, actors continued to struggle to accommodate diverse ideals of sovereignty and international political organization within the rhetoric of self-determination. Chapter 4 explores the immediate post-colonial era during which time questions over the legal implications of self-determination as an ongoing norm were scrutinised and developed against the backdrop of new battles to redefine the sovereign state. For newly independent states self-determination as a corollary to the principle of non-interference arguably provided one means to reinforce their newfound independence and to promote the accommodation of new forms of internal governance within the international sphere. Simultaneously, another reinvention of self-determination was taking place, one enmeshed with new sovereign expectations. Western Powers increasingly began to promote democratic governance and individual human rights within the ambit of self-determination, as the new standards of political legitimacy. The international human rights regime was increasingly framed as a reaction to the "negative sovereignty" of post-colonial states, whose categorical statehood left them without the "capacity of a government to provide political goods to its citizens."[65] In this formulation 'internal' self-determination becomes the new expectation of statehood from which states draw their international legitimacy.

Despite attempts to redirect self-determination towards the internal functioning of the state, however, the end of the Cold War underlined that the rhetorical and legal power of self-determination to challenge the hermetic seal of statehood could not entirely be contained. Many of the key conflicts in the world continue to be framed in terms of claims of self-determination. Chapter 5 examines the ongoing debate around the implications of self-determination

---

64 Brad Roth, *Sovereign Equality and Moral Disagreement: Premises of a Pluralist International Legal Order* (Oxford: OUP, 2011).

65 Robert Jackson, *Quasi States: Sovereignty, International Relations and the Third World,* (Cambridge: CUP 1990) 24; 76.

for sovereignty and international stability, especially after the Cold War. With the unfreezing of the Cold War blocs came a profusion of new claims to statehood and autonomy, based upon a broader conception of 'peoples' entitled to self-determination. The contingency of new self-determination claims upon recognition have taken place against a backdrop of debate over the concept of sovereignty and increasing scrutiny over forms of governance, particularly human rights protection. In this context a shift of emphasis to the association between self-determination and democratic governance, along with a commitment to human rights and minority rights, has assumed new relevance to the standards of sovereign equality in our time. Given that as Martti Koskenniemi put it, "the discourse of national self-determination contains little that is self-evident or on which everyone can agree," debates have turned to what the ethical standards of self-determination could mean with regard to the construction of the modern state.[66] For indigenous peoples in particular self-determination's normative and legal power offers an important platform to renegotiate their historic exclusion from sovereign rights and privileges.

## 4 Approach

The book concentrates on the central encounters in which self-determination was contested, redefined and operationalized by different actors within a wider historical trajectory. The motivation for the selection of these key encounters was their proximity to major shifts in state formation and imperial collapse: following World War I, with the decolonisation movements after World War II and their after-effects, and with the end of the Cold War. In each moment, I explore the main points of discussion and modes of articulation surrounding the meaning and application of self-determination as a legal idea offered by various groups of actors. While the overlap between political and legal articulations and argumentation of self-determination are difficult to distinguish, my primary focus is on the claims and practices of self-determination as a framework or basis for legal claims. However, this exploration is not carried out through a legal doctrinal lens, but rather a socio-legal one. That is, I

66 Lee C. Buccheit, *Secession: The Legitimacy of Self-Determination* (New Haven: Yale University Press, 1978); Allen Buchanan, "Toward a Theory of Secession," 101 *Ethics* (1991) 322–342; Allen Buchanan, *Secession: The Morality of Political Divorce from Fort Sumter to Lithuania and Quebec* (Boulder, Colorado: Westview Press, 1991); Allen Buchanan, "Democracy and Secession" in Margaret Moore, ed., *National Self-Determination and Secession* (Oxford: OUP 1991) 14–33.

am less concerned with the legality of such claims, but rather how self-determination was interpreted and applied to pursue different legal strategies and expectations. In this respect, the study draws upon ideas of socio-legal theory that are generally associated with the work of Pierre Bourdieu, and the idea of depicting law as a 'social space'.[67] The central condition of this investigation is the need to account for the contested dynamics of self-determination within a wider legal and political history, by avoiding both a teleological and linear narrative, and also a monolithic depiction of international law as a socially closed phenomenon.[68] That is that we approach law as the product of a struggle to give it meaning, a struggle always taking place in a certain socio-political and legal structures which themselves are changing over time, and one which is not necessarily contained within the orthodox approach to international law.

To move beyond traditional doctrinal limits, I utilize a broadened legal landscape within which to examine these articulations, one that combines the traditional sites and sources of international legal activity (institutions, courts, legal source material) with other political and social settings in order to provide a complex and contextualized account. This is rooted in a concern not only to underline the contingency of events and how international legal developments are embedded in their specific places and moments, but an open-ended approach to the question of 'where international law can be said to lie'.[69] Looking beyond international law's perceived boundaries, both

---

67 Pierre Bourdieu, 'The Force of Law: Toward a Sociology of the Juridical Field', trans. Richard Terdiman, *Hastings Law Journal* 38 (1987), 805.

68 This point is also addressed by Anne Peters: "Concepts change over time. They are no more solid than the period or context in which they originated. Therefore, the analysis of a legal concept should include a reflection about the social and political context of the concept, and the political agenda behind it, about the 'speakers' and the 'addressees', and about the shifting meaning of a concept in the course of time. Surely a legal historian should not limit him- or herself to concepts found in legal documents. Other concepts too can be of legal relevance. Such a distinction can help to identify blind spots in the law, or illustrate the blurred boundary between the spheres of law and politics" *in* Bardo Fassbender, Anne Peters (eds) *Oxford Handbook of the History of International Law* (Oxford: OUP, 2012) 12.

69 Anne Orford, 'The Past as Law or History? The Relevance of Imperialism for Modern International Law' *NYU IILJ Working Paper* 2012/2, at 10; The classic example here is the 'structuralist' phase of the work of Kennedy and Koskenniemi. See David Kennedy, 'Critical theory, structuralism, and contemporary legal scholarship', (1986) 21 *New England Law Review* 209; David Kennedy, *International legal structures* (1987), David Kennedy, 'A new Stream of International legal scholarship' (1988) 7 *Wisconsin International Law Journal* 1; Koskenniemi, *From Apology to Utopia: The Structure of International Legal Argument* (Cambridge: CUP 1989); Martti Koskenniemi, *The Gentle Civilizer of Nations: The Rise and Fall of International Law 1870–1960* (Cambridge: CUP, 2001).

conceptually and methodologically, towards the periphery, I draw on existing 'turn to history' scholarship.[70] which has sought to move outside the restrictive boundaries of doctrine, chronicling the indeterminacy and politicization of legal ideas and questioning the methodological and theoretical constraints of the classical relationship between history and international law, which in the words of Jennifer Pitts include:

> ... aspirations to the status of a science, a dependence on stylised histories populated by founding fathers and origins myths, a reliance on sovereignty as a foundational principle, a tendency to regard empires and imperialism as historically superseded and also 'incidental to the discipline proper', and a blindness to their own participation in structures and discourses of racialized hierarchy[71]

The tendency of international legal history to set out "in advance the parameters of the discipline (in terms of its subjects and sources, its actors and modes of engagement),"[72] is perhaps best reflected in the tendency of classical historical accounts to draw primarily on doctrine, judicial decisions, treatises, and the writings of prominent international law practitioners as their historical source material. This "ready-made methodology" of the sources doctrine, as Rose Parfitt has underlined, has particular implications for the practice of writing international legal history. Feed the past into this "legal historiographical machine" as she terms it, and consciously or not a relatively uniform product is bound to emerge – namely a "history of rules developed in the European

70 The expression historiographical turn refers to a constant and growing need on the part of international lawyers to review the history of international law and to establish links between the past and the present situation of international norms, institutions and doctrines. The work of Martti Koskenniemi has, in this respect, been instrumental to a historical reorientation of the entire discipline international law, see Martti Koskenniemi, *From Apology to Utopia: The Structure of International Legal Argument* (Cambridge: CUP, 1989); Martti Koskenniemi, *The Gentle Civilizer of Nations: The Rise and Fall of International Law 1870–1960* (Cambridge: CUP, 2001). For an account of the various strands see Miriam Bak McKenna and Matilda Arvidsson, "The turn to history in international law and the sources doctrine: Critical approaches and methodological imaginaries," *Leiden Journal of International Law* (2019), pp. 1–20.

71 Pitts (2017: 283).

72 Matthew Craven, 'Introduction: International Law and Its Histories,' in M. Craven, M. Fitzmaurice and M. Vogiatzi (eds.) *Time, History and International Law* (Leiden: Brill, 2006) at 8.

state system since the 16th century which then spread to … the entire globe."[73] This raises critical questions about method and the appropriate relationship between history and law in international law. Discard the methodology dictated by the classic approach to sources, as Parfitt explains, "and the possibility of "challenging Eurocentrism" emerges – but at the risk of dissolving the specifically international legal character of the historical undertaking."[74] To completely reject these categories and vocabularies of preceding histories would be reductive, argues Koskenniemi, and would deprive lawyers of the "shared imagination" provided by these historical associations.[75]

To identify the discourses, practices and conceptions, both domestically and internationally, of self-determination, and locate that within a broader legal, political and social context, I have relied on a wide range of primary and secondary sources.[76] This includes various official legal texts – covenants, treaties, resolutions, judicial decisions – along with a variety of legal academic texts and judicial documents. I have supplemented this legal source material with primary and secondary sources and literature pertaining to the surrounding historical context including official documents, historical accounts and studies written by prominent scholars. I have drawn on material associated with a wide range of actors - lawyers, diplomats, bureaucrats, activists – as well as the analysis and historical accounts of scholars from various fields. This includes available verbatim records from meetings within relevant bodies, correspondence among national delegates and the League's or UN representatives, relevant petitions, pamphlets, newspapers' articles, official documents, official statements, annual reports and recommendations. With regards to the various domestic contexts that I study, I have largely relied upon official statements and speeches, as well as on legal documents.

The study does not strive for a comprehensive historical account, rather, it opts to critically recount the tensions that have accompanied self-determination's trajectory within a wider legal and political historical progression and explore how as a legal idea it was defined and more generally structured over time by the competing input of actors. Moreover, drawing on the sociology of knowledge, I have sought to integrate structural concerns – of race, gender, empire and nation – into my account, in order to move beyond what Jouannet

73 Rose Parfitt, 'The Spectre of Sources', (2014) 25 EJIL 297, (reviewing B. Fassbender and A. Peters (eds.), *The Oxford Handbook of the History of International Law* (Oxford: OUP, 2012) 299.

74 Parfitt, (2014) at 299.

75 Koskenniemi, in Fassbender and Peters, (2012) at 945.

76 Andrew Fitzmaurice, 'Context in the History of International Law' (2018) 20 *Journal of the History of International Law* 5, 6–7.

and Peters call the "methodological primacy of technicism (doctrinalism) and pragmatism in international legal scholarship."[76] Pushing against the functionalism and pragmatism of many international legal accounts which attempt to posit smooth or evolutionary histories, I instead dwell on the "ambiguity and ambivalence" of self-determination's circulation.[77] By taking as its starting point the adversarial nature of international law as a field which is produced at the crossroads of a set of different agendas and actors, we can observe how self-determination as a norm is impacted and transformed by these stakes. Through this broader conceptual framework, the history of self-determination is re-examined to reveal the contestations and points of conflict both within and outside of the existing mainstream discourse.

While the narrative in this book has both a strong legal and international focus, this does not signify that these were the sole or primary articulations of self-determination during these periods. Numerous other actors across different contexts have shaped and formed discourses of self-determination. However, the focus of this book is the history of resistance and transformation of global society driven by the legal redefinitions and reformulations of self-determination. It should also be stressed that the book does not go into comprehensive depth about the motivations and mechanics of these movements for resistance, but rather zooms in on the role that self-determination as a legal argument played in such moments. In taking self-determination as a discursive anchor point, I hope that this focus will reveal something about how self-determination as a legal idea has helped to create the conditions for global transformation.

---

76 Emmanuel Jouannet and Anne Peters, 'The Journal of the History of International Law: A Forum for New Research', (2014) 16 *Journal of the History of International Law* 1, at 2.

77 Nathaniel Berman, *Passion and Ambivalence: Colonialism, Nationalism and International Law* (Leiden: Brill, 2012) at 44.

CHAPTER 1

# Self-Determination: Hierarchies of Empire

The adoption of General Assembly Resolution 1514, the "Declaration on the Granting of Independence to Colonial Countries and Peoples" on December 14, 1960, by 89 votes to 0, with 9 abstentions all from colonial powers, was a watershed moment in the delegitimisation of empire. In the space of the fifteen years after the founding of the UN, anti-colonialists had successfully launched a challenge to colonial rule, refashioning self-determination as a right that entailed the independence of colonial peoples. Rupert Emerson, writing in 1965, described its adoption as "almost an amendment of the Charter."[1] The declaration affirmed the right to self-determination and called for an immediate end to all forms of colonial rule, declaring it a violation of human rights. "This session" the Somalian representative stated at the time, "may well go down in history as the "Assembly of Freedom" and our declaration, as a "Declaration of Freedom," would rank with the great Charters of mankind: the Magna Carta, the Declaration of Independence, the Declaration of the Rights of Man, and the Charter of the United Nations."[2] Barely a decade before, Herbert Morrison, the deputy leader of the progressive British Labour Party, echoing the sentiments of the vast majority of Western powers, had argued that granting independence to colonial peoples would be "like giving a child of ten a latch-key, a bank account and a shot-gun."[3] Colonial peoples had therefore been assiduously excluded from the ambit of restoration of sovereignty and self-government championed by the 1941 Atlantic Charter, and later the United Nations Charter which created the blueprint for the post-war order. As Alex Quaison-Sackey, Ghana's representative to the United Nations later stated: "If indeed Africa was a forgotten continent at the time of the promulgation of the

1 Rupert Emerson, "Colonialism, Political Development, and the UN," 19 *International Organization* (1965) 484–503 at 487.

2 Verbatim Records of the General Assembly Plenary Meeting, 945th session, 13 December 1960, A/PV. 945, para. 26.

3 Quoted in William Louius, *Imperialism at Bay, 1941–1945: The United States and the Decolonization of the British Empire* (New York: OUP 1978) 14.

 | DOI:10.1163/9789004479197_003

Charter…the Declaration calling for an immediate end to colonialism in all its territories has redressed the balance."[4]

To understand how this momentous shift came about, and moreover, how it was that self-determination was to assume a central role in the legal framing of decolonization, this chapter distills some of the main historical antecedents that made it possible, indeed necessary, for the anti-colonial movement to centre their revolutionary legal claims to independence around self-determination. In the face of fierce opposition, anti-colonialists were able to renegotiate the existing normative bases of international law and state sovereignty which enabled imperial rule. Reframing self-determination as a fundamental freedom from non-domination and right to self-rule - ultimately crystalizing self-determination as a right – and elevating colonial peoples to the status of rights holders – anti-colonialists were able to prompt a critical rupture in existing forms of territorial control and legitimacy which had excluded them from equal sovereignty in the international system. Beginning in 1945, with self-determination's inclusion in the Charter in articles 1 and 55[5] as one of the founding principles of the UN, anti-colonialists set about teasing out an international legal framework which would give credence to the rights of colonial independence and sovereign equality as an essential part of the principle of non-domination within international society.

Self-determination's inclusion in the Charter – and indeed the deliberately vague formulation in which it appears – in turn rests on a complicated history of political thought regarding foundational notions of sovereign legitimacy which in 1945 at least were considered critical to the establishment of a new world order. "Where would many of us here be if it were not for a principle of self-determination?" asked the Egyptian delegate.[6] To rule out self-determination as the basis of the new international order would be, in the words of the Rapporteur "reverting to previous conditions which lead to many wars…we would be in the same way breathing the air of our enemies, and it is

4 Alex Quaison-Sackey quoted in Steven Jensen, *The Making of international Human Rights: The 1960s, Decolonization, and the Reconstruction of Global Values* (New York: CUP, 2016) 65.

5 The final text of the UN Charter provides in Article 1(2) that one of the purposes of the United Nations is: *To develop friendly relations among nations based on the principle of equal rights and self-determination of peoples, and to take other appropriate measures to strengthen universal peace*. Article 55 of the Charter further states that the UN shall promote goals such as higher standards of living, full employment, and human rights "[w]ith a view to the creation of conditions of stability and well-being which are necessary for peaceful and friendly relations among nations based on respect for the principle of equal rights and self-determination of peoples."

6 Rapporteur, Cmttee. I/1, 15 May, 396.

not fragrant air and we would not like to breathe it."[7] This chapter takes up the question of how self-determination and its normative connection to the independence and sovereign equality of states came to occupy such a central role in contemporaneous political thought, which ultimately influenced its inclusion as one the founding principles of the new international order in the Charter.

Rooted in a longer history of western political thought, this process sees the melding of several conceptual ideas of political organization originating in the 17th century with the linguistic framing of 'self-determination' – or *Selbstbestimmung* - coined by German nationalists in the 18th century. The backdrop to this development sees the emergence of two interlinked institutional and legal forms that structured the distribution of political authority in Europe and its non-European territories prior to decolonization: the institution of sovereignty and the institution of empire.[8] This process saw the simultaneous advancement of ideas of sovereign legitimacy centred around the notion of popular sovereignty and later nationalism, as a means of expanding the existing system of dynastic rule on the one hand, and the construction and formalization of an international system of law prefaced upon strategies of sovereign exclusion on the other.

The two centuries prior to self-determination's inclusion in the Charter, saw its emergence as an idea tied inextricably with the emergence of the juridical state and struggles to modify and define the notion of the sovereign, firstly through the idea of popular sovereignty and later the notion of national self-determination. "If sovereignty," as Andrew Hurrell notes, "has provided the basic institutional framework of the society of states, it was national self-determination that came ever more to provide the political power and the moral meaning to the idea of an international society."[9] The first part of this chapter sketches the earliest phase of this process, when the nascent international community, itself undergoing unprecedented institutionalization from naturalism to positivism, was confronted with self-determination as a normative contention concerning the function and identity of territorial distribution and authority, notably in John Locke's and Jean-Jacques Rousseau's writings on popular sovereignty. Nevertheless, while the concept of self-determination was therefore emancipatory in origin, alongside political equality and equality of rights, it was so almost exclusively at the level of rhetoric. Crucially, it did not challenge the existing power structures of Europe, which remained centred on the four great empires – German, Austro-Hungarian, Ottoman and

---

7 Rapporteur, Cmttee. I/1, 15 May, 12.
8 Reus-Smit (2013: 153).
9 Andrew Hurrell, *On Global Order*, (Oxford: OUP, 2007) 121.

Russian – nor the arbitrary division of the world into states according to the interests of Western elites. The untold counterpoint to the development of self-determination is that the reallocation of territorial sovereignty was prefaced upon the simultaneously shifting dichotomy between sovereign and non-sovereign peoples and strategies of exclusion, particularly of non-European peoples. Imperial domination structured international society was to assume a central role in the development not only to regimes of sovereignty, but to the international legal structures that came to govern them.

## 1 Sovereignty and Empire

Classic accounts of international law situate the Westphalian formula of *cuius regio eius religio*[10] as the basis of the establishment of the model of independent and sovereign states, and its defining principles, including non-interference, territorial integrity and the notion of the balance of power.[11] This transition involved two interrelated processes - the centralisation and demarcation of authority, and the rationalisation and consolidation of hierarchy.[12] At this moment, it is argued, European society transforms from a system of atomized princely states loosely connected by the republica Christiana, into an international society based on separate, independent and equally sovereign entities.[13] For most scholars, the right of states to decide unilaterally upon their internal political affairs becomes a fundamental expression of their status as

---

10 First stated in the Treaty of Augsburg of 1555.

11 In 1758, Emmerich de Vattel wrote in *The Law of Nations* that: Europe forms a political system in which the nations inhabiting this part of the world are bound together by their relations and various interests into a single body. It is no longer, as in former times, a confused heap of detached parts, each of which had but little concern for the lot of others, and rarely troubled itself over what did not immediately affect it. The constant attention of sovereigns to all that goes on, the custom of resident ministers, the continual negotiations that take place, make of modern Europe a sort of republic, whose members – each independent, but all bound together by a common interest – unite for the maintenance of order and the preservation of [state] liberty. This is what has given rise to the wellknown principle of the balance of power, by which is meant an arrangement of affairs so that no state shall be in a position to have absolute mastery and dominate over others. Vattel, *The Law of Nations; or, Principles of the Law of Nature Applied to the Conduct and Affairs of Nations and Sovereigns* (Chitty, Joseph, trans.), (Philadelphia: T. and J. W. Johnson and Co, 1863).

12 Christian Reus-Smit, *The Moral Purpose of the State: Culture, Social Identity, and Institutional Rationality in International Relations* (Princeton: Princeton University Press, 1999) 99.

13 Robert Jackson, 'Sovereignty in World Politics: A Glance at the Historical and Conceptual Landscape', *Political Studies* 47 (1999), 435–439.

autonomous political entities in the international political system.[14] By the beginning of the eighteenth century, as Osiander notes, European monarchs were "essentially…self-determining actors, none of which was entitled to dictate to others."[15] This relationship between sovereignty and independence has come to characterize accounts of statehood in modern international law.[16]

The accuracy of this account has been the subject of sustained critique by historians and international lawyers alike, not least for its narrow geographical focus to the exclusion of non-European forms of rule.[17] As many critical

---

14 Stephen Krasner, "Compromising Westphalia," 20(3) *Int'l Security* 115 (1995–1996) Krasner crystallises sovereignty in four different, yet interrelated, ways which reflect this reality. He sees it, first, as the taking of decisions related to regulation of territorial borders, as well as decisions related to people and goods crossing those borders. Actions taken by sovereigns in the name of the state on the international plane are further seen as manifestations of sovereignty (and the conceptual basis for treaty-making and a parallel system of international law). Finally, Krasner presents a conception of the 'Westphalian model' of sovereignty whereby political life is based on the concepts of territoriality and autonomy governed by domestic political authorities. This certainly was something completely new in the historical development of public international law.

15 Andreas Osiander, 'Sovereignty, international relations, and the Westphalian myth', *International Organization*, 55.2 (2001), 439. For the classical narrative of self-determination the consecration of the internal and external laid the foundations for development of self-determination as a doctrine See James Summers, *Peoples and International Law: How Nationalism and Self-Determination Shape A Contemporary Law of Nations* (Dordrecht: Martinus Nijhoff, 2007); Leo Gross, *The Peace of Westphalia, 1648–1948, 42 American Journal of International Law* 20 (1948).

16 In common with many other international lawyers, Jennings and Watts, in their Oppenheim's International Law, include sovereignty as one of the four constituent elements of the state, holding that '[s]overeignty in the strict and narrowest sense of the term implies…independence all around, within and without the borders of the country. Robert Jennings and Arthus Watts. Eds. *Oppenheims's International Law 9th ed* (London: Longman, 1992) 32; Similarly. Crawford states that independence is 'the central criterion of statehood'. Using the Island of Palmas Arbitration (1928) and the *Austro-German Customs Case* (1931) as precedents, Crawford concludes that independence is the ability of a state's institutions of government to exercise exclusive control over its internal affairs. The recognition of this quality by other states is not a statement of approval or disapproval of the government or people, merely an acknowledgement of legal standing. By this explanation, the society of states is the collection of political entities that mutually recognize the right to independence over matters deemed to be internal and base their equal legal standing on this premise (Crawford: 1979, 48).

17 For such critiques of the Westphalia narrative, see e.g., Derek Croxton, 'The Peace of Westphalia of 1648 and the Origins of Sovereignty', *International History Review* 21(3) (1999) 569–592; Osiander (2001); Benno Teschke, *The Myth of 1648: Class, Geopolitics and the Making of Modern International Relations*, (London: Verso, 2003); Matthew Craven, 'On Foucault and Wolff or from Law to Political Economy', *Leiden Journal of International Law* 25 (2012) 627–645; Turan Kayaoglu, *Legal Imperialism: Sovereignty and Extraterritoriality*

accounts have drawn attention to, moreover, the creation and formalization of an international system of law and sovereignty was also prefaced upon strategies of sovereign exclusion which were deeply interlinked with the expansion of European empires.[18] In his seminal work *Imperialism, Sovereignty, and the Making of International Law*, Anthony Anghie argued how modern conceptions of sovereignty were interwoven with European empires' subjugation of non-European peoples, and continued to be foundational for international legal thought.[19] At the time of the early colonial period, inter-polity law defined political entities as either enemies or members of the republica.[20] With the discovery of the 'New World', Anghie observed, the question arose as to how non-Christian indigenous populations would fit within this dichotomy. Contemporaneous jurists such as Francisco de Vitoria and Hugo Grotius, therefore offered a new dichotomy, which was to become a cornerstone for the modern international legal order–the distinction between sovereign and non-sovereign prefaced upon a corresponding set of sovereign characteristics and duties.[21]

A new theory of secular natural law proposed by Vitoria, which centred around the vital issues of property and title, paved the way for the incorporation of indigenous peoples into the European international legal order. Vitoria's depiction of a universal law of nations not only posited its binding nature for indigenous peoples owing to their capacity for reason, but simultaneously marked their social and political practices as violations of that very law.[22] In Carl Schmitt's words:

> [T]his amounted to a rejection of a particular type of argument put forward at that time ... [that] presented the natives as savages and barbarians ... in order to place them outside the law and to make their land free for appropriation[23]

*in Japan, the Ottoman Empire and China*, (Cambridge: CUP 2010); Turan Kayaoglu, 'Westphalian Eurocentrism in International Relations Theory', *International Studies Review* 12(2) (2010) 193–217.

18 See Anghie (2005); Mieville (2005: 156) Recently, Rose Parfitt's *The Process of International Legal Reproduction* has also explored how a hierachical understanding of individuals shaped a hierarchy between sovereign states and non-sovereign colonies. Rose Parfitt, *The Process of International Legal Reproduction* (Cambridge: CUP, 2019).

19 Anghie (2005: 2–3).

20 Mieville (2005: 173).

21 Anghie (2005); See also Reus-Smit (1999: 157) and Getachew (2019).

22 Anghie (2005: 15).

23 Carl Schmitt, "The Land Appropriation of a New World," 109 *Telos*, 44–5.

Vitoria also posited a new theory of sovereignty prefaced upon a new conception of sovereign legitimacy – the right to wage war, a right only legitimately exercised in Victoria's account, by the Spanish as Christian emissaries.[24] Were this not the case, he argues, "even Turks and Saracens might wage just wars against Christians, for they think they are thus rendering God service."[25] During this period, as Anghie underlines, "the most characteristic and unique powers of the sovereign, the powers to wage war and acquire title over territory and over alien peoples are defined in their fullest form by their application to the non-sovereign Indian."[26] From this point onwards, this distinction between those who could claim sovereignty and those who could not, became a defining feature of international society; a dynamic which would later give rise to a new kind of moral justification for colonial expansion, which extended non-sovereignty into the metric of civilization, and the division between 'civilised' peoples and 'non-civilised.'[27]

## 2 Popular Sovereignty and the Age of Revolution

As state consolidation grew throughout Europe, debates surrounding sovereignty shifted towards a new focus. French jurist and political philosopher, Jean Bodin's theory of absolute, consolidated and indivisible sovereignty in his *Six Books of the Commonwealth* became a defining account of sovereign authority, giving rise to a a theory of political legitimacy as a prerequisite for stable political authority.[28] Bodin's theories of 'unequal sovereignty' also presented a new approach that allowed him to extend sovereign authority beyond the realm of Christian sovereigns to some non-European states.[29]

24 The prince is the entity in whom all power is vested: for the prince only holds his position by the election of the State. Therefore, he is its representative and wields its authority; aye, and where there are already lawful princes in a State, all authority is in their hands and without them nothing of a public nature can be done either in war or in peace. Vitoria later concludes: 'Such a state, then, or the prince thereof, has authority to declare war and no one else.' Quoted in Anghie (2005: 24).

25 Victoria, quoted in Anghie (2005: 18).

26 Anghie (2005: 28). See also Antony Anghie, "Franciso de Vitoria and the Colonial Origins of International Law" 5 *Social and Legal Studies* 3 p. 335.

27 Martti Koskenniemi, The Gentle Civilizer of Nations: The Rise and Fall of International Law 1870 – 1960. (New York: CUP, 2001) 127–31.

28 Jean Bodin, *The Six Books of a Commonwealth,* K. D. McRae, ed., (Cambridge: Harvard University Press, 1962) bk. I, ch. VIII, 84.

29 Bodin describes the monarchs of 'France, Spain, England, Scotland, Ethiopia, Turkey, Persia and Moscovy' as 'sovereign absolutely', Jean Bodin, *The Six Books of a Commonwealth*

> We have already said that an absolute sovereign is one who, under God, holds by the sword alone. If he holds of another he is not sovereign. But this raises a difficulty. If those who hold anything at all of another in faith and homage are not sovereigns, there are hardly any sovereign princes in the world. On the other hand if we concede that those who do so hold in faith and homage are sovereigns, we are in effect saying the vassal and his lord, the servant and his master, are equals in honour, power, and authority[30]

In the next decades, new political thought began to redefine the "moral purpose of the state,"[31] transforming it from divinely ordained social order to the idea of a social contract. The idea of the 'consent of the governed' became a defining feature of sovereign legitimacy. It is here, at least in historical retellings of self-determination's ascent, that political theories of self-determination began to crystalise in political philosophers John Locke's and Jean-Jacques Rousseau's accounts of popular sovereignty.

Locke's account of the natural state of man – as "perfect freedom" and "equality"[32] gave rise to a new standard of legitimacy, whereby the societal contract forged by individuals entrusting the government with the power to rule was also liable for revision, should they fail to uphold their trust.[33] Locke's conception of popular sovereignty, and the related liberal and republican attributes of parliamentary regimes representing the will of the governed, was prominent in the Age of Revolution (1770–1850) – bookended by the French and American Revolutions on one side and the Revolutions of 1848 on the other. Increasingly the idea of 'the people' as the legitimate unit of political organization becomes central to discussions of sovereignty and the state, and to the link between internal and external sovereignty.[34]

---

(McRae, Kenneth Douglas, ed.), (Cambridge: Harvard University Press, 1962). 114.

30 *Ibid* Chapter IX.

31 Reus-Smit (1999: 88).

32 Locke (1690).

33 Luke Glanville *Sovereignty and the Responsibility to Protect*, (Chicago: University of Chicago Press, 2014) 63.

34 This is exemplified in Pufendorf's definition of the State as a 'compound Moral person, whose will being united and tied together by those covenants which before passed amongst the multitude, is deemed the will of all, to the end that it may use and apply the strength and riches of private persons towards maintaining the common peace and security' (Pufendorf, *On the Law of Nature and Nations*, Bk VII, c 2, s 13).

Revolutionary change in Europe tied to notions of popular sovereignty had begun to occur as early as the mid seventeenth century, with the Glorious Revolution of 1688 and the attempted Corsican revolution of 1729. In 1774, the Russian and the Ottoman Empires, agreed in Article 3 of the Treaty of Kutchuk-Kainardji that "all the Tartar peoples ... shall without any exception, be acknowledged by the two Empires as free nations, and entirely independent of every foreign power, governed by their own sovereign...elected and raised to the throne by all the Tartar peoples."[35] A series of slave rebellions in the Caribbean, until recently treated as sidebars to this period, also drove forth demands for emancipation from alien rule. The Haitian revolution (1791–1804) established the first independent nation in the Caribbean and the first black republic in the world. Rather than drawing on proto ideas of liberal freedom, however, the Haitian and Caribbean revolutions were composed of multiple political strands such as "ethnic-based identities and hierarchies, slave royalism, radical republicanism, peasant consciousness, early forms of pan-Africanism, and working-class internationalism."[36]

Motivated by the "crimes of tyranny," on one side, and by the "progress of liberty," on the other,[37] the Atlantic Revolutions have come to represent a key moment in self-determination's history – and in defining its content and implications. Despite the lofty rhetoric posited by the revolutionary leaders, in reality the goals of the revolutions were driven largely by mercantilist demands and were closely interwoven - political self-government, rejection of the *ancien regime*', and in the case of the American Revolution, free trade and escaping their debts to English merchants.[38] Nevertheless, the rhetorical framing of the revolutions – the idea of a link between the people and the sovereign, and that the consent of the governed should be based upon a respect for individual choice - was a dominant feature of both revolutions. The American Declaration of 1776, by which the thirteen British colonies declared their independence citing the "repeated injuries and

35 Treaty of Kutchuk-Kainardji, July 21, 1774, M.S. Anderson (ed.), *Documents of Modern History: The Great Powers and the Near East 1774–1923* (London: Edward Arnold, 1970), 9–14 quoted in Fabry (2010: 25).

36 Steven Havn, 'Slave Rebellions and Mutinies Shaped the Age of Revolution', *Boston Review*, April 23, 2021.

37 L. Huberman, *Man's Worldy Goods* (New York: Monthly Review Press, 1936), 137.

38 See Joan Hoff "From Sarajevo to Sarajevo" in Michael Hogan (ed), *The Ambiguous Legacy: US Foreign Relations in the America Century* (Cambridge: CUP, 1999).

usurpations"[39] committed by the Crown, and the French Declaration of the Rights and Man and Citizen of 1789, each sought to establish concrete legal meaning to the abstract philosophical concept of natural rights. In the case of America, the doctrine of popular sovereignty is seen to facilitate the legal transfer of sovereignty from the British Crown to the people of the American colonies.[40] Indeed, the view of sovereignty passing to the people and from them to the states were confirmed in such early American law cases as *Penhallow* v. *Doane,*[41] *Ware* v. *Hylton*[42] and *Chisholm's Executors* v. *Georgia.*[43]

This rupture in sovereignty as a space within which to assert a claim to national independence becomes of particular importance in later legal constructions of self-determination. Although, as Joan Hoff writes, the normative concept of self-determination in the context of the American Revolution had little to do with the evolution of domestic democracy and the creation of new rights and freedoms, and everything to do with providing a its leaders with "a domestic and foreign policy image to assert their claims to independence."[44] It is

39 'By declaring that "these United Colonies are ... Free and Independent States [and] ... have the full power to levy war, conclude peace, contract alliances, establish commerce, and do all other acts and things which Independent States may of right do," [Declaration of Independence §35] the Declaration announced America's intention to be included within the family of nations. The Declaration was, essentially and legally, an assertion of sovereignty constituted by the law of nations as much as a political instrument to separate from England.... American intellectuals, grounded in the philosophies of the day, viewed the law of nations as constituting sovereignty.' (D. Sylvester, "International Law as Sword or Shield? Early American Foreign Policy and the Law of Nations," 32 *New York University Journal of International Law and Politics* 1 (1999), 9–10.

40 The depiction of the Revolution as an act of sovereignty passing from England to the people of the colonies is also depicted in Story's commentary of the Declaration of Independence: "It was emphatically the act of the whole people of the united colonies, by the instrumentality of their representatives, chosen for that among other purposes.... It was an act of original, inherent sovereignty by the people themselves, resulting from their right to change the form of government, and to institute a new one, whenever necessary for their safety and happiness... It was ... the achievement of the whole for the benefit of the whole. The people of the united colonies made the united colonies free and independent States, and absolved them from all allegiance to the British crown. The Declaration of Independence has accordingly always been treated as an act of paramount and sovereign authority, complete and perfect per se, and ipso facto working an entire dissolution of all political connection with, and allegiance to, Great Britain. And this, not merely as a practical fact, but in a legal and constitutional view of the matter by courts of justice." *Commentaries on the Constitution of the United States* 250–251 (1891).

41 (1795), 3 Dalil. 53 (per Patterson and Iredell JJ.).

42 (1796), 3 DalI. 199 (per Chase J.).

43 (1793), 2 Dali. 419 (*per* Jay C.J.)

44 Joan Hoff "From Sarajevo to Sarajevo" in Michael Hogan (ed.), *The Ambiguous Legacy: US Foreign Relations in the America Century* (Cambridge: CUP, 1999) 199.

perhaps telling, as Howard Zinn notes, that while the American revolutionaries "were moved by the militancy of slaves in the 1770s to attack slavery as they expanded the arguments for human freedom," the fear of slave rebellions on their own shores was listed amongst the crimes of King George, declaring that he had "excited domestic insurrections amongst us."[45] Nor were the rights of man upon which the revolution were based extended to slaves within the new United States. Furthermore, as Bernard Lewis notes, the claim that the American Revolution was the first great movement against anti-imperialism also falls flat, given that "the colonized in the U.S. were the Native Americans, not British settlers" and that the American Revolution was engineered and fought "not by Native American nationalists but by British settlers, and, far from being a victory against colonialism, it represented colonialism's ultimate triumph—the English in North America succeeded in colonizing the land so thoroughly that they no longer needed the support of the mother country."[46]

In contrast to the American Revolution, the new liberal order installed by the French Revolution was underpinned by the idea of the 'nation,' which was to become the central foundation for claims to political legitimacy and territorial authority in the coming century.[47] In the words of Abbé Sieyès: "The Nation exists before all things and is the origin of all. Its will is always legal, it is the law itself…"[48] The French revolutionaries furthered the American application of the sovereignty discourse but focussed its effects internally as a means of consolidating the new republic. The nation was affirmed as the holder of sovereignty, allowing the National Assembly to claim the right to exercise sovereignty on behalf of the nation, as the nation's authentic representative. By equating the French people with the nation, revolutionary leaders sought to

---

45 Howard Zinn, *A People's History of the United States 1492-Present* (New York: Harper Collins, 1995) 72.

46 Bernard Lewis, "The Revolt of Islam," *The New Yorker*, 19 November 2001, p. 54. Quoted in Ebere Nwaubani, "The United States and the Liquidation of Colonial Rule in Tropical Africa 1941–1963" 43 *Cahiers d'Etudes Africaines* (2003) 505–552. Similarly, he notes "the claim by Anglo-America that they were the first to win independence from British rule would have been analogous to Ian Smith and his kinsmen in then Rhodesia asserting that their unilateral declaration of independence in 1965 was intended to end British colonial rule in the territory."

47 As the Declaration states in article III: "The principle of sovereignty resides essentially in the Nation; no body of men, no individual, can exercise authority that does not emanate expressly from it" See *Declaration of the Rights of Man and Citizen*, August 27, 1789, John Hall Stewart (ed.), *A Documentary Survey of the French Revolution* (New York: The Macmillan Company, 1951), 114.

48 Quoted in Alfred Cobban, *The Nation-State and National Self-determination* (London: Collins, 1969), 165.

impede any internal threats to their legitimacy by fostering a sense of national cohesion. In other words, as Chimene Keitner notes "the indivisibility of sovereignty reinforced the indivisibility of the nation, the entity said to possess it…and that indivisibility, that imperative of unity, and that automatic self-legitimation were claimed by the leaders of the (re)constituted state once it had been affirmed, or they had defined it, as national."[49]

During the Napoleonic period, the doctrine of popular sovereignty would also come to figure in the French Revolutionary State's efforts to provide legitimacy and cohesion to its strategy of expansion, through the use of plebiscites as an expression of popular will to decide the population's fate;[50] although more often than not the will of the people was obtained by systematic repression.[51] The use of plebiscites declined by the late nineteenth century, replaced by forceful annexations, as well as the new phenomenon of satellite or puppet states.[52] The controversy surrounding the annexation of Corsica became a high-profile cause for proponents of nationalism, with both Jean-Jacques Rousseau and Edmund Burke declaring the action a violation of national self-determination and comparing the transfer of a nation without its consent to "trees on an estate" or like "herds of cattle, without consulting [the people's] interests or their wishes."[53]

There was also another implication of rise of the nation, one that Edmund Burke was quick to underline in his Reflections on the Revolution.[54] In replacing the traditional structure of dynastic rule, social rights were no longer rooted

---

49 Chimene Keitner, *The Paradoxes of Nationalism: The French Revolution and its Meaning for Contemporary Nation Building*, (New York: State University of New York Press, 2007) 72.

50 Plebiscites were held in the Papal enclaves of Avignon and the Comtat Venaissin, in July 1791, and in the Sardinian territories of Savoy and Nice in September 1792 and January 1793, S. Wambaugh, *A Monograph on Plebiscites with a Collection of Official Documents* (New York: Carnegie Endowment for International Peace, 1920) 33–40.

51 In Belgium the will of the people there for union in spring 1793 was obtained by systematic repression. See Summers (2007: 103).

52 After 1870 there were only two plebiscites: that of Saint Batholemew in 1877 between France and Sweden and the case of the separation of Sweden from Norway in 1905. The annexations included the Prussian take-over of Hanover (1866), Schelswig (1868), and Alsace-Lorraine (1871).

53 Quoted Hoff (1999: 204).

54 Burke's criticised the "abstract principles" of the French Revolution: "It has been the uniform policy of our constitution to claim and assert our liberties, as an entailed inheritance derived to us from our forefathers, and to be transmitted to our posterity; as an estate specially belonging to the people of this kingdom, without any reference whatever to any other more general or prior right." Edmund Burke, "Reflections on the Revolution in France, and on Proceedings in Certain Societies in London Relative to that Event" in *The Works of Edmund Burke* (London: George Bell & Sons., 1876) vol. II, 307.

in social and religious orders, but rather accrued through national citizenship. This congruence between individual and national rights created immediate problems for the vast number of peoples who fell outside the ambit of political and sovereign protection – particularly minorities and stateless persons.[55] The contradictions and exclusionary dynamics of political citizenship, linked both to racial and ethnic hierarchies, was nowhere more evident than in the United States, where African American subjects were denied civic rights and participation.[56] As Hannah Arendt concluded, "the whole question of human rights was quickly and inextricably blended with the question of national emancipation; only the emancipated sovereignty of the people, of one's own people, seemed to be able to ensure them."[57] The lack of national rights became synonymous with the lack of individual rights, and with more and more groups excluded from rights protection, demands for independence only grew.[58]

## 3 National Self-Determination, Imperial Expansion and the Civilizing Mission

The rise of 'principle of nationality' began to alter notions of state legitimacy, raising the link between nationality, popular sovereignty and territorial authority, and coalescing into a new rhetorical framing: *Selbstbestimmungsrecht.*[59] Growing demands for national emancipation and the establishment of new nation-states was to transform the European continent between 1830 and 1878. However, several other interrelated processes during the nineteenth century were to highlight the ideological and political limits of the new standard of

55 Hannah Arendt, *The Origins of Totalitarianism* (George Allen & Unwin, London, 1958) 292.

56 Getachew (2019: 20).

57 Arendt (1958: 293).

58 *Ibid.*

59 See e.g. Johann Kaspar Bluntschli: "This is the basis of nationality as a practical principle in politics; it is not content with the State protecting national language, custom, and culture, but demands that the State itself should become national. Absolutely stated, it comes to this: Every People has a call and a right to form a State. As mankind is divided into a number of Peoples, the world must be divided into the same number of States." J. K. Bluntschli, *The Theory of the State* (Oxford: Clarendon Press, 1885) 95; Marx and Engels too believed that the establishment of nation-states was a vital step in the historical evolution towards a socialist society: 'Since the proletariat must first of all take political control, raise itself up to be the class of the nation, must constitute itself the nation, it is still nationalistic, even if not at all in the bourgeois sense of the term' see Eric Hobsbawm, 'Marx, Engels and Politics', in E. J. Hobsbawm (ed.) *The History of Marxism: Volume One: Marxism in Marx's Day* (Bloomington: Indiana University Press 1982), 249.

territorial organisation and the inequality of national rights that lay at its core: the rise of emancipation of the American colonies, imperial expansion in Africa, and the rise of theories of racial superiority.

As Martti Koskennemi explains, the role of nationalism as a consolidating factor for territorial states also rose in parallel to the development of the industrial state.[60] According to Ernest Gellner, the increasing deatomization of the industrial society due to social mobility and the demands of industrial economy necessitated the introduction of new strategies of social cohesion and internal consolidation – which had not been necessary in the agrarian state.[61] National identity – based primarily on language and ethnicity, was seen as the basis for new forms of solidarity and political coherence – and the ultimate source of representative authority.[62] Moreover, this shared identity was coalescing in the nation-state was seen to be the most effective basis for representative government – and indeed for satisfying the purpose of government itself.[63] Without a national character," argued Francis Lieber, "States cannot obtain that longevity and continuity of political society which is necessary for our progress."[64] Unification of national groups into their "own" nation states therefore became one of the key drivers of statehood.

Around this time, the term *Selbstbestimmungsrecht* attained prominence in the work of German nationalists.[65] Originating in the work of Immanuel Kant, the term was grounded in an individual attainment of reason, or as Kant puts its "knowledge of himself through self-determination in space and time."[66] Later in the writings of Johann Gottlieb Fichte, like his contemporary

60 Koskenniemi (1993: 251).

61 Ernest Gellner, *Nations and Nationalism* (Oxford: Basil Blackwell 1983) 10–11.

62 However, as Eric Hobsbawm has shown, many of the emerging national identities of the nineteenth century were carefully crafted by national elites to elicit popular support. Eric Hobsbawm, *Nations and Nationalism Since 1780: Programme, Myth, Reality* (Cambridge: CUP, 1990) 24–31.

63 As John Stuart Mill noted in his work Considerations on Representative Government: "Free institutions are next to impossible in a country made up of different nationalities. Among a people without fellow feeling, especially if they read and speak different languages, the united public opinion, necessary for the working of representative government, cannot exist" J. S. Mill, "Representative Government" in *Utilitarianism, Liberty, Representative Government* (London: J. M. Dent & Sons 1954) at 361.

64 Francis Lieber, *Fragments of Political Science on Nationalism and Inter-Nationalism* (New York: Charles Scribner & Co., 1868) 22.

65 Eric D. Weitz, 'Self-Determination: How a German Enlightenment Idea Became the Slogan of National Liberation and a Human Right', *The American Historical Review*, 120 (2), (2015) 462–496, 464.

66 Immanuel Kant, "Aus dem Nachlaß, April 1800–Februar 1803," VII. Konvolut, VI. Bogen, 4. Seite, in Karsten Worm and Susanne Boeck, eds., *Kant im Kontext II: Werke, Briefwechsel*

Giuseppe Mazzini, the possibility of the self-determination of the individual was linked to that of the nation. An individual, Fichte asserted, only becomes self-determining in conjunction with others – his 'people' – it was therefore only through national self-determination – and thereby the attainment of statehood – that this collective destiny could be satisfied.[67] The inherent tensions between the individual and the group in the formulation were, however, largely sidelined in Fichte and Manzzini's work. As Eric D Weitz notes, "in all their writings, they sailed over the intrinsic tensions between individual and group rights and the difficult problem of what to do with non-nationals who lived within the borders of the new national state."[68] Nor were the rights of self-determination to be extended to all within the political community. On the subject of the women's equal rights, for example, Fichte argued that women's capacity for self-determination extended only to freely entering into a marriage of her choice, after which time her husband self-determined for her. "The husband represents her entirely, from the state's point of view, she is completely annihilated by her marriage … In the eyes of the state, her husband becomes her guarantee and her legal guardian; in all things, he lives out her public life, and she retains only a domestic life."[69] A woman, he continued "cannot even think about exercising her rights directly on her own."[70]

While this collectivist understanding of self-determination would not attain broader rhetorical prominence until the turn of the twentieth century, emergent nationalist rhetoric began to take hold and a series of revolutions followed throughout Central and Eastern Europe in 1848–49, as ethno-national groups began to makes demands for emancipation from imperial regimes.[71] While these movements were largely unsuccessful, claims to national self-determination led to the creation of the states of Italy, Germany and Hungary. "We will not attempt any alliances with kings" wrote Giuseppe Mazzini in 1832, shortly after forming the "Young Italy" movement for independence and Italian unification, "we will only deal with other peoples, never with kings."[72] The transformative impact of nationalism was described by Fredriech von Gentz:

---

*und Nachlaß. Komplettausgabe* (CD-ROM, Berlin, 2003).

67 Weitz (2015: 469–470).

68 *Ibid.*

69 G. Fichte, *Foundations of Natural Right: According to the Principles of the "Wissenschaftslehre"*(1796), ed. Frederick Neuhouser, trans. Michael Baur (Cambridge, CUP 2000). Quoted in Weitz (2015: 476).

70 *Ibid.*

71 Arendt (1958: 232).

72 Giuseppe Mazzini, "On the Superiority of Representative Government", in S Recchia and N Urbinati (eds.), *A Cosmopolitanism of Nations: Giuseppe Mazzini's Writing on Democracy,*

> The interior of all European countries without exception is wracked by a burning fever, companion or forerunner of the most violent convulsions the civilized world as known since the end of the Roman empire. It is struggle, it is war to the death between old and new ways, between the old and the new social order[73]

Within the growing socialist movement, self-determination was also emerging as a central political idea. In his *Critique of Hegel's Philosophy of Right* (1843) Karl Marx proposes self-determination as a synonym for collective autonomy, with the "people" as its source. In Marx's eyes, the crystallization of national consciousnesses would pave the way for the overthrowal of empire, both within Europe and in the colonies, which would in turn create the conditions for the adoption of international socialism.[74] As Weitz explains "Marx and Engels leapt with enthusiasm at the signs of burgeoning national movements—the Irish against the English, the Poles against the Russians, the Italians against the Habsburg Empire."[75] In 1896, the Socialist International included an article on "self-determination for all peoples" within its program. This position was not without its critics, however. Rosa Luxembourg criticized the nationalist platform, arguing that efforts to forge emancipatory connections across borders could be derailed if national independence became the sole objective of self-determination.[76] The practical contradictions of such an approach could not be satisfied – not least how could the great national and ethnic diversity of Europe be neatly divided into political units – who could be said to constitute the nation? And indeed, rising national consciousnesses also rose in parallel

*Nation Building and International Relations* (Princeton: Princeton University Press, 2009) 43–44.

73 Quoted in Mark Mazower, *Governing the World: The History of an Idea*, (New York: Penguin, 2012) 271.

74 Weitz (2015: 481).

75 Weitz (2015: 482).

76 According to Luxemburg's account of the contradiction national independence and anti-capitalist struggle using the example of her native Poland, see Deborah Whitehall 'A Rival History of Self-Determination', *EJIL* 27(3) (2016) 719–743.
"In order to win independence for Poland, the Polish proletariat would not only have to break the grip of the three most powerful governments in Europe but would also have to be strong enough to overcome the material conditions of existence of its own bourgeoisie. In other words, despite its position as an enslaved class, it would have to take the position of a ruling class at the same time and to use its rule to create a new class state, which, in turn, would be the instrument of its further oppression." Quoted in Deborah Whitehall 'A Rival History of Self-Determination', EJIL 27(3) (2016) 719–743 at 727.

to increased national and ethnic tensions and inevitably conflict. The model of the nation and the correlation between the boundaries of the nation and the state could rarely be satisfied in practice, inevitably creating new minority enclaves which led to more tensions.[77] By the time of the Balkan Wars of 1912, ethnic cleansing had emerged as a deliberate military strategy in the pursuit of a homogenous nation state.

Outside the European content, however, it was a different story altogether, where the imperial project had become re-oriented around the notion of the civilizing mission. For many European intellectuals, including Mazzini and John Stuart Mill, the appeal to self-government did not extend to people who were not 'ready' or 'advanced' enough for self-rule.[78] Mazzini argued that Italy, once free, should acquire colonies of its own, in order to participate in "the great civilising mission suggested by our times" and he recommended that it "invade and colonise the Tunisian lands when the opportunity presents itself."[79] From the mid-nineteenth century onwards the growth of European empires had brought more than 450 million people in Africa and Asia under direct colonial rule. This rapid expansion, and the conflicts that inevitably followed over territorial control and conquest, meant that by the end of the nineteenth century, international law was forced to seek a common framework to resolve them.[80]

By this time the rise of positivist ideas of international law led to increasing systematization of legal regimes and a re-evaluation of classical ideas, including notions of sovereignty. In opposition to the earlier idea of a natural law universal legal order, the new positivist incarnation with the nation state at its core, claimed that international law was the exclusive province of civilized societies – the "family of nations."[81] For positivists sovereignty came primarily to imply control over territory. As Lawrence states:

> International Law regards states as political units possessed of proprietary rights over definite portions of the earth's surface. So entirely is its conception of a state bound up with the notion of territorial possession

---

77 Arendt (1958: 233).

78 See e.g. Duncan Bell, "John Stuart Mill on Colonies" *Political Theory* 38 (1) (2009): 36–64.

79 Giuseppe Mazzini, "On the Superiority of Representative Government," in S Recchia and N Urbinati (eds) *A Cosmopolitanism of Nations: Giuseppe Mazzini's Writing on Democracy, Nation Building and International Relations* (Princeton: Princeton University Press, 2009) 28.

80 William Grewe, *The Epochs of International Law* (Berlin: Walter de Gruyter, 2000), 295.

81 Anghie (2005: 27).

> that it would be impossible for a nomadic tribe, even if highly organised and civilized, to come under its provisions.[82]

Territorial control, came to be the defining quality of the sovereign. The problem of colonial powers was that many non-European states could easily fulfil this criterion.[83] Therefore, a new qualifying demand was added – the standards of civilization; a standard that would give rise to a new hierarchical ordering of sovereignty.[84] As Lauren Benton explains: "At the top were assumed to stand the civilized – Europeans, or former European settler colonies. Below them stood 'barbaric' powers like the Ottomans and the Chinese that had an institutional history and some state capacity. At the bottom were the 'savage' peoples of Africa and the Pacific."[85] As Lawrence commented in 1895:

> there are many communities outside the sphere of International Law, though they are independent states. They neither grant to others, nor claim for themselves the strict observance of its rules. Justice and humanity should be scrupulously adhered to in all dealings with them, but they are not fit subjects for the application of legal technicalities. It would, for instance, be absurd to expect the king of Dahomey to establish a Prize Court, or to require the dwarfs of the central African forest to receive a permanent diplomatic mission.[86]

This system of differentiated sovereign hierarchies manifested itself in the distinctions between States enjoying full membership and those enjoying merely partial membership in the family of nations with the attendant rights and powers.[87] To gain full membership of to the family of nations, moreover,

82 T. J. Lawrence, *The Principles of International Law* (Boston DC: Heath and Co, 1895) 136.

83 As Alexandrowicz points out: "All the major communities in India as well as elsewhere in the East Indies were politically organised; they were governed by their Sovereigns, they had their legal systems and lived according to centuries-old cultural traditions." C.H. Alexandowitz, *An Introduction to the History of the Law of Nations in the East Indies* (Oxford: Clarendon Press, 1967) 14.

84 Anghie (2005: 27).

85 See Lauren Benton, 'From International Law to Imperial Constitutions: The Problems of Quasi-Sovereignty', *Law and History Review* 26(3) (2008) 595–619 at 598.

86 Lawrence (1895: 58).

87 See Henry Wheaton, *Elements of International Law* ([1866] Oxford: Clarendon Press, 1936); Lassa Oppenheim, *International Law: A Treatise* (London: Longmans, Green & Co. 1905).

was dependent upon States demonstrating the hallmarks of 'civilization' in the European optic.[88]

This division would also become central to the expansionist practices of the European nation states. Territories unable to satisfy the criteria of civilization were categorized as terra nullius and susceptible to territorial acquisition. While denounced as a "self-serving myth,"[89] the idea of the "civilizing mission" came to underpin colonial expansion.[90] According to Joseph Hornung, a Swiss lawyer, civilized states were to accept "the hegemony and trusteeship of the strong… in the interests of the weak" and to this end, Hornung continued, colonialism was justified.[91] This joined other legal modes of of acquisition of territory under classical international law including the "discovery" doctrine as affirmed in an 1823 US Supreme Court decision.[92] The core of the decision was the "discovery" doctrine gave rights of ownership to the European sovereigns who "discovered" the land and converted the indigenous owners into tenants.

One imperial region where ideas of national self-determination were able to pave the way for independence, as Mikulas Fabry has shown, was Central and South America.[93] Between 1810 and 1830 the birth of twelve new countries was linked, at least tangentially, to the language of self-determination. Venezuela's proclamation of independence, was made under "the authority held from the virtuous inhabitants of Venezuela"[94] The Declaration of Independence of the

---

88 See John Westlake. *Chapters on the Principles of International Law* (Cambridge: CUP, 1894). 141–3.

89 During the Napoleonic Wars, the French philosopher Charles Fourier denounced civilization as a self-serving myth and called for philosophers to treat all mankind equally.

90 For the discussion of the 'civilizing mission' claim of colonial administrations during the 19th century, see: Lauren A Benton, *Law and Colonial Cultures: Legal Regimes in World History, 1400–1900* (Cambridge: CUP, 2002); Jennifer Pitts, *A Turn to Empire: The Rise of Imperial Liberalism in Britain and France* (Princeton: Princeton University Press 2006); Josep Maria Fradera, *The Imperial Nation: Citizens and Subjects in the British, French, Spanish, and American Empires* (Princeton: Princeton University Press 2018). On the lineage of the 'civilizing mission', see: Anthony Pagden, *Lords of All the World: Ideologies of Empire in Spain, Britain and France c.1500–c.1800* (New Haven Yale University Press 1995); Jürgen Osterhammel, Europe, the 'West' and the Civilizing Mission (German Historical Inst 2006).

91 Joseph Hornung "Civilises et barbares" (1885) as analyzed in Martti Koskenniemi, *The Gentle Civilizer of Nations: The Rise and Fall of International Law, 1870–1960* (Cambridge: CUP, 2002) 129–30.

92 Johnson v. M'Intosh, 1 U.S. (8 Wheat.) 543 (1823).

93 Miklas Fabry, *Recognizing States* (Oxford: OUP, 2010) Chapter 2.

94 See *Declaration of Independence of the Confederated Provinces of Venezuela*, July 5, 1811, BFSP, Vol. 1, part 2, pp. 1108–13. On the influence of the *US Declaration of Independence*, see also David Armitage, *The Declaration of Independence: A Global History* (Cambridge: Harvard University Press, 2007) 118–22.

United Provinces of the Rio de la Plata was anchored in "the unanimous will of the people," Peru's in "the general will," and Guatemala's in "the general wish of the people of Guatemala." Chile's proclamation stated that the citizens had in "the first act of a free people" irrevocably consented to Chile being "a free, independent and sovereign state." The deputies of Bolivia's parliament heralded independence "in the name and absolute authority of their worthy electors."[95] The creation of new states also presented many practical problems – particularly over territorial division. To prevent the rise of multiple, conflicting claims to territory, the leaders of the newly formed republics gradually agreed to accept all political communities that managed to establish themselves *de facto* within the administrative divisions drawn by the Spanish crown.[96] The principle of *uti possidetis juris* was applied – derived from Roman property law – meaning "as you possess, so you may possess" ensuring that new states were to inherit whatever borders they had under colonial law and were not entitled to territory beyond them.[97] In addition, recognition practices surrounding the new states were made contingent on a number of conditions falling under the 'standard of civilization' rubric, most notably abolition of the slave trade.[98] Thus while colonial territories could gain de facto independence, the emerging international legal order ultimately conditioned the success of such action through recognition. The influence of geopolitical concerns in the process of recognition has also been underlined. Adam Watson for instance argued that:

> after the Napoleonic Wars Britain actively supported the independence of Latin America: both for economic reasons, in order to open the doors

---

95 In addition, the famous sentence in Art. 3 of the 1789 Declaration of the Rights of Man and the Citizen – "sovereignty resides essentially in the nation" – can be found, either verbatim or slightly altered, in the early constitutional documents of Venezuela, the United Provinces of the Rio de la Plata, Chile, Colombia, Peru, Mexico, Bolivia, and Uruguay. References to "the rights of the man and the citizen" were inserted into the constitutions of Guatemala and the Dominican Republic. All of these constitutions then entrenched popular representation as one of the main principles of their government. See BFSP, Vols. 6 (1816–19), 8 (1820/1), 9 (1821/2), 10 (1822/3), 11 (1823/4), 13 (1825/6), and 14 (1826/7).

96 See Santiago Torres Bernárdez, "The *Uti Possidetis Juris* Principle in Historical Perspective," in Konrad Ginther et al., *Völkerrecht zwischen Normativen Anspruch und Politischer Realität* (Berlin: Duncker & Humblot, 1994) 417, 424.

97 Fabry (2010: 51). For a detailed description of how the advent of *uti possidetis juris* in Latin America undermined the right of conquest, see Sharon Korman, *The Right of Conquest: The Acquisition of Territory by Force in International Law and Practice* (Oxford: Clarendon Press, 1996), 234–8.

98 George Canning to Henry Chamberlain (Confidential), January 12, 1825, Webster, *Britain and the Independence of Latin America,* Vol. 1, p. 253.

> of that continent to what was then the world's most expansive economy, and for strategic reasons, in order to establish new and supposedly democratic states there to balance what were considered in London the reactionary tendencies of the Holy Alliance.[99]

By the late nineteenth century, the processes of imperial expansion had reached their peak, underpinned by new racial theories of hierarchy.[100] The "colour-line" as W.E.B Du Bois dubbed it expanded racial segregation and domination from a domestic to a global scale and was central to the rapid expansion of colonialism in Africa.[101] The 1885 Berlin Conference framed the scramble for Africa in terms of the need to "initiate the indigenous populations into the advantage of civilization," and "to regulate the conditions most favourable to the development of trade and civilization in certain regions of Africa."[102] The result was the removal of any existing forms of African autonomy and self-governance and the consecration of largely arbitrary colonial boundaries. Within less than two decades, British colonial possessions increased by 4.5 million square miles and 66 million inhabitants, the French nation gained 3.5 million square miles and 26 million people, the Germans won a new empire of a million square miles and 13 million natives, and Belgium through her king acquired 900,000 square miles with 8.5 million population.[103] By the beginning of the twentieth century almost half the globe was divided amongst the powers of Europe. However, as Andrew Hurrell notes, "the successful development of empire, however, carried with it the seeds of its own destruction."[104] Rising demands to dismantle these Empires, would see the expansion of self-determination into an international political and legal principle, and radically alter the nature of international society.

---

99 Adam Watson, *The Evolution of International Society*, (London: Routledge, 1992) 266.

100 Getachew (2019: 22).

101 W.E.B Du Bois "To the Nations of the World" in *W.E.B. Du Bois: A Reader*., ed. David Levering Lewis (New York: Henry Holt, 1995) 639.

102 'General Act of the Berlin Conference on West Africa', 26 February 1885. At http://african-history.about.com/od/eracolonialism/l/bl-BerlinAct1885.htm.
See Duncan Hall, *Mandates, Dependencies and Trusteeship* (Carnegie Endowment Fund for International Peace, Washington, 1948) 103.

103 These figures are quoted by Carlton J. H. Hayes, *A Generation of Materialism*, (New York: Harper and Brothers 1941) 237.

104 Hurrell (2007: 276).

CHAPTER 2

# Renegotiating Sovereignty in the Interwar Period

By the dawn of the First World War the saturation of imperial hierarchies had seemingly reached their breaking point. In Europe, the conflicts sparked by fractious national and ethnic groups had risen to a crescendo, while critics of empire such as Vladimir Lenin condemned "the barbarous policy of bourgeois civilization," calling for an end to imperial exploitation.[1] In a war essentially fought over empire, therefore, self-determination emerged as a political factor of great strategic value for challenging existing territorial arrangements, and, as the war progressed, as a means of propagating new visions of sovereignty and political legitimacy in the post-war international order. As we have seen in the previous chapter, self-determination had emerged from its intellectual origins in early enlightenment thought to a broadly defined political justification for national emancipation and sovereign rights. These intellectual and conceptual roots were to give the idea a legitimacy (and a resonance) that few other political ideas could claim. The fact that the meaning and scope of self-determination were hardly defined was not problematic; on the contrary, its wide appeal was deeply intertwined with its conceptual ambiguity.

As this chapter will explore, this period saw the emergence of self-determination as a broader normative value in discussions of the state system, as well as its political appropriation of self-determination by different actors in the pursuit of a number of political and normative causes; a process which became an important precursor to the increasing circulation and resignification of self-determination in the anti-colonial project. Legally, self-determination would also emerge from this period as a strategic tool to challenge positivist ideas of unfettered international legal sovereign authority and reconstruct the juridical state, which would in its own way enable for the radical reconstruction of the international order after World War II. Rhetorically, the many meanings of self-determination that would emerge from this period in the hands of different actors, would highlight the discursive and political malleability of the principle.

For Lenin self-determination contained a revolutionary clarion call for dismantling "imperialist" nations; a cause that was also inextricably bound up

1 V. I. Lenin, "Declaration of Rights of the Working and Exploited People," in *Collected Works* (Moscow: Foreign Languages Publishing, 1946) vol. 26 at 424.

 | DOI:10.1163/9789004479197_004

with the struggle for class solidarity.[2] The Soviet leader claimed that the desire for national self-determination was a worldwide phenomenon that European imperialists attempted to suppress. It was imperative, Lenin argued, that socialist ideals of self-determination look "towards East, towards Asia, Africa, and the colonies, where this movement is a thing of the present and the future."[3] Independent nationhood, he argued, was to play a crucial role in the process of socialist development. It is therefore unsurprising that self-determination emerged at the centre of the Bolshevik debate on post-war political reorganisation – couched in the language of revolutionary anti-imperialism and calling for an end to the imperialist state structure.

Against this backdrop of political upheaval and demands for national emancipation on the European continent and abroad, self-determination also rose to prominence in the political rhetoric of the Allied powers, most notably Woodrow Wilson. Wilson's vision of a post-war order was one in which national self-determination would replace "decadent, violent power-politics with simple, pacific, and rational first principles."[4] In Wilson's new liberal international order, state power would be superseded by nationality as the core principle of political legitimacy. "Self-determination is not a mere phrase but an imperative principle of action", Wilson opined in his address to Congress in early 1918.[5] Wilson's recalibrated sovereign statehood elevated ideas of community and national identity, determined largely by religious and linguistic characteristics as the new principle of political organization, in order to ensure lasting peace and order. The idea that sovereignty was something that inhered in a 'people' rather than something imposed externally, was in many ways a revolutionary proposal.

Like previous appeals to self-determination in the eighteenth and nineteenth centuries, however, its application was met with immediate conditioning. Though the League upheld the independence of the newly established

2 V. I. Lenin, "The Right of Nations to Self-Determination" in V. I. Lenin, Collected Works (Moscow: Foreign Languages Publishing, 1946) vol. 1, pp. 564–611 at 572. See Bill Bowring, "Burial and Resurrection: Karl Renner's controversial influence on the "National Question" in Russia," in E. Nimni (ed.), *National-Cultural Autonomy and its Contemporary Critics* (London: Routledge, 2005).

3 V. I. Lenin, "The Revolutionary Proletariat and the Right of Nations to Self-Determination" in V. I. Lenin, Collected Works (Moscow: Foreign Languages Publishing, 1946) vol. 1 407–14 at 407.

4 Nathaniel Berman, *Passion and Ambivalence, Colonialism, Nationalism, and International Law* (Leiden: Martinus Nijhoff, 2012) 128.

5 Woodrow Wilson, "Address to a Joint Session of Congress, February 11, 1918" in The Papers of Woodrow Wilson (PWW), ed. Arthur S Link (Princeton: Princeton University Press, 1984) 46: 318–24, 321.

European nations such as Hungary, Czechoslovakia, and Yugoslavia, overarching diplomatic demands gave way to the elevation of national independence. Population transfers, arbitrary territorial re-organisations and disappointed national aspirations marked the period, and self-determination was glaringly absent from the final text of the League of Nations Covenant. Wilson's new vision of national sovereignty, moreover, did not apply to lands outside Europe. The previous standard of civilization of the previous century was replaced with a mandate system that effectively repackaged European imperialism and the standard of civilization for the post-war climate. This new qualifying standard – fitness for sovereignty – was even extended to independent countries which had been admitted to the League as independent states - Haiti, Ethiopia, and Liberia.[6]

Within classical accounts, this period is largely identified as emblematic of the failure of self-determination to achieve legal status, particularly its inability to transition from Wilson's *Fourteen Points* to the post-war peace treaties of the League of Nations Covenant. The period's nexus to the colonial invocation of self-determination is therefore largely seen as an anomaly, relevant only by reference to the principle's "imperfect"[7] application and failure to achieve judicial status, rather than its impact on shifting ideas of statehood and sovereignty.[8] As I will argue, however, this period is an important precursor to self-determination's legal and political mobilization by anti-colonialist activists to reframe the principle in support of their own cause.[9] Even as Wilson and Jan Smuts, architect of the Mandate system, offered a version of self-determination that was seemingly incompatible with colonial independence,[10] the entanglement of self-determination with new international legal ideas of internal and external sovereignty, particularly in the Mandate system, was to lay the

---

6 For a discussion of the differentiated regimes of sovereignty applied during this time see Rose Parfitt, "Empire des. Negres Blancs: The Hybridity of International Legal Personality in the Abyssinia Crisis of 1935–1936," *Leiden Journal of International Law* 24 (2911) 849–72; Parfitt (2019); Arnulf Becker Lorca, *Mestizo International Law: A Global Intellectual History 1842–1933* (Cambridge: CUP 2014), 277–78.

7 Thomas Franck argues that self-determination "was imperfectly applied" during this time. Thomas Franck, The Power of Legitimacy Among Nations (Oxford: OUP, 1990) 154 and Michla Pomerance refers to the Wilsonian "double standard" Pomerance (1982: at 1–14).

8 Michla Pomerance writes: 'Thus, after conclusion of the Peace Settlement, "self-determination" remained in law essentially what it had been before then a right of revolution, a matter of self-help'. Pomerance (1982: 7).

9 See for instance Manela (2007: 24–37).

10 For an extended discussion of the manner in which Wilson and Smuts sought to neutralize the revolutionary potential of self-determination see Getachew (2019: 40–52).

groundwork for the principle's strategic mobilization after the Second World War. As Nathaniel Berman has argued, the application of self-determination through plebiscites and the minority protection regimes posed a crucial challenge to existing notions of legitimate statehood and of sovereignty, where domestic political structures and state action could be conditioned (in theory at least) by an internationally sanctioned regime.[11] It also opened a key legal space where marginalised groups which had been kept apart from international law, could assert their rights as a matter of international concern and assume limited standing in international society.[12] Self-determination's political malleability, as the broader manner in which self-determination emerged in discussions of state sovereignty and the construction of the juridical state during this period – including by international jurists in the *Aaland Islands* decision – would open up an important legal space from which to challenge the legitimacy of colonial rule in the next.

## 1 Self-Determination as Political Strategy

Throughout the War the revolutionary potential of self-determination as a principle of national emancipation was harnessed by both the Allies and the Central Powers and amongst ethnic groups, who sought to advocate for their independence. Representatives of many national and ethnic groups approached the Allied and Central powers with the hope of obtaining official support – while also hoping to bolster public sympathy for their causes.[13] On 11 April 1918, the 'Congress of Oppressed Nationalities' met in Rome to discuss their common plight. The main achievement of the Congress was the drafting of a joint statement to the Allied War Council, pledging the nationalities present to struggle for the break-up the Austro-Hungarian Empire and for the creation of independent states.[14] However, the Balkan conflicts had also highlighted how demands of national emancipation could quickly become bound up in elements of ethnic cleansing, forced deportation and population

---

11 Nathaniel Berman, "'But the Alternative is Despair': European Nationalism and the Modernist Renewal of International Law" 106 *Harvard Law Review* (1993) 1792–1903.

12 *Ibid.*

13 C.A. Macartney, *National States and National Minorities* (Oxford: OUP, 1938), 179–211.

14 Raymond Pearson, *National Minorities in Eastern Europe, 1848–1945* (London: Macmillan, 1983), 117–189.

exchange.[15] The expulsion and extermination by Turkey of 2 million Armenians in 1915, for example, was largely ignored by the Allied and Central Powers.[16]

The Central Powers lent their support to Irish and Flemish separatists, along with the separatist claims of Lithuania, the Finns and the Baltic provinces.[17] The Allies too proclaimed national independence and self-determination as principle of territorial organisation as one of their war aims.[18] A memorandum issued by the British Foreign Office in 1916 announced that one of the UK's 'chief objects' of the war "is to ensure that all the states of Europe, great and small, shall in the future be in a position to achieve their national development in freedom and security."[19] Tellingly, as Thomas Musgrave notes, they qualified the statement by noting that pledges already made to their allies might be "difficult to reconcile with the claims of nationalities." The Allies had promised substantial territorial concessions to potential allies such as Italy, Romania and Bulgaria in return for military assistance.[20] In 1917 the British Foreign Secretary, Arthur Balfour, in an attempt to rally international Jewish support for the allied cause, also promised a Jewish national home in Palestine.[21]

Building upon earlier socialist pronouncements on self-determination, demands for national emancipation had also assumed a central position in Bolshevik political theory. The Bolshevik articulation of self-determination, however, was directed as a political challenge to existing forms of imperial rule - wherever they occurred. Denouncing World War I as an "imperialist war," Lenin called for an end to both empire and capitalism which were in his eyes two sides of the same coin.[22] For Lenin imperialism was not simply a policy of

15 See Norman Naimark, *Fires of Hatred: Ethnic Cleansing in Twentieth-Century Europe* (Cambridge: Harvard University Press, 2002) 17.

16 Thomas D. Musgrave, *Self-Determination and National Minorities* (Oxford: Clarendon Press, 1997) 15.

17 *Ibid.*

18 *Ibid.*

19 Lloyd George *The Truth About Peace Treaties* (1938) Vol 1. 31 at 32 quoted in Musgrave (1997: 16).

20 *Ibid.*

21 H. W. V. Temperley, *A History of the Peace Conference of Paris* (London: Henry Frowde & Hodder & Stoughton, 1924) vol. VI at 1703.

22 Lenin saw five 'basic features' as central. (1) The concentration of production and capital developed to such a high stage that it created monopolies which play a decisive role in economic life. (2) The merging of bank capital with industrial capital, and the creation, on the basis of this "finance capital", of a financial oligarchy. (3) The export of capital, which has become extremely important, as distinguished from the export of commodities. (4) The formation of international capitalist monopolies which share the world among themselves. (5) The territorial division of the whole world among the greatest

the stronger powers, but a central aspect of capitalism itself.[23] This stemmed from his theory of imperialism whereby the "super-profits" generated from capitalist exploitation outside the national sphere allowed the national ruling class to "...economically bribe the upper strata of 'its' workers..." and divide the proletariat thus causing it to abandon revolutionary ambitions.[24] The liberation of national groups, including those living under colonial rule, to determine their own destiny freely, including a right of secession or autonomy if they so desired, was in Lenin's mind a structured attack against imperialist capitalism. In a 1922 letter to the Soviet Foreign Minister, he wrote that the war had intensified the liberation movement of oppressed and colonial people, arguing that the "right of all people to secession and self-rule" must be recognised.[25]

National self-determination also presented a strategic possibility to elicit support for the Bolsheviks from the various nationalities against Tsarist Russia and its oppressive policies of "russification."[26] As Lenin posited in the years before the Bolshevik Revolution, Tsarist Russia was "a prison of nations," and a socialist revolution based on nationalist and socialist principles was more likely to succeed than one based on socialism alone. Lenin was quick to acknowledge that this might lead to problems, but the newly liberated national entities would be better suited to the evolution of class-consciousness, thereby ultimately stimulating the desire for unification into a single socialist society. Following the revolution, the provisional government expressed an immediate change in policies towards its various nationalities as evidenced by the declaration of 29 March 1917: "the purpose of free Russia [was] not domination over other peoples ... but the establishment of a durable peace on the basis of the self-determination of peoples."[27] The new policy led to declarations of autonomy of a number of ethnic groups: Northern Caucus in May 1917, Ukraine in June 1917 and the Finns in July 1917.[28] Later, on 15 November 1917, the Bolsheviks issued the Declaration on the Rights of People of Russia, which guaranteed "the right of self-determination up to an including the separation and the formation of the independent state, the abolition of all national privileges

---

capitalist powers is completed.' V.I. Lenin, *Imperialism: The Highest State of Capitalism*, (New York: International Publishers, 1939) 89.

23 G. Lukacs, *Lenin: A Study in the Unity of His Thought* (London: New Left Books, 1970) 43–4.

24 V.I. Lenin, *Imperialism: The Highest State of Capitalism*, (New York: International Publishers, 1939) 89.

25 Lenin, *Foreign Policy*, 421 Quoted in Cassese (1993: 16).

26 Musgrave (1997: 19).

27 A. J. Mayer, *Political Origins of the New Diplomacy, 1917–1918* (New Haven: Yale University Press, 1959) 75.

28 Musgrave (1997: 17).

and restrictions, and freedom of national minorities to develop." In the December 1917 Brest-Litovsk treaty, self-determination was incorporated, declaring in Article 3 "to determine the future of these territories (Poland, Courland and Lithuania) in agreement with their population," while Article 6 recognised the independence of Ukraine.

For observers, the Russian Revolution heightened concerns about the spread of revolutionary change throughout Europe. US Secretary of State Robert Lansing, while somewhat sympathetic to the cause of national independence, nevertheless argued that "the necessities of preserving an orderly world require that there should be a national authority with sovereign rights to defend and control the communities within national boundaries."[29] The threat of revolutionary change also hovered over Europe's colonial holdings, with demands for independence emanating from Egypt, India, China and Korea. Against this backdrop, the Western allies turned to an articulation of self-determination as an expression of their own vision of a new liberal democratic international legal order, which would contain the threat of revolution.[30]

In his support for the Allied cause Wilson remarked that the US had entered the war to fight "for liberty, self-government, and the undictated development of all peoples."[31] National aspirations were, in Wilson's words, "to be accorded the utmost satisfaction that can be accorded them without introducing new or perpetuating old elements of discord and antagonisms that would likely in time break the peace of Europe and consequently the world."[32] In January 1918 Wilson delivered his famous *Fourteen Point* plan, in which he laid out his vision of post-war order. While he did not explicitly mention self-determination in the speech, it was clear the principle lay at its core, however it was also a far less revolutionary application he had in mind. With his intellectual roots lying firmly in liberal democratic theory, Wilson's articulation of self-determination, while centred on nationality, was primarily a commitment to the principle of 'the consent of the governed.' "Peoples may now be dominated and governed only by their own consent" he stated in a February 1918 speech before the US Congress. This led to three of the central interlocking elements of his proposed post-war settlement: (1) a scheme whereby identifiable peoples were to be

29 Robert Lansing, *The Peace Negotiations: A Personal Narrative* (Boston: Houghton Mifflin, 1921) 412.

30 Michla Pomerance, "The United States and Self-Determination: Perspectives on the Wilsonian Conception" 70 *American Journal of International Law* (1976) 1–27 at 25.

31 Woodrow Wilson, 'Speech to Congress for a Declaration of War Against Germany', 2 April 1917 [http://www.archives.gov/historical-docs/todays-doc/index.html?dod-date=402].

32 W. Ofuatey-Kodjoe, *The Principle of Self-Determination in International Law.* (New York: Nellen Pub. Co., 1977) 82.

accorded Statehood; (2) the fate of disputed border areas was to be decided by plebiscite; and (3) those ethnic groups too small or too dispersed to be eligible for either course of action were to benefit from the protection of special minorities regimes, supervised by the Council of the new League of Nations.[33] Wilson argued that the readjustment of borders of Italy, Montenegro, Rumania and Serbia should take place according to "clearly defined lines of nationality." While the need for the autonomous development of peoples under the Ottoman and Austro-Hungarian Empires was mentioned in points eleven and twelve.

Unlike Lenin, Wilson was vague about the concreteness of the principle's extension to colonial peoples, and he shied away from any suggestion of an automatic right to independence.[34] For Wilson, the question of the capacity for self-governance was at the core of the question of independence; however, there was also a heavily racialized element to this consideration.[35] On the question of the Philippines, Wilson was in favour of granting independence but only after a suitable period of tutelage, which he considered necessary for a people whose character and constitutional development was not ready for the task of self-government.[36] He noted however, that this would largely be impossible given that "no one can form a community or be wisely subjected to common forms of government who are as diverse and as heterogeneous as the people of the Philippine Islands."[37] Wilson thus extends the right to self-determination to colonial peoples whilst simultaneously suggesting that the full realization of this right was largely impossible; a position that would come to characterize the position adopted in the Mandate System.

While less revolutionary in outlook than Lenin's formulation, Wilson's self-determination nevertheless implied a radical reframing of the underlying logic of the state system, and the link between political legitimacy and the people (at least for some). This new normative proposal for the legitimate units of political authority, posed critical questions for not only the state order, but for

33 Anthony Whelan, "Wilsonian Self-Determination and the Versailles Settlement" 43 *J. C. L. Q.* (1994) 99–115 at 102.

34 Derek Heater, *National Self-Determination: Woodrow Wilson and His Legacy* (New York: St. Martin's Press, 1994) 24–25.

35 For a longer discussion of Wilson's racialized views of self-determination see Getachew who notes that Wilson and Smuts repurposed self-determination "it in ways that supported unequal integration and preserved a structure of racial hierarchy within the league" (2019: 40, Chapter 2).

36 *Ibid.*

37 Woodrow Wilson, 'The Ideals of America', in *The Papers of Woodrow Wilson*, Arthur S Link (ed.) (Princeton: Princeton University Press, 1972) 225.

the existence of imperial rule. Berman locates Wilsonian self-determination within the liberal national tradition which "assumed that each nationality should be a political unit under an independent constitutional government which would put an end to despotism, aristocracy, and ecclesiastical influence, and assure to every citizen the broadest practicable exercise of personal liberty, political, economic, religious and educational… [It] assumed, moreover, that each liberal national state in serving its true interests and those of its citizens would be serving the true interests of humanity at large and that 'true interests' could best be served by national policies of freetrade, anti-militarism, anti-imperialism, and international co-operation and peace."[38] Wilson's draft for the Covenant of the League of Nations appealed heavily to the liberal democratic roots of self-determination, providing:

> The Contracting Parties unite in guaranteeing to each other political independence and territorial integrity but it is understood between them that such territorial arrangements, if any, as may in future become necessary by reason of changes in present racial and political relationships, pursuant to the principle of self-determination and also such territorial adjustments as may in the judgment of three-fourths of the delegates be demanded by the welfare and manifest interest of the people concerned, may be effected if agreeable to those peoples; and that territorial changes may in equity involve material compensation. The Contracting Powers accept without reservation the principle that the peace of the world is superior in importance to every question of political jurisdiction or boundary.[39]

Wilson's appeal to self-determination thus saw the principle as a just way to achieve peace in a world of discord and violence. It also raised the concerns of many, not least Robert Lansing, who noted that the phrase was "loaded with dynamite,"[40] particularly its threat to European colonial rule. "When the President talks of 'self-determination' what unit has he in mind? Does he mean a race, a territorial area, or a community? … The more I think about the President's declaration as to the right of 'self-determination,' the more convinced

38 Berman quoting *Carlton J.H. Hayes, The Historical Evolution of Modern Nationalism* 120–163 (1931) (discussing liberal nationalism) at 41.

39 See KJ Partsch, 'Fundamental Principles of Human Rights: Self-Determination, Equality and Non-Discrimination' quoted in Karel Vasak and Philip Alston, 1. *The International Dimensions of Human Rights* (Westport: Greenview Press, 1982) 63.

40 Robert Lansing, *The Peace Negotiations: A Personal Narrative* (Boston: Houghton Mifflin, 1921) 97.

I am of the danger of putting such ideas into the minds of certain races. It is bound to be the basis of impossible demands on the Peace Conference and create trouble in many lands. What effect will it have on the Irish, the Indians, the Egyptians, and the nationalists among the Boers? Will it not breed discontent, disorder and rebellion?"[41] Wilson later conceded that he had not foreseen the problematic nature of his promise of self-determination: "When I gave utterance to those words ('that all nations had a right to self-determination') I said them without the knowledge that nationalities existed, which are coming to us day after day... You do not know and cannot appreciate the anxieties that I have experienced as the result of many millions of people having their hopes raised by what I have said."[42] Ultimately, however, the entire provision was dropped; self-determination was not mentioned in the League Covenants; and the "heart of the Covenant," Article 10, referred only to the necessity of respecting and preserving "as against external aggression the territorial integrity and existing political independence of all Members of the League. The decision to omit self-determination in the final Covenant, did not however dampen the claims of the many national groups who had pinned their hopes on Wilson's earlier assertions.

## 2 Post WWI Resettlement and "The New International Law"

When states gathered at Versailles in 1919, the language of self-determination had moved centre stage to become a guiding principle of the post-war settlement. As Eric Weitz sardonically notes, "antiwar socialists, leaders from various belligerent countries, pacifists, and even, before the end of the war, the German occupiers of Eastern Europe all bandied about 'self-determination.'"[43] "The days of the Treaty of Vienna are long past" declared the British Prime Minister, "we can no longer submit the future of European civilization to the arbitrary decisions of a few negotiators striving to secure by chicanery or persuasion the interests of this or that dynasty or nation...government with the consent of the governed must be the basis of any territorial settlement in this

41 Ibid 412.

42 Quoted in H.W. V (ed.) *A History of the Peace Conference of Paris (Six Volumes)*, (London: Henry Frowde & Hodder Stoughton, 1924) 429.

43 Eric D. Weitz, 'Self-Determination: How a German Enlightenment Idea Became the Slogan of National Liberation and a Human Right', *The American Historical Review*, 120 (2), (2015) 462–496.

war."[44] However, it was not clear how both national interests and concerns about world order would be accommodated. As Manley O' Hudson wrote in 1923:

> When President Wilson proclaimed his integral programme, condensed in his fourteen points, and the justice principle for all the peoples and all nationalities, that they have a right to live under identical conditions of freedom and security, be they strong or weak, the war became for millions of combatant men (...) a real crusade for the liberation of oppressed people. Later, by accepting these principles as the base of the armistice, Allied States found themselves morally compelled to undertake a wide project of territorial readjustment that would naturally arouse the most extravagant hopes among numerous European peoples[45]

Despite the lofty rhetoric, it soon became apparent that the conflicting interests of the Allied and Associated Powers, together with the logistical problems of territorial reorganisation would derail this promise to a large extent.[46] Hurst Hannum, commenting on this process notes that "it should be underscored that self-determination in 1919 had little to do with the demands of the peoples concerned, unless those demands were consistent with the geopolitical and strategic interests of the Great Powers."[47]

During discussions a number of different expectations and understandings of self-determination were posited by delegates. The Bolshevik ideal of self-determination as a catalyst for global revolution had largely been superseded by the Wilsonian variety, but glimpses were still present. Post-imperial states, including Japan, questioned the institutional boundaries of self-determination, demanding the recognition of the equality of nations and races in international law.[48] Other states were more reticent. Some supported the application of the principle, although this support was tempered by geopolitical concerns against the shifting power politics of post-war Europe, along with concerns that the principle would create problems within imperial holdings.

---

44 Statement of British War Aims by Prime Minister Lloyd George, January 5, 1918, Scott, *Official Statements of War Aims and Peace Proposals*, 228–9.

45 Quoted in Maja Spanu, *The Idea of Self-Determination: Hierarchy and Order after Empire* (PhD thesis 2014, European University Institute) 69.

46 *Ibid.*

47 Hurst Hannum, *Autonomy. Sovereignty, and Self-Determination: The Accommodation of Conflicting Rights*, rev. ed., (Philadelphia: University of Pennsylvania Press, 1996) 28.

48 Spanu (2014: 10).

Nevertheless, the decision to allow a number of communities to form their own states, and the wider use of plebiscites constituted a significant development in an international system according to Berman, which had "formerly left to sovereign discretion how (and indeed whether) to take into account the wishes of the people."[49] This application of the principle of self-determination in the post-war environment (albeit imperfectly applied), not only offered a broader endorsement of nationalism, but also a major reconsideration of pre-war views regarding sovereignty and political legitimacy.[50] International society now imposed clear expectations on both the constitution of states and the nexus between their political institutions and their populations at the domestic level. Moreover, the creation of minority regimes and protections, critically raised the issue of civic and political rights from a purely internal issue to a matter of international oversight.[51]

The creation of the League of Nations, in the eyes of many inter-war jurists, also posed a direct challenge to the idea of international law as a state centred institution, concerned only with the relations between states – underpinned by the notion of unfettered and primary sovereign authority.[52] Under this system groups and communities who could not could themselves become states (colonies, nations, minorities) were denied any formal international legal status, organised under the notion of international legal personality.[53] The shift towards a broadening of the international community with the creation of the League, along with other international organizations, indicated a step away from this earlier model of "state-centred positivism" towards an international law which reflected more diffuse sources of authority.[54] This was hardly coincidental. For it was, in their optic, precisely this earlier form of sovereign organisation that had led to the events of the First World War.[55] As Benedict

49 Nathaniel Berman, "Modernism, Nationalism, and the Rhetoric of Reconstruction," 4 *Yale Journal of Law & the Humanities* (1992) 351–379 at 366.

50 See, e.g, Frederick C. Hicks, *The New World Order: International Organization, International Law, International Cooperation* (New York: Doubleday, Page & Company 1920).

51 Spanu (2014: 62).

52 Anghie (2005: 126).

53 This position was surmised by Lassa Oppenheim in his classic Treatise of 1905: *The conception of International Persons is derived from the conception of the Law of Nations. As this law is the body of rules which the civilised states consider legally binding in their intercourse, every state which belongs to the civilised states, and is, therefore, a member of the Family of Nations, is an International Person*Oppenheim (1905: 99) quoted in Matthew Craven & Rose Parfitt "Statehood, Self-Determination and Recognition" in Malcolm D. Evans, ed. International Law. (Oxford: OUP, 2018).

54 *Ibid.*

55 Berman (1993: 1802).

Kingsbury points out, inter-war jurists were keenly aware of "the importance in international relations of the links between sovereignty and domestic structures,"[56] and that the form of government within a state had a decisive impact on the peace and stability of the international system.[57] Nationalism was a force to be reckoned with, rather than simply repressed, given, as one commentator put it, it had caused "more destruction than powder and gas."[58] Therefore, while acknowledging the problematic aspects of nationalism, they also realised its necessity in the new international legal order. This process not only saw the widespread use of plebiscites but also included the creation of three internationally administered regions, which imposed demands on the states administrating them: Danzig and Upper Silesia, regions claimed by Poland and Germany; and the Saar, a region claimed by France and Germany.[59]

While in theory the application of the plebiscitary model, and the reorganisation of national boundaries raised the prospect of international law's reconstructed idea of the nation state, linked in some degree to representative authority, in practice this was easier said than done. It became immediately clear that to align the borders of the new states with those of the (ethnic) nations would largely be impossible for historical and demographic reasons. Not only was the idea of the 'nation' a highly subjective one, in most cases the problem of the dispersed and varied nature and identity of most national and ethnic groups in Europe means that making nation and state congruent was "utterly impracticable."[60] For example, in the case of Czechoslovakia, recourse was made to two different interpretations of nationality– historical national identity in the states of Bohemia and Moravia, and ethnic national identity in Austrian Silesia.[61] Strategic concerns also played a major role. The decision to partition the latter with Poland, which led to the creation of large Polish and German minorities, was done on the basis of "strategic necessities and viable statehood" for the newly created state.[62] These minorities were also subject

56 Benedict Kingsbury, 'Sovereignty and Inequality', 9 *European Journal of International Law* (1998) 599 at 608 (referring to judicial decisions and arbitral awards).

57 Anghie (2005: 134).

58 René Johannet, Preface to Louis Le Fur, Races, nationalités, états, at III (1922); quoted in Berman (1993: 1802).

59 The League regime for Upper Silesia was the most complex of these regimes. The region was partitioned between the two states after an 'expert' interpretation of the results of an internationally supervised plebiscite. It was then placed under a fifteen-year international regime designed to ensure the temporary unity of the region, a system overseen by international adjudicatory and administrative bodies.

60 Hobsbawm, (1992: 131–41).

61 Sir Ivor Jennings, *The Approach to Self-Government* (Cambridge: CUP, 1956) 55–6.

62 Franck (1990: 156).

to automatic state denationalization under Article 91 of the Versailles Treaty, stripping them of their German nationality.[63] This debate over the conflicting interpretations of the 'nation' was to play out in several cases before the Permanent Court of International Justice, throughout the 1920s and 30s.[64]

The inconsistencies and seeming arbitrariness of the approach quickly raised the ire of many national groups. The result, Hannah Arendt explained, "was that those peoples to whom states were not conceded, considered the Treaties an arbitrary game which handed out rule to some and servitude to others."[65] Critically, the outcome also left a large number of minorities in the new states.[66] One of the largest minorities to emerge was ethnically German, who were now spread across Poland, Romania and Czechoslovakia. To counter these problems minorities rights and protection regimes were proposed to ensure a balance between ethnic interests and national order.[67] The minority treaties would safeguard the rights of national communities who found themselves geographically cut off from the 'kin State', by requiring the new and expanded states of central Europe to provide civil rights and a certain cultural autonomy to minority groups.[68] This also included "a number of group rights relating to language, education and cultural [*and religious*] institutions." As the PCIJ in the Minority Schools in Albania case explained, the aim of the scheme was:

> [T]o secure for certain elements incorporated in a State, the population of which differs from them in race, language or religion, the possibility of living peacefully alongside that population and co-operating amicably

63 *Treaty of Versailles* art. 91, June 28, 1919.

64 Acquisition of Polish Nationality, Advisory Opinion, 1923 P.C.I.J. (ser. B) No. 7, at 6 (Sept. 15); Greco-Bulgarian "Communities," Advisory Opinion, 1930 P.C.I.J. (ser. B) No. 17, at 4 (July 31).

65 Hannah Arendt, *Imperialism* (New York: Harvest, 1968), 150.

66 James Summers, *Peoples and International Law: How Nationalism and Self-Determination Shape a Contemporary Law of Nations* (Dordrecht: Martinus Nijhoff, 2007) 114.

67 Woodrow Wilson tried unsuccessfully to include an article on minority rights in the League Covenant. Instead, minority protection took the form of a series of separate treaties and declarations centred on the League. The peace treaties of Versailles, St. Germain, Trianion, Neuilly-sur-Seine and Lausanne all contained articles on minority protection. Specific minorities treaties were agreed with Poland, Czechoslovakia, Yugoslavia, Romania, Greece and Lithuania. Bilateral agreements were concluded between Germany and Poland over Upper Silesia, and Sweden and Finland over the Aaland Islands. Moreover, in their accession to the League, Albania, Lithuania, Latvia, Estonia and Iraq made declarations on the protection of minorities. Berman (1988: 368).

68 Claude (1955: 12–30).

> with it, while at the same time preserving the characteristics which distinguish them from the majority, and satisfying the ensuing special needs.[69]

The Court noted that the scheme contained two key and interlocking objectives: first, complete equality between nationals of the State belonging to racial, religious or linguistic minorities and other nationals; and, secondly, "to ensure for the minority elements suitable means for the preservation of their racial peculiarities, their traditions and their national characteristics." These objectives were interlinked, the Court said, arguing that there could be no true equality between the majority and a minority if the latter was deprived of the institutions enabling it to preserve its special characteristics.[70] Signatories were required not only to integrate the guarantees into their domestic legislation, but to give assurance that minority protection would be viewed as an obligation of international interest, under the guarantee of the League of Nations.[71]

While no direct enforcement mechanism was provided for, many inter-war lawyers nevertheless understood the system and its degree of international oversight, in terms of the broader departure from unfettered sovereignty, one in which the political legitimacy of the state would be defined along lines of protection and good treatment of domestic populations.[72] Indeed, numerous delegations at the Paris Peace Conference, in particular those of the successor states of the Empires, were against these specialised treaties, arguing that it was a violation of their national sovereignty. As the president of the Romanian delegation argued: "If minorities realise that the freedoms that they enjoy are

---

69 *Minority Schools in Albania* (Advisory Opinion), PCIJ (1935) Series A/B, No. 64, 17.

70 The System comprised a number of different elements. Special minorities clauses were incorporated in the Peace Treaties concluded with four of the States vanquished in the First World War: Austria; Bulgaria; Hungary, and Turkey. Complete minorities treaties were signed by the Principal Allied Powers, in 1919 and 1920, with five States: Poland (in a Convention with Poland, the Free City of Danzig) also undertook, in 1920, to apply within its territory provisions similar to those of the Polish minorities treaty; Czechoslovakia; Romania; the Serb-Croat-Slovene State; and Greece. Five other new States made appropriate Declarations before the Council of the League of Nations: Albania in 1921; Lithuania in 1922; Latvia in 1923; Estonia in the same year; and Iraq in 1932. In regard to two States, the Minorities System was applied only to certain districts having a special status: Finland, in respect of the Aaland Islands (under a Finnish Declaration before the Council of the League of Nations in 1921); Germany, in respect of Upper Silesia (under a Convention concluded with Poland in 1922.

71 From Helmer Rostling's "Protection des minorités par la Société des Nations," in Revue Internationale de la Croix-Rouge, Year: 4; n. 39; 15 March 1922. 203. section 41, Dossier 7727. R1648. LNA, Geneva.

72 Berman (1992: 351).

guaranteed to them not by the state to which they belong, but by the protection of an external presence, the foundations of the state will be undermined."[73] In this sense, the Minority Treaties can also be understood as offering a new form of sovereign conditioning, one very much in line with previous ideas of sovereign hierarchy. By demanding that newly created states abide by the demands of minority protection, as Maja Spanu has explored, the treaties can also be understood as a new set of criteria for entry into statehood in postwar international society. In other words, as tools of "international disciplining," the treaties would establish the conditions for what good domestic order within the new states should be.[74] These conditions, however, just like in previous periods, were to be decided by the more 'mature' members of international society.

## 3 The Aaland Islands Dispute

That emerging ideas surrounding self-determination, particularly of minority groups, offered a radical reconditioning to both the internal and external constitution of a sovereign state was also evident in the two decisions emanating from the Aaland Islands dispute.[75] The decisions - the first extended legal discussions of self-determination – engaged with questions of both the legitimacy of the plebiscitary model as well as the minority protection scheme.

In the aftermath of the fall of the Russian empire in 1917 and Finland's declaration of independence from Russia, a plebiscite was held by the Aaland islanders expressing their desire to re-join Sweden.[76] The islands' strategic importance to Finland, however, led to a dispute with Sweden, which was submitted to two international commissions, the Commission of Jurists

73 Quoted in Spanu (2014: 80).

74 Spanu (2014: 54). See Also Maja Spanu "The Hierarchical Society: The Politics of Self-Determination and The Constitution of New States after 1919" *European Journal of International Relations, 26* (2), 372–396.

75 For a longer discussion of the case see Berman (1988).

76 James Barros, *The Aland Islands Question: Its Settlement by the League of Nations* (New Haven: Yale University Press, 1968). See also Norma Padelford and K. G. A. Anderson, "The Aaland Islands Question" 33 *American Journal of International Law* (1939) 65–87; Phillip Brown, "The Aaland Islands Question" 15 *American Journal of International Law* (1921) 268–72; Cassese (1995:.27–31); Sarah Wambaugh, *Plebiscites Since the World War with a Collection of Official Documents* (Washington: Carnegie Endowment for International Peace, 1933) vol. 1 at 515–8.

and the Commission of Rapporteurs.[77] The Council first asked the Commission of Jurists whether the dispute was a matter of "domestic jurisdiction" and therefore outside the Council's competence. While Finland had not officially become a state at the time of the referendum, it argued that given that it exercised effective control over the Islands, the rights of domestic jurisdiction barred the Council from making any recommendations for the dispute's resolution. Finding that they could not resolve the competence question without resolving the substance of the dispute, they turned to the question of whether the Islanders had the right to hold a plebiscite in order to decide their political future according to the principle of self-determination.

While reiterating sovereign rights over territory, and that "under normal conditions…International Law leaves entirely to the domestic jurisdiction of the state" the issue of whether a particular group is to be granted the right to "determine its own political fate,"[78] the Jurists found that the League of Nations had jurisdiction because Finland was not definitely constituted as a state when the conflict arose. While sovereignty provides the "essential basis" of law, they note, where it is lacking, that is to say, in cases where states were, "not yet fully formed or… undergoing transformation or dissolution" then the situation becomes "obscure and uncertain from a legal point of view." In this setting, they argue, international law is empowered to step in and mediate the dispute.[79] Specifically, under such circumstances:

> The principle of self-determination of peoples may be called into play. New aspirations of certain sections of a nation, which are sometimes based on old traditions or on a common language and civilisation, may come to the surface and produce effects which must be taken into account in the interests of the internal and external peace of nations.[80]

Self-determination in this reasoning act as a kind of "tie breaker", allowing law – which primarily leaves to sovereign discretion matters of internal constitution – to engage with matters of secession and sovereignty.[81] In this sense,

---

77 *Report of the International Commission of Jurists Entrusted by the Council of the League of Nations with the Task of Giving an Advisory Opinion upon the Legal Aspects of the Aaland Islands Question*, League of Nations Official Journal, Special Supplement No. 3, (October 1920).

78 *Ibid* 5.

79 Berman (1988: 74–76).

80 *Ibid* 6.

81 According to Nathaniel Berman self-determination arises in 'moments of rupture': "The discourse of self-determination flourishes in the conceptual and real hiatuses in

as Berman argues, "the opinion draws an essential connection between the questions of self-determination and that of a new kind of international legal competence" which was developing, allowing it enquire into the internal and external constitution of the state.[82]

Following the conclusion of the Jurists' report, the League Council created the Commission of Rapporteurs to once again examine the Aaland question. The relationship between sovereignty and self-determination also lay at the heart of the Rapporteurs' deliberations.[83] Despite conceding that "the Islanders feared Finnish even more than Russian domination" the Rapporteurs concluded that "the right of sovereignty of the Finnish State over the Aaland Islands is incontestable and that their present legal status is that they form part of Finland."[84] In a widely quoted statement, the Rapporteurs considered that:

> To concede to minorities, either of language or religion, or to any fractions of a population the right of withdrawing from the community to which they belong, because it is their wish or good pleasure, would be to destroy order and stability within States and to inaugurate anarchy in international life; it would be to uphold a theory incompatible with the very idea of the State as a territorial and political unity.[85]

Crucially, however, this statement is prefaced by somewhat of a caveat. While the Rapporteurs considered that it was not possible to admit "as an absolute rule" regarding the rights of minorities to secede, they also expressed an awareness that situations may arise in which it would be unwarranted to insist that a minority stay within the boundaries of the state.

> The separation of a minority from the State of which it forms a part and its incorporation in another State can only be considered an exceptional

international society. Rather than being positioned on one side or another in the law/sovereignty dilemma, it weaves a textured discourse between them. In this way, its very marginality to normal international law enables it to occupy a privileged conceptual role in international law, illuminating law's basic conceptual dilemmas." Berman (1988: 72–76). Moreover, according to Koskenniemi, the distinction between "normal" and "abnormal" situations has since been at the core of most juristic discussion about the legal significance of the right of self-determination. Koskenniemi (1994: 254).

82 Berman (1988: 74).

83 *The Aaland Islands Question: Report Submitted to the Council of the League of Nations by the Commission of Rapporteurs*, (League of Nations Doc. B7 [C] 21/68/106, (April 1921) at 27.

84 *Ibid* 22.

85 *Ibid* 22.

> solution, a last resort when the State lacks either the will or the power to enact and apply just and effective guarantees[86]

Hence, the Rapporteurs not rule out the possibility of of secession as a last resort, for instance, in cases of persistent and extreme oppression of a group.[87] In this respect the Rapporteurs also draw a link between self-determination and the tempered notion of state sovereignty embodied in the minority protection regimes. Self-determination may not have given the Islanders a right to separate but it bound Finland to "enact and apply just and effective guarantees of religious, linguistic and social freedom."[88] These were supplemented by a number of recommendations offered by the Rapporteurs to be included in the autonomy arrangement, which would be monitored by the League. However, the Rapporteurs were quick to warn that if these arrangements were not fulfilled it would be forced to reconsider its protection of Finnish sovereignty.[89]

While the Rapporteur's recourse to minority protections in theory offered a solution to the ongoing tensions surrounding national claims, the problem was that in practice there was little international oversight.[90] The League refused to admit individual complaints and virtually none ever made it to the Council which could transfer the matter to the Permanent Court of International Justice. Between 1922 when the Court was established, and 1939 when the Minority System came to an end, only 16 petitions reached the Court, out of 930 that were filed, while the Committee-of-Three deemed that 758 were simply not receivable.[91]

Discontent amongst states about the demands of the Minority Treaties, coupled with the lack of enforcement, led to states gradually abdicating from their commitments.[92] In the interwar period, the fragility of the various solutions to minority protection and the issue of national aspirations became increasingly evident. The difference in treatment meted out to different groups created the problem of the "named and unnamed minorities, protected and unprotected people."[93] In the case of the rising problem of anti-Semitism in states

86 *Ibid* 28.

87 *Ibid* 28.

88 *Ibid* 28.

89 *Ibid* 34.

90 Berman (1988: 368).

91 Christian Tams and Malgosia Fitzmaurice, *Legacies of the Permanent Court of International Justice*, (Leiden: Brill, 2013) 130.

92 Musgrave (1997: 55).

93 Caroline Fink, *Defending the Rights of Others, The Great Powers, the Jews, and International Minority Protection, 1878–1938*. (Cambridge: CUP 2004) 73.

the League largely dodged the issue. When the issue of the persecution of the Jewish minority in Yugoslavia was raised before the Committee, it refused to consider the issue noting that "it [was] desirable to limit conversation to the case of those minorities as to which it might be suggested that special treatment was desirable."[94]

A worrying rhetorical trend emerged alleging that minorities posed a threat to internal stability of the state, leading to both the expulsion of several groups, as well as the rise in transfer of populations.[95] Indeed, minority recognition grew in parallel to patterns of deportation.[96] The practice of minority transfer had begun soon after the creation of the treaties, grounded in the view as stated in a 1915 memorandum that, "the stability of national frontiers delineated according to ethnic criteria could best be secured through the removal of inassimilable ethnic minorities."[97] These included two major arrangements, one between Greece and Bulgaria and the second between Greece and Turkey – each with devastating effects for the populations involved.[98] In the aftermath of the 1929 financial crisis schemes of forcible mass resettlement and large-scale deportation grew. The breakdown of the minority protection was complete when Poland formally renounced its minority treaty in 1934.[99]

These developments showcased the limitations of the new sovereignty regime, as states retreated behind the buffer of domestic jurisdiction in their treatment of sub-state groups, often invoking the rhetoric of self-determination to do so. In the case of Benito Mussolini's rise to power in Italy, self-determination was also increasingly coupled with a state's fundamental

94 Marilyn Lake, and Henry Reynolds. *Drawing the Global Colour Line: White Men's Countries and the International Challenge of Racial Equality*. (Cambridge: CUP 2008) 335.

95 The *Convention Between Greece and Bulgaria Respecting Reciprocal Emigration* of 1919 was concluded for the explicit purpose, not of conferring minority rights but rather of carrying out a voluntary and reciprocal transfer of national minorities. Later the *Convention concerning the Exchange Greek and Turkish Populations* of 1923 laid down the compulsory exchange of nearly two million members of their national minorities; a practice that seemed to point to the relatively stopgap nature of minority treaties where nationally cohesive states was the preferred option. Hans Morgenthau "The Paradoxes of Nationalism" 46 *Yale Review* (1957) 489–90 at 487.

96 Eric Weitz, "From the Vienna to the Paris System: International Politics and the Entangled Histories of Human Rights, Forced Deportations, and Civilizing Missions." *The American Historical Review* 113, no. 5 (2008): 1313–43.

97 Fink (2004: 47).

98 For an in-depth discussion see Umut Özsu, *Formalizing Displacement: International Law and Population Transfer* (Oxford: OUP 2014).

99 See Patrick Thornberry, *International Law and the Rights of Minorities* (Oxford: Clarendon Press, 1991) 47.

right to expansion.[100] This gave rise not only to the intensification of its colonial efforts in Libya and its claims to the border regions from the collapsed Austro-Hungarian Empire, but it also extended to its infamous invasion and occupation of Ethiopia. As Rose Parfitt has explored, Italy's actions involved a highly legalistic case before the League of Nations in which it argued that its actions were justified on the grounds of Ethiopia's failure to meet the conditions of its League membership (which were conditions uniquely placed on Ethiopia due to widespread uncertainty over its 'Civilizational' development).[101] In the case of Germany, the Versailles settlement and its conditions were contested as a violation of the sovereignty of the German nation and its peoples.[102] The Nazis ultimately inscribed the principle of self-determination in their first party platform, and throughout the 1930s Nazis and their sympathisers demanded the unification of the German people under the principle of nationality.[103] Or as Eric Hobsbawm later reflected, Hitler was possibly the most "logical Wilsonian nationalist."[104]

## 4 Quasi-Sovereigns: The Mandate and Trusteeship System

A very different idea of law and sovereignty found expression in the creation of the Mandate and Trusteeship system. From the start of the Peace Conference, it was made abundantly clear that colonial powers were unwilling to give up their overseas possessions. However, the question of what to do with the colonies and territories formerly under the authority of the defeated imperial powers – Germany and the Ottoman Empire - remained unresolved. As Neta Crawford notes, "annexation could not be allowed if the victors, especially Woodrow

---

100 According to Mussolini:

> For Fascism, the growth of empire, that is to say the expansion of the nation, is an essential manifestation of vitality, and its opposite a sign of decadence. Peoples which are rising, or rising again after a period of decadence, are always imperialist; any renunciation is a sign of decay and of death. Fascism is the
> doctrine best adapted to represent the tendencies and the aspirations of a people, like the people of Italy, who are rising again after many centuries of abasement and foreign servitude.

Mussolini 1934, 16 in Parfitt (2017: 117–118).

101 Parfitt (2017: 117–118) and Parfitt (2019: 327–334) See also Getachew (2019: 62–67).

102 Vagts (1996: 687–688).

103 See Alfred Cobban, *The Nation-State and National Self-determination* (London: Collins, 1969) 93.

104 See Ruth E. Gordon "Some Legal Problems with Trusteeship" 23 *Cornell International Law Journal* (1995) 301, 317.

Wilson and Lloyd George, were to be bound to their wartime rhetoric."[105] Yet equally to grant these territories independence would expose the Allies own colonial holdings to criticism. Rather than extending the principle of political independence to colonial regions, therefore, the League converted them into a set of quasi-sovereign entities, to be ruled by 'trustees', with the express understanding that they weren't fit to govern themselves.

While the creation of the scheme in many ways placed the renegotiation of absolute sovereignty at centre stage by tasking States with obligations regarding the treatment of colonial peoples, in reality it largely operated as a stopgap to the issue of the disrupted colonial sovereignty of the Axis powers, furthering colonial expansion over the "backward" peoples and territories brought under the regime.[106] While recognising colonial peoples' latent capacity for self-rule but deferring its realization because of their "backwardness," the Mandate System provided a means of circumventing independence for colonial peoples, whilst not entirely abdicating from the principle of self-determination. In this respect, as Getachew has explored, the Mandate System representing an articulation of self-determination very much in line with the one proposed by Wilson – one compatible with the institution of empire through the addition of a set of deviations and restrictions that would restrain the principle's revolutionary potential.[107] The underlying justification of the scheme was presented in 1918 by G.L. Beer, who was later chief of the colonial division of the US delegation to the Paris Peace Conference:

> Under modern political conditions apparently the only way to determine the problem of politically backward peoples, who require not only outside political control but also foreign capital to reorganize their stagnant economic systems is to entrust the task of government to that state whose interests are most directly involved...If, however, such backward regions are entrusted by international mandate to one state, there should be

105 Wilson declared at the Peace Conference: 'We are done with the annexations of helpless peoples meant by some Powers to be used merely for exploitation.' Neta Crawford, *Argument and Change in International Politics: Ethics, Decolonization and Humanitarian Intervention*, (Cambridge: CUP, 2002) 261. See also Ruth Cranston, *The Story of Woodrow Wilson: Twenty-Eighth President of the United States, Pioneer of World Democracy* (New York: Simon & Schuster, 1945) 318.

106 Mandatories were required to promote 'self-government' and 'well-being', and to supervise such matters they were obliged to submit an annual report to the League Council. See P. E. Corbett, 'What is the League of Nations?' 5 *British Yearbook of International Law*, 126–136.

107 See Getachew (2019: 41–52).

> embodied in the deed of trust most rigid safeguards to both protect the native population from exploitation and also to ensure that the interests of other foreign states are not injured…But far more important than any arrangement of this character to secure the interests of the European and American states in such backward countries is the necessity of clearly defined provisions to protect the natives from exploitation.[108]

Subsequently, South African statesman General Jan Smuts, later South African Prime Minister and a key advocate of racial segregation, also proposed a Mandate system in his plan for a League of Nations declaring that "the German colonies in the Pacific and Africa are inhabited by barbarians, who not only cannot possibly govern themselves, but to whom it would be impracticable to apply any ideas of political self-determination in the European sense."[109] Like Wilson, Smut's articulation of self-determination was one prefaced on the extension of the principle to colonial peoples under the ambit of political tutelage and improvement, whilst maintaining that colonial subjects would never realize democratic self-government in a European sense – thus ensuring the maintenance of empire. For Smuts it was the "old Empires" – the Austro-Hungarian and Ottoman – based on "the inequality and bondage and oppression of the smaller national units" that lay at the root cause of WWI – and not the more recent iterations, which he said were based on "principles of national freedom and political decentralization."[110]

The broad, primary goal of the Mandate System was to prevent the exploitation of the native peoples; its secondary goal was to promote their well-being and development.[111] According to Smuts, it would be based on principles of "no annexation and the self-determination of nations."[112] In practice, however,

108 George Louis Beer, *African Questions at the Paris Peace Conference* (New York: Macmillan, 1923) 424–425.

109 Jan Smuts, *The League of Nations: A Practical Suggestion* (London: Hodder & Stoughton, 1918), quoted in Duncan Hall, *Mandates, Dependencies and Trusteeship* (Washington: Carnegie Endowment Fund for International Peace, 1948), 13.

110 J. C. Smuts, "The League of Nations: A Practical Suggestion" in D. H. Miller ed., *The Drafting of the Covenant* (New York: G. P. Putnam's Sons, 1928) vol. 2, 11.

111 Hall (1948: 94).

112 Jan Smuts, *The League of Nations: A Practical Suggestion* (London: Hodder & Stoughton, 1918), quoted in Hall (1948: 10). Although the powers had publicly voiced opposition to territorial annexation as a proper end of victory, secret arrangements had in fact been made by Great Britain, France and Japan prior to the armistice. These arrangements provided, among other things, that three British Dominions were to have the right to annex, respectively, German South West Africa, New Guinea and German Samoa. South Africa was to receive the first of these.

the scheme was largely based on the metric of the standards of civilization. These colonies and territories were, in the words of Article 22 of the League Covenant, "inhabited by peoples not yet able to stand by themselves under the strenuous conditions of the modern world" – and thus self-determination would have to be adjusted to this end. It was decided that "tutelage of such peoples should be entrusted to advanced nations who by reason of their resources, their experience or their geographical position can best undertake this responsibility."[113] Reflecting perceived differences in development and levels of civilization, Article 22 created three classes of Mandate. In the language of the Covenant, and according to the mandatory agreements, the former lands of the Ottoman Empire became Class A mandates, having reached a "stage of development" where they, with some assistance, would soon be "able to stand alone." The Class B mandates, were "at such a stage, that the Mandatory must be responsible for the administration of the territory under conditions which will guarantee freedom of conscience and religion, subject only to the maintenance of public order and morals, the prohibition of abuses such as the slave trade, the arms traffic, the liquor traffic…" The Class C Mandate territories were those which, "owing to the sparseness of their population, or their small size, or their remoteness from the centre of civilisation … can be best administered under the laws of the Mandatory as integral portions of its territory, subject to the safeguards above mentioned in the interests of the indigenous population."

Thus, as Anghie explains, the mandate system continued to support a world divided between civilised and uncivilised, where sovereignty would be earned through the development of certain social and political infrastructure.[114] Indeed, speaking in 1919 Lloyd George noted that "there was no large difference between the principles of the Mandate System and those of the Berlin Conference."[115] Writing in 1930 Quincy Wright compared the relationship between mandatory power and mandate territory to the guardianship of a minor, with the mandate territory to be educated for self-government.[116] Judge McNair's depiction of the "sacred trust" embodied in the mandate system in the 1950 South-West Africa advisory opinion is also worth noting:

---

113 See William Bain, *Between Anarchy and Society: Trusteeship and the Obligations of Power* (Oxford: OUP, 2003), 107.

114 Anthony Anghie, 'Colonialism and the Birth of International Institutions: Sovereignty, Economy and the Mandate System of the League of Nations', (2002) 34 NYUJILP513.

115 Duncan Hall, "The Trusteeship System," 24 *British Yearbook of International Law* 33, 37 (1947).

116 Quincy Wright, *Mandates Under the League of Nations* (Chicago: University of Chicago Press, 1930) 11.

> Nearly every legal system possesses some institution whereby the property (and sometimes the persons) of those who are not sui juris, such as a minor or a lunatic, can be entrusted to some responsible person such as a trustee or tuteur or curateur. The Anglo-American trust serves this purpose, and another purpose even more closely akin to the Mandates System, namely, the vesting of property in trustees, and its management by them in order that the public or some class of the public may derive benefit or that some public purpose may be served. The trust has frequently been used to protect the weak and the dependent...[117]

To cross the threshold from 'uncivilized' to 'civilized', moreover, was largely out of the reach of most of the mandate territories – and in fact only one territory – Iraq managed to terminate its mandate.[118] This followed months of negotiations with Permanent Mandates Commission which issued strict guidelines as to when a territory could be considered sufficiently "prepared." The *General Conditions to be fulfilled before the Mandate Regime can be brought to an End in respect of a Country placed under that Regime* recommended that a candidate meet the following *defacto* conditions:

a. It must have a settled government and an administration capable of maintaining the regular operation of essential government services;
b. It must be capable of maintaining its territorial integrity and political independence;
c. It must be able to maintain the public peace throughout the whole territory;
d. It must have at its disposal adequate financial resources to provide regularly for normal government requirements;
e. It must possess laws and a judicial organization which will afford equal and regular justice to all.

For inter-war scholars, however, the central dilemma of the mandate system was the issue of sovereignty, and indeed of the mandate's general status under international law.[119] While it was clear that the Axis powers had lost their titles

117 *Ibid* 130.

118 Fabry (2010: 151).

119 The general view among states at that time was that Native communities had no status in international law and as such could not possess any rights of statehood See, e.g., *Island of* Palmas *Case* (P.C.A., 1928), 2 *Reports of Int. Arb. Awards,* 829. 888; *Status of Eastern Greenland* (P.C.I.J., 1933), Series A/B, No. 53, 3 Hudson, World *Court Reports,* 151, 171.

to their colonial possessions as a result of the peace settlement,[120] the issue of where sovereignty over the mandates was vested was never resolved. The proposed candidates included the League, the mandatory power and the mandated territory, which was considered to hold a sort of "latent sovereignty" that would emerge in its actualised form upon the termination of the mandate.[121] ICJ Judge Baron McNair would later articulate the notion of "sovereignty in abeyance:" "The doctrine of sovereignty has no application to this new system. Sovereignty over a Mandated Territory is in abeyance; if and when the inhabitants of the Territory obtain recognition as an independent State ... sovereignty will revive and vest in the new State."[122] This issue in particular was to assume great importance in the period after the abolition of the League and the transition to the system of Trusteeship and attempts by various states to absorb their former mandates.

Despite the maintenance of the civilising mission which lay at the core of the Mandate System, its construction, Neta Crawford argues, was nevertheless a significant challenge to unbridled European imperial power, indicating at least a significant shift in attitudes towards colonialism.[123] While the issue of sovereignty over the mandates was never fully resolved, it was clear that Mandate powers did not acquire such territories as 'colonies' in the classical sense and were subject to a moderate degree of international oversight. These new institutional practices worked in many way to deconstruct colonial rule. As Edward Grigg told members of the British House of Commons in 1935, "The attack on our position in Africa is not, in my opinion, coming from Africans or from anybody outside ourselves. It is coming from within our own ranks ... If that kind of propaganda goes on it will undermine the peace of the Colonial Empire, not because of its effects in Africa, but because of its great effect upon ourselves."[124] As Crawford notes "the Mandate system grew to be more than its framers – or the mandatory powers – intended, ultimately striking a wedge in the colonial system."[125]

And indeed, Algerian, Vietnamese and Tunisian nationalist movements seized on the concept of self-determination to formulate their claims for self-government.[126] As Erez Manela has argued, the "Wilsonian moment" had prompted numerous activists, politicians and intellectuals from colonial

---

120 See PMC VI sess. 121–124.

121 Anghie (2005: 147).

122 *International Status of South-West Africa,* ICJ Reports 1950, No. 10, p. 128 at p. 150 (11 July) (Separate opinion of Judge McNair).

123 See Neta Crawford., *Argument and Change in World Politics: Ethics, Decolonization, and Humanitarian Intervention* (Cambridge: CUP, 2002).

124 Edward Grigg, quoted in R.D. Pearce, *The Turning Point in Africa: British Colonial Policy 1938–48* (London: Frank Cass, 1982) 12.

125 Crawford (2002: 264).

126 *Ibid* 242.

territories to adopt the rhetoric of self-determination to ground their aspirations "that resonated with a wider, international discourse of legitimacy."[127] From India, Egypt and Korea, letters and petitions making claim to self-determination from groups and individuals around the world made their way to the delegates of the Peace conference – the bulk addressed to Wilson himself.[128] One of the most notable examples, was the petition by a young Ho-Chi-Minh – entitled "The Claims of the People of Annam" in support of the Indochinese cause against the French, which quoted the American Declaration of Independence.[129]

Between the two world wars, the Pan-Africanism, Pan-Arabism and Pan-Islam movements began to grow in strength. These movements draw upon Lenin's account of self-determination and its call for the liberation of colonial peoples, which was also gaining force with the founding of the Communist International. At its founding meeting in March 1919, delegates asserted that the League was a system based on the preservation of colonial exploitation and colonial exploitation "meant only to change the commercial label of colonial slavery."[130] The Second Pan-African conference endorsed a declaration stressing racism as a problem and proposed 'self-government' for Africans. During the Third Pan-African Congress in 1923 demands were made that Africans have a "voice in their own governments ... access to land and its resources ... trial by juries of their peers under established procedures of law ... development of Africa for the benefit of Africans, and not merely for the profit of Europeans."[131] Writing after his return from Europe, W.E.B. Du Bois argued that "the one new Idea of the World War – the one which may well stand in future years as the one thing that made the slaughter worthwhile – is an Idea which we are likely to fail to know because it is today hidden under the maledictions hurled at Bolshevism."[132] It would be the revolutionary potential of this idea that anti-colonial activists would take forward into the next era - a refashioning that would now concentrate on the legal framework of the international system to secure liberation.

127 Manela (2007: 221).

128 Manela (2007: 4–5).

129 *Ibid.*

130 "Extracts from the Theses on the International Situation and the Policy of the Entente Adopted by the First Comintern congress" in *The Communist International: 1919–1943, Documents 1*, 42.

131 Quoted in George Padmore, *Pan-Africanism or Communism* (Garden City, NY: Anchor Books, 1971), 108–109.

132 Quoted in Getachew (2019: 52).

CHAPTER 3

# "One World" - Anticolonialism at the UN

If the "fat, pale continent"[1] of Europe had been the first key battleground of self-determination's normative and legal implications, then from the 1940s onwards, decolonisation in Asia and then crucially Africa was to assume central stage in these debates.[2] While the great project of internationalism, governance and the codification of universally recognised rights and freedoms was spearheaded by the United Nations, a gradual disillusionment with international law was also manifesting. It its perhaps ironic then that as international relations scholars galvanized their scepticism towards the previous era's recourse to applying universal moral standards to the behaviour of states,[3] it was precisely these standards which were instrumental in effecting a wholesale change to long-standing legal and political notions of sovereignty in the face of reluctant colonial powers who continued to deny colonial people their claim to independence.[4]

While self-determination had been diminished by the events of the Second World War, its continuing political appeal ensured that it remained prominent in the new international order. Having been included in the Atlantic Charter and its demands for the restoration of sovereignty and self-government,[5] self-determination was invoked as one of the founding principles of the United

---

1 Preface to Franz Fanon's *The Wretched of the Earth* (New York: Grove Press, 1963).

2 I borrow this phrase from the text of the Fifth Pan-African Congress: "We demand for Black Africa autonomy and independence, so far and no further than it is possible in this "One World" for groups and peoples to rule themselves subject to inevitable world unity and federation." "The Challenge to the Colonial Powers," in *History of the Pan African Congress: Colonial and Coloured Unity; A Program of Action*, ed. George Padmore (1947; London: Hammersmith Bookshop, 1963), 5.

3 See Hans J. Morgenthau, *Politics Among Nations: The Struggle for Power and Peace*, 4th ed (New York: Alfred A Knopf, 1967).

4 See D. A. Low, *Eclipse of Empire* (Cambridge: CUP, 1993); Geoffrey Barraclough, *An Introduction to Contemporary History* (Harmondsworth: Penguin, 1967), ch. 6; R. F. Holland, *European Decolonization, 1918–1981* (London: Macmillan, 1985); John Gallagher in *The Decline, Revival and Fall of the British Empire* (Cambridge: CUP, 1982), 73–4; Nicholas Tarling, *The Fall of Imperial Britain in South-East Asia* (Oxford: OUP, 1993); John Darwin, *The End of the British Empire: The Historical Debate* (Oxford: Basil Blackwell, 1991).

5 The Atlantic Charter signed by Winston Churchill and Franklin Roosevelt in August 1941 stated, in part, that they "desire to see no territorial changes that do not accord with the freely expressed wishes of the peoples concerned." Under article 3 of the Atlantic Charter both leaders committed to "respect the right of all peoples to choose the form of government

 | DOI:10.1163/9789004479197_005

Nations Charter in articles 1 and 55.[6] Like its early invocations during the interwar period, it was framed in broadly ambiguous terms. The ambit of its application, moreover, remained both limited and far from binding in nature. Importantly, self-determination was framed in a manner that did not imply independence for colonial peoples, and which could easily bolster the continuation of a system of unequal sovereignty in the international system. Indeed, as Mark Mazower has explored, despite the egalitarianism and appeal to universal, the UN system was committed to upholding the structures that underpinned empire and the interests of the great powers.[7] This was confirmed in the Charter itself, which extended the Mandate system through the Trusteeship system where colonial holdings were renamed "non-self-governing territories."

In subsequent decades, however, anti-colonialists successfully transformed the hollow universality of self-determination in the Charter into a legal platform for decolonization.[8] As this chapter will argue, anti-colonialists harnessed the legal vagaries of the Charter's formulation and granted new meaning to its legal and normative components – culminating in formulation of a legal right to decolonization with the passing in 1960 of resolution 1514 by the General Assembly. Framed in the language of "political will" and "autonomy from external interference," self-determination, reinvented as a demand for non-domination and equality, and justified on universal grounds in the name of international stability and human rights, cemented the anti-colonialist challenge to both the normative and legal beliefs that had underpinned colonial rule, primarily the exclusion of colonial peoples deemed 'unfit' for independence from the sovereignty regime.[9] The position that it was the colonial powers themselves who would govern and ultimately decide the fate of their territories, was gradually dismantled and replaced by resounding belief that colonialism was an illegitimate form of rule, contrary to the human rights of

under which they will live," and "to see sovereign rights and self-government restored to those who have been forcibly deprived of them."

6 Antonio Cassese, *Self Determination of Peoples: A Legal Appraisal* (New York: CUP 1995), 37.

7 Mark Mazower, *Governing the World: The History of an Idea*, (New York: Penguin, 2012) 150–51.

8 This claim is supported by many scholars, including Christian Reus-Smit "Post-1945 Decolonisation" in *Individual Rights and the Making of the International System* (Cambridge: CUP, 2013), Maja Spanu (2014: Chapter 5), and more recently Adom Getachew (2019: Chapter 3).

9 As Ryan Irwin has argued to pose their anti-colonial challenge, actors engaged with "concepts of sovereignty, freedom, and development" and used "discourses of human rights, racial equality, and nationalism to expand their authority [within the organization]." Ryan Irwin, "A Wind of Change? White Redoubt and the Postcolonial Moment, 1960–1963," *Diplomatic History* 33( 5) (2009): 898.

colonial peoples, and the broader goals of international peace and security.[10] These demands were to provide the foundation for the anti-colonial claim to decolonization, one which was directed towards a broader transformation of the international system.

This chapter examines the legal mobilization of self-determination to create the conditions for decolonization at the international legal level, giving rise to a new sovereign standard in which sovereign equality and independence from imperial domination would be the hallmarks. Self-determination's elevation to a 'right' of colonial peoples - marked a revolutionary development in international law and politics. International law had never before granted *a priori* right of sovereignty to a state by mere virtue of its status.[11] These efforts were primarily fought out in the newly created UN forums for human rights, which emerged as critical forums for the reinvention of self-determination by newly independent states – which had largely been excluded from efforts to reform the international system and its underlying values during the drafting of the Charter.[12]

The link between the role of human rights in anti-colonial self-determination has been increasingly debated in recent years. Several scholars support the view that anti-colonial self-determination was deeply attached to human rights,[13] while others dispute this claim.[14] These discussions join other debates about the role of ethical arguments such as self-determination in delegitimizing empire through the appeal to statehood during this period.[15] However, this assessment fails to account for the full extent of the anti-colonial claim to

10 See Getachew (2019: 89).

11 Fabry (2010: 157).

12 Heather, A. Wilson, *International Law and the Use of Force by National Liberation Movements* (Oxford: Clarendon Press 1988). 61.

13 See Reus-Smit (2013) and Burke (2010).

14 In Jan Eckel's words, 'those activists and states that did base their claims on human rights did not so much express their commitment to universal norms as appropriate them for their specific anticolonial policies'. Andreas Eckert similarly argues that 'commitment to human rights remained rhetorical, however, often sacrificed in the name of ideology, traditions or institutions Jan Eckel, 'Human rights and decolonization: new perspectives and open questions', *Humanity: An International Journal of Human Rights, Humanitarianism, and Development*, 1.1 (2010), 113; Andreas Eckert, 'African nationalists and human rights, 1940s and 1970s', in Stefan-Ludwig Hoffmann (ed.), *Human Rights in the Twentieth Century* (Cambridge: CUP 2011), 284.

15 Daniele Archibugi, for example, argues that during this time self-determination "was interpreted mainly as the right of peoples to become states, a reiteration of the conceptual and legal categories used to reorganize European society after World War I." Daniele Archibugi, 'A critical analysis of the self-determination of peoples: a cosmopolitan perspective', *Constellations*, 10.4 (2003), 494.

self-determination, which had larger aspirations for normative and institutional change in the international system. Post-colonial framings of self-determination were, I argue, were indeed linked to human rights as a means of propagating decolonial action, but they were also enmeshed in and linked to a broader project that was directed towards the reinvention of both the content and implications of human rights, as well as the international system as a whole. These efforts involved the reinvention and crystallization of self-determination not only as a rule demanding the sovereign equality of colonial peoples, but towards a more ethical international order, in which an ongoing right to self-determination would safeguard and strengthen the independence of all peoples, including in the economic field.[16]

## 1 Self-Determination and the New World Order

When the delegates assembled to draft the United Nations Charter in San Francisco in April 1945 there was a "general feeling" that some explicit reference to self-determination should be made in the Charter.[17] Keen to rehabilitate self-determination from its wartime circulation by Nazi and Fascist leaders, the allied leaders Churchill and Roosevelt pushed for a refinement of its moral foundations that returned it to its liberal roots. They were joined by the Soviet Union, who remained bound to their ideological commitments to self-determination as a tool of anti-imperialism. Numerous statements were made in support of self-determination, with many underlining its necessity "for progress and for development" and in strengthening the goal of universal peace.[18] As "one of the guiding ideas of peace and solidarity among nations and of a conciliation and cooperation… it should be definitely planted among

16 For discussions of the continuing reinvention of self-determination during the 1960 and 70s see for instance Brad Simpson, 'Self-Determination, Human Rights, and the End of Empire in the 1970s', 4:2 *Humanity* (2013) pp. 239–26. In Getachew's study, *Worldmaking after Empire: The Rise and Fall of Self-Determination* (Princeton: Princeton University Press 2019) she demonstrates, against the standard view of decolonisation as a moment of nation-building in which the anticolonial demand for self-determination culminated in the rejection of alien rule and the formation of nation-states, that anticolonial nationalism was a form of *worldmaking*.

17 Cassese (1996: 38); United Nations (UN), Documents on the United Nations Conference on International Organization (United Nations Information Organization, New York, 1945), Vol. 3, 146–148.

18 Report of Rapporteur of Committee 1 to Commission 1/1, 1 June, 17.

the foundations of the Charter of the United Nations" argued the Yugoslavian representative.[19]

Ultimately, among the purposes of the UN spelled out in articles 1 and 55 of the Charter is the promotion of "equal rights and self-determination of peoples."[20] The precise dimensions of the principle, however, remained loosely defined. Many states sought to highlight its relationship to human rights, whilst a majority opinion emerged that self-determination should be understood and promoted as self-government. The representative from Panama called attention to the intertwined nature of human rights and self-determination and called for the creation of a "declaration of human rights" that would enshrine self-determination and self-government as "essential human rights."[21]

It was however firmly stressed that "the principle conformed to the purposes of the Charter only insofar as it implied a right of self-government… and not the right of secession."[22] From this, argues Cassese, it was clear that self-determination was not an "independent value," but was subordinate to the larger aims of peace and security "with the obvious consequence that it might and indeed should be set aside when its fulfilment would give rise to tension and conflict among states."[23]

This was nowhere more evident than in the treatment of colonial peoples. While the Atlantic Charter had renewed calls for self-government and "right of all peoples to choose the form of government under which they will live" – this did not, Churchill insisted, apply to territories of the British Empire.[24] In September 1941 Churchill hastened to place a caveat upon the Charter, telling the House of Commons that the Atlantic Charter was directed towards restoring "the sovereignty, self-government and national life of the States and nations of

19 Report of Rapporteur of Committee 1 to Commission 1, June 13, 1945, UNCIO, vol. 6, 455.

20 The final text of Article 1(2) provides that one of the purposes of the United Nations is: "To develop friendly relations among nations based on the principle of equal rights and self-determination of peoples, and to take other appropriate measures to strengthen universal peace." Article 55 of the Charter further states that the UN shall promote goals such as higher standards of living, full employment, and human rights "[w]ith a view to the creation of conditions of stability and well-being which are necessary for peaceful and friendly relations among nations based on respect for the principle of equal rights and self-determination of peoples."

21 UN, *Documents*, Vol. 6, 215.

22 UN, *Documents*, Vol. 6, 296.

23 Antonio Cassese, "The Helsinki Declaration and Self-Determination,' in Thomas Buergenthal (ed.), *Human Rights, International Law and the Helsinki Accord* (Allanheld, Osmun & Co., Montclair, 1977) 84.

24 Parliamentary Debates, Fifth Series, vol. 374, House of Commons, Official Report, eighth vol of Sess 1940–41, pp 68–69 quoted in Cassese (1995: 37).

Europe under the Nazi yoke" and was "quite a separate problem from the progressive evolution of self-governing institutions in regions whose peoples owe allegiance to the British crown."[25] "I have not become the King's First Minister in order to preside over the liquidation of the British Empire," he later said.[26] In correspondence with the deputy prime minister, the Secretary of State for the Colonies remarked:

> The truth, I suppose, is that we do not think the Atlantic Charter at present applicable in its entirety to Colonial territories. There is, for instance, the principle of self-determination, which finds a prominent place in the Charter. Can it possibly be said that the African Colonies are fit for the application of this principle? Or the West Indies? Or the Pacific Islands? ...The Atlantic Charter was originally intended, as I understand it, to be concerned primarily with the European countries at present overrun by Hitler. They are adult nations, capable of deciding their own fate. No doubt, the time may come when even the most backward of our Colonies [will] also become adult nations. But at present they are children and must be treated as such[27]

Rene Pleven, secretary for the French colonies was equally adamant that the French would not give up their colonies:

> At this very moment, when France is certainly more aware than ever of the importance of her Empire....a new doctrine is being put forward whereby colonial responsibilities should be assumed no longer by those nations who for centuries carried them out...but by some international organization which, one has to assume, is credited with the cardinal virtue of justice...and of competence and diligence. Neither the interests nor the wishes of the colonial populations would be served by a reform

---

25 *Ibid.*

26 In 1940 the British Labour Party announced its view that:
*For colonial peoples, Labour demands that everywhere they should move forward, as speedily as possible, towards self-government. In the administration of colonies not yet ready for self-government the interests of the native population should be paramount, and should be safeguarded through an extension and strengthening of the Mandate System. There must be equal opportunity of access for all peaceful peoples to raw materials and markets in these colonial territories.* Quoted in Morgan, *The Official History of Colonial Development*, vol. 1, xxvii. (Macmillan, London, 1980).

27 Secretary of State for the Colonies, Cranborne, to Deputy Prime Minister Atlee, 14 January 1943, in Porter and Stockwell, eds., *British Imperial Policy*, 142.

> which would transfer to a caretaker organization, acting under a collective name, the continuation of the colonizing work which is liberating the primitive societies from the great calamities which are ravaging them and which are called: disease, ignorance, superstition, tyranny.[28]

In 1943 Britain drafted a Joint Declaration on colonial policy with the US, promising that "Parent" or "Trustee" states would "guide and develop the social, economic and political institutions of the Colonial peoples until they are able without danger to themselves and others to discharge the responsibilities of government."[29] The US in its official policies on the question of dependent peoples declared in 1942 that it would support the plight of dependent peoples for emancipation as long as those peoples were "prepared and willing to accept the responsibilities of liberty" and "show themselves worthy of it and ready for it."[30] This position was carried forward in the UN Charter, which established the Trusteeship System and Trusteeship Council, which contained the same general philosophy as that which had guided the text of Art. 22 and the Mandate System.

As Neta Crawford has argued, the establishment of the Trusteeship System at the UN attempted to offer a new legitimacy to colonialism.[31] In her estimation, the scheme did envisage eventual decolonisation of specific territories, however, in 1945, this was a distant scenario. Like, the Mandate system before it, it essentially operated on the rationale that many colonial territories were "either incapable or deficient in power of self-government" and it was the duty of the "advanced" nations to guide them to attain the capacity to "govern themselves."[32] In the planning of the post-WWII international order, this rationale was reframed using the language of "responsibilities." This relationship of tutelage was also confirmed in the wording of the article:

> Members of the United Nations which have or assume responsibilities for the administration of territories whose peoples have not yet attained

---

28 Quoted in WR Louis *Imperialism at Bay, 1941–1945: The United States and the Decolonization of the British Empire* (Oxford: OUP 1978). 14–15.

29 Quoted in Morgan, *The Official History of Colonial Development*, vol. V, (London: Macmillan, 1980), 8.

30 The War and Human Freedom" (a radio broadcast by Cordell Hull on 23 July 1942), *Department of State Bulletin*, 25 July 1942, 642.

31 Crawford (2002: 312–313).

32 Jan C Smuts, *The League of Nations: A Practical Suggestion* (London: Hodder and Stoughton, 1918); See also Ruth B Russell, *A History of the United Nations Charter: The Role of the United States 1940–1945* (The Brookings Institution 1958) 75–91.

> a full measure of self-government recognise the principle that the interests of the inhabitants of these territories are paramount, and accept as a sacred trust the obligation to promote to the utmost, within the system of international peace and security established by the present Charter, the well-being of the inhabitants of these territories [...]

As a voluntary system, however, the UN had no competence to include colonial holdings, which were deemed domestic affairs. Nor was any real supervisory machinery provided other than for the eleven territories that were formally put under international supervision of the UN. Many states stressed that they considered intervention into colonial matters a breach of non-intervention and interference in their domestic jurisdiction.[33] Moreover, the scheme only provided the vague aim of self-government to these peoples at the end of their tutelage period. As indicated by Rupert Emerson, commenting on the state of mind that prevailed during the drafting, Huntington Gilchrist, a conference staff member, remarked that "independence was not mentioned as a goal, for the simple reason that no colonial power except the United States looks upon it as a normal and natural outcome of colonial status."[34]

The contradictory role that self-determination had assumed in the Charter, affirming the rights of independence and self-governance, whilst simultaneously applying a caveat for colonial peoples, also reflected the contradictory role the principle played in the broader post-war climate. While democratic rights and national aspirations of subject peoples was linked to the stability of the new system, the major powers also sponsored the division of Germany, along with Korea, Palestine and Vietnam. Allied powers also expressed an acceptance of the revival of population transfer as a necessary element of post-war settlement.[35]

33 As France stated in 1945 "nothing under consideration by the Trusteeship Committee shall authorise the United Nations to intervene in matters which [were] essentially within the domestic jurisdiction of any state." Quoted in William Bain, *Between Anarchy and Society Trusteeship and the Obligations of Power*. (Oxford: OUP 2003), 123.

34 Huntington Gilchrist", Colonial Questions at the San Francisco Conference," 39 *The American Political Science Review*, 5 (1945) 987 quoted in Rupert Emerson, *Colonialism, Political Development, and the UN, International Organization*, Vol. 19, No. 3, *The United Nations: Accomplishments and Prospects* (Summer, 1965), 486.

35 See Churchill, Speech on the Russo-Polish Border, House of Commons, December 12, 1944 in Holborn (ed), War and Peace Aims Vol II 537–540; Report to Minister Masaryk and the Government from Benes, dated June 7th 1943: 'He [Rossevelt] agrees to the transfer of the minority population from Eastern Prussia, Transylvania and Czechosolvakia' Reproduced in E Benes, Memoirs of Dr Eduard Benes (London: George Allen Unwin, 1954) at 195. Czech foreign minister Eduard Benes argued in 1942 that "it will be necessary after

One place in which self-determination was conspicuously absent during the immediate post-war period was in the debates over human rights – particularly during the drafting of the Universal Declaration of Human Rights (UDHR). An earlier proposal by the Soviet delegate to add a right to self-determination to the Declaration was roundly rejected, for fear it would stoke demands for colonial emancipation.[36] René Cassin, one of the architects of the human rights regime, was opposed to any suggestion that self-determination was a human right, accusing proponents of the right to self-determination of "reversing the order of the Charter" and "transforming the end into the means since, according to them, peoples should be granted the right to self-determination in order that they should be enabled to enjoy essential political rights and fundamental freedoms."[37] To Cassin, a proponent of the liberal human rights tradition, human rights were predominantly individual in nature. The "rights of peoples," were collective rights, and therefore had no place within the UDHR in his estimation. Despite the absence of self-determination from the UDHR, however, the creation of the human rights regime was still received as an important moment for anti-colonial efforts. As Andreas Eckert writes anti-colonialists, such as Nigerian nationalist leader Eyo Ita, considered that "the UDHR provided a new yardstick with which peoples of all lands could measure the success or failure of their political system.... To him, the UDHR was a direct condemnation of imperialism in all its forms. Its universal language ushered a new global era..."[38]

## 2 Contesting Empire at the UN

For anti-colonialists the immediate post-war period seemed to present an impasse to anti-imperialism. Lacking both normative and legal force the anti-colonial lobby could do little to advance their claims to independence, as relations between colonial powers and their dependencies was still a matter firmly

this war to carry out a transfer of populations on a very much larger scale than after the last war." Quoted in I. Claude, *National Minorities* (Cambridge: Harvard University Press, 1955) 74.

36 Quoted in G.I. Tunkin *Theory of International Law* (London: Wildy, Simmons and Hill Publishing, 1970), 69.

37 Commission on Human Rights, First Session, Summary Record, 4th meeting, 28 January 1947, E/CN. 4/SR. 4, noted in Zuijdwijk, Ton, *Petitioning the United Nations*: A Study in Human Rights (Hampshire: Gower, 1982) 4.

38 Andreas Eckert, "African Nationalists and Human Rights, 1940s-1970s" in Stefan Ludwig Hoffmann (ed.), *Human Rights in the Twentieth Century* (Cambridge: CUP 2011).

within domestic competence. With the absence of any clear legal basis for decolonisation, and with no real supervisory role of the UN prescribed under chapter XI, any attempt on the part of a colonized people to break free from its colonial mother country without the consent of the colonial power was unjustified.

In broader international political circles, decolonization was not an imminent concern, either from the major powers or the colonial powers themselves. Roger Louis notes that during this period "the general policy of the American government, in pursuit of security, tended to support rather than break up the British Imperial system."[39] During the May 1950 tripartite foreign ministers' (France, Britain, United States) meeting in London, the US reiterated its belief in the "progressive development of all dependent people towards self-government and where conditions are suitable towards independence," noting that "we believe that there must be an orderly, guided development of these people towards political maturity which only time and patience can provide."[40] The glaring tensions, however, between the broader appeal to self-determination and equality (both individual and sovereign) promoted in the foundational documents of the UN, and the maintenance of the colonial system were becoming difficult to deny.

Within the next few years, 25 new states were to join the UN (among them Egypt, Iraq, Lebanon, Saudi Arabia and Syria), half of which were former colonies, which slowly began to tip the power balance within the UN. This influence – not to mention voting strength - in the General Assembly was also bolstered by the 'frozen' nature of the Security Council by the early 1950s due to Cold War tensions.[41] Their new standing in the international community, underpinning by formal state equality, provided a platform from which to launch their formal attack on remaining colonial rule. With the backing of

---

39 WR Louis *Imperialism at Bay, 1941–1945: The United States and the Decolonization of the British Empire* (Oxford: OUP 1978) 567–68.

40 Policy paper prepared by the Bureau of Near Eastern, South Asian, and African Affairs, "Future of Africa," 18 April 1950, *FRUS, 1950*, vol. 5 (1978), 1524–1538. Further, at the July 1950 Anglo-American colonial policy talks, John Hickerson, the United States assistant secretary for UN Affairs, assured the British that the United States "was not out to break up the [British] Empire. We consider it as a great force for stability" Summary Record of Colonial Policy Talks with the UK, 5 July 1950, File 350, Accra Consulate, Classified General Records, 1950–52, Box 5 (National Archives (NA), Washington DC). Cited in Nwaubani (2003: 524)

41 For example, the Security Council passed a mere five resolutions a year on average in the early 1950s, representing a sharp decline from the years just before and reflecting the inability to develop consensus in the very body that was meant facilitate international compromise and harmony. During the first 6 years of the UN, the USSR used its veto in the Security Council no fewer than 47 times.

these newly independent states the UN began to reject the position that colonial matters were not a matter of international oversight.[42] For example, in the case of Indonesia, attempts by the Netherlands to reclaim control over the colony were treated as a matter of international concern, despite Dutch claims that it was a domestic matter, protected by its right to control over its domestic jurisdiction. It was successfully argued by a number of states that the Dutch armed intervention in their former colony was a threat to international peace and security, which ultimately warranted the UN Security Council's intervention. Crucially, in a sign of things to come, these states also cited the Indonesian's right to self-determination as the justifiable basis under international law to support Indonesia's claim.[43] In the face of angry protests by the Administering Powers, the UN ultimately became involved in a number of colonial disputes, including those in the French North African colonies, Cyprus, and Angola. The UN also pledged that Libya should become independent no later than January 1, 1952, and that Somaliland should also gain its independence by 1960. The case of Libya, as Mark Mazower notes, was a key illustration of the assertiveness of the Assembly, as it defeated efforts by the British, Americans and French to divide Libya into three trusteeships.[44]

With no precise legal framework to guide practice, and with the limitations of the Trusteeship system which tipped the balance in favour of colonial powers, however, there was no real recourse to enforce decolonial change. UN supervision was limited to the eleven territories listed in the Trusteeship Council and in the case of non-self-governing territories was entirely dependent upon the administering authority submission. The arbitrariness of this position was highlighted by a representative for India who noted:

> … the division of dependent areas into non-self-governing territories and trust territories was merely an accident of history; the former were the possessions of the victors of the two world wars and the latter those of the defeated.[45]

---

42 Rupert Emerson, "Colonialism, Political Development, and the UN," *International Organization,* Vol. 19, No. 3, *The United Nations: Accomplishments and Prospects* (Summer, 1965), 489.

43 See, for instance, Egypt's argument on the application of the UN principle of self-determination to the situation that was taking place in Indonesia in S/PV.14, 'The Indonesian Question', 10 February 1946 at 200–09.

44 Mazower (2012: 257).

45 Quoted in Harold Karan Jacobson, "The United Nations and Colonialism: A Tentative Appraisal" *International Organisation* 16(1) (1962) 38.

While 74 countries had initially been submitted as Non-Self-Governing Territories under Chapter XI of the Charter, as early as 1949 several administering territories has ceased transmission with regards to several of countries.[46] Spain and Portugal denied that their overseas territories fell within the scheme, while in the case of South West Africa, South Africa went so far as to indicate that it intended to annex the territory.[47] Moreover, a number of states had begun to alter their constitutional relationships with their colonies, in order to exclude them from the ambit of Article 73 or prepare plans to absorb them into their national territory.[48]

As a consequence, the General Assembly began to actively assert its competence to decide whether or not a territory was non-self-governing in 1949 by resolution 334(IV), also setting up a committee "to examine factors which should be taken into account in deciding whether any territory is or is not a territory whose people have not yet attained a full measure of self-government." Additionally, a number of other resolutions were adopted regarding the question of territorial status.[49] In Resolution 742(VII) it declared that "a decision may be taken by the Assembly on the continuation or cessation of the transmission of information required by Chapter XI of the Charter." However, any attempt to extend the measure of supervisory function exercised by the UN, for example to direct the listing of non-self-governing territories, was repeatedly criticized on the basis of a violation of Article 2(7).

The way forward lay in the creation of an enforceable right to decolonization in which self-determination would provide the normative and legal platform for action. Self-determination, with its central position in the UN Charter, represented an obstruse yet powerful normative argument with which to challenge the legitimacy of empire. Self-determination already enjoyed broad support amongst most states, as evidenced by the drafting of the Charter, and had been evoked consistently throughout the War and immediate post-War period as the grounding principles of international peace and security. Therefore, highlighting the inconsistency of the broader appeal to self-determination as the right to self-government given its denial to the people living under colonial rule became the centerpiece of anti-colonial efforts to delegitimate empire.

46 David Raic, *Statehood and the Law of Self-Determination* (The Hague: Kluwer, 2000) 203.

47 Steven Hillebrink, *The Right of Self-Determination and Post-Colonial Governance: The Case of the Netherlands Antilles and Aruba* (London: TMC Asser Press, 2008) 13.

48 The French Constitution of 1946 reaffirmed the integration of AOF and AEF into the French republic. In the period 1946 to 1955, the French republic attempted to fully integrate the territories into the French state by gradually recognizing equal legal status for all the inhabitants of the French colonies.

49 GA Resolutions 567(VI); 648(VII); 742(VIII).

The backdrop for these developments was the debates surrounding the drafting of the Covenants on Human Rights during the drafting by the Third Committee and the UN Human Rights Commission between 1950 and 1955. Post-colonial and other "Third World" states called for the insertion of a clause on self-determination in order to provide "moral and legal support to peoples aspiring to political and social independence."[50] This, Reus-Smit argues, marked the beginning of the use by post-colonial delegates of human rights language as "revolutionary discourses," to challenge hegemonic understandings of world order.[51] By grafting self-determination to the emerging human rights agenda, moreover, colonial peoples could position themselves as entities accruing international rights, even where they were denied these by their Administering Powers.[52] The appeals to this new international legal standing was also joined by new demands framed in the language of self-determination. These were in keeping with their recalibration of the international order and the post-imperial state, directing self-determination towards safeguarding and strengthening the sovereignty, including from non-intervention, as well as grafting self-determination to economic sovereignty and rights.[53]

The decision to take advantage of the growing human rights agenda from which to launch their reinvention of self-determination was not only strategic but also vital. Having largely been excluded from a role in laying down the foundational principles of the new UN system during the drafting of the UN Charter, the debates surrounding the Covenants gave them a new possibility to shape the values of the international order. It was also vital, as it became clear that opponents of colonial independence sought to hijack debates for their own interests. The previous year colonial powers had sought to insert a special colonial clause in the Covenants to exclude colonial territories and non-self-governing territories from the application of universal human rights.[54] This, it was argued, was justified on the basis of cultural difference and level of advancement.[55] As noted by the Belgian delegate:

---

50 United Nations, *Yearbook of the United Nations 1951*, 485.

51 Christian Reus-Smit, "Human Rights in a Global Ecumene," *International Affairs* 87(5) (2011): 1205–18 at 1212.

52 Reus-Smit (2013: 151–192).

53 In 1952 Chile introduced a proposal in the Human Rights Commission for the inclusion of a right of "permanent sovereignty," or economic self-determination into the draft Covenant, Chilean Draft, (E/CN.4/L.24) Comm.HR, Report 8th Session, 14 ESCOR (1952) Supplement No. 4, p. 8, para. 67.

54 Burke (2010: 116).

55 Belgium, 5 GAOR (1950) 3rd Cmmttee, 292nd mtg, (A/C.3/SR.292) para 133.

> [Human] rights presupposed a high degree of civilisation (and) were often incompatible with the ideas of people who had not reached a high degree of development. By imposing those rules on them at once, one ran the risk of destroying the very basis of their society. It would be an attempt to lead them abruptly to the point which the civilised nations of today had only reached after a lengthy period of development[56]

This argument was roundly rejected, with the Egyptian delegate noting that it "was only too reminiscent of the Hitlerian concept which divided mankind into groups of varying worth."[57]

The debates regarding self-determination's inclusion in the Covenants that took place over the following years highlighted the ongoing reluctance by Western states to support either self-determination or the broader process of decolonization. The UK delegate argued that Article 1 of the covenants held the potential for "tragic consequences" if it were adopted.[58] Self-determination could not, it was argued, be implemented in the same manner as other rights contained within the Covenants,[59] rather it was of necessity a slow and gradual process which should be kept apart from any provision on the subject in an international treaty.[60] Most Western states reiterated their position that under the 'sacred trust' placed on States responsible for non-self-governing territories by the UN Charter administering powers were to nurture colonial peoples, raising them up to the point where they were ready for independence.[61]

The arguments regarding preparedness for sovereignty were dismissed by anti-colonialists, who highlighted the inherent conflict in this line of reasoning, given colonial powers' economic and political interests in maintaining these territories. As one state put it "If the colonial Powers had not been able to bring their colonial peoples to an adequate stage of development in two centuries, they would be unlikely to be able to do so in the two ensuing decades."[62] While Saudi Arabia mounted a stinging attack on the continued fallacy that underpinned justifications for colonial rule:

56 A/C.3/SR.292 (1950). Quoted in Moyn, *The Last Utopia*, 96.

57 Quoted in Burke (2010: 120).

58 GAOR 3rd Cmmtte, 401st meeting, 24 January 1951, A/C.3/SR. 401, para. 23.

59 See Denmark, UN Doc. A/C.3/SR 644 para 3.

60 See UK UN Doc A/C.3/SR.309 para 59.

61 United Nations, *Yearbook of the United Nations 1952* (New York: UN Office of Public Information, 1952), p. 441.

62 Yugoslavia, 7 GAOR (1952) 3rd Cmttee., 448th mtg., (A/C.3/SR.448) para. 24.

> The metropolitan States averred that, if they were to withdraw from the territories under their control, the peoples of those territories would cut one another's throats, the fallacy of that argument had been proved by experience but even if it were true, that risk was preferable to their position of subjugation.[63]

In rejecting the claims of colonial powers, anti-colonialists began to draw a direct line between colonialism and the violation of not only human rights and human dignity, but the broader aims of the international system contained in the UN Charter. A crucial part of this process, as Adom Getachew and Daniel Philpott have shown, was the depiction of colonialism as a form of racial oppression, "holding that colonialism by its very nature subordinated Asian, African, and Central American peoples to European rulers, implying their inferiority and perpetuating their domination."[64] Colonization, anti-colonialists argued, was "a state of subjection to another power little better than slavery," with dependent peoples experiencing a violation of personhood that denied them basic human dignity and made the achievement of their individual human rights impossible.[65] If the Covenants were to ensure true universality of equality, then self-determination for all people was an absolute necessity. Emphasizing the ongoing nature of the right at the core of the international human rights system, anti-colonialists stressed that independence in and of itself was not the ultimate goal. National liberation "was not an end in itself," they argued, but rather "a means essential, as the experience of centuries had shown, for ensuring those very human rights with which the Third Committee was concerned."[66] Invoking the language of international peace and security contained within the UN Charter, anti-colonialists highlighted the incompatibility of colonial rule with the principles of sovereign equality and peace amongst nations, arguing that this system endangered the stability of the new world order. As Getachew explains, "as long as hierarchy remained a feature of international society, equality was limited to existing states.... this partial recognition of equality created conditions for the violent subjugation of colonized peoples and for imperial competition between states."[67] This line of argumentation was to become a fixture of the anti-colonial lobby's strategy in

---

63 Saudi Arabia, 6 GAOR (1951) 3rd Cmttee., 398th mtg., (A/C.3/SR.398) para. 37.
64 Getachew (2019: 89) and Philpott (2001: 15).
65 Yearbook of the United Nations, 1952 (New York: United Nations Organization, 1952) p. 442.
66 GAOR 3rd Cmmtte 401st meeting, 24 January 1952, A/C.3/SR. 401, para. 45.
67 Getachew (2019: 89).

the following years, as their efforts towards removing the remnants of colonial rule ramped up, eventually leading to demands for the right to armed resistance and self-defence to counter imperial intervention.

The ongoing dimension of the right was also stressed, with many states linking self-determination to the rights of other groups under foreign domination,[68] highlighting the situations in Korea,[69] Palestine,[70] Kashmir[71] and Eastern Europe.[72] The Philippines recognised that: "Another important aspect of the problem of self-determination was an increasing consciousness of the plight of formerly sovereign peoples, who had lost everything as a result of the Second World War save the outward trappings of independence…. "[73] The interdependence between self-determination and the ongoing enjoyment of human rights was highlighted, particularly "a people's right to adopt representative institutions and freely to choose the form of government which it wished to adopt."[74] The link to economic self-determination, which would assume prominence in the 1970s, was also drawn, as the right of nations to "permanent sovereignty over their natural wealth and resources."[75]

Ultimately, the Third Committee adopted the draft article 1 by 33 votes to 12, with 13 abstentions in November 1955, and self-determination was adopted into the draft Covenants:

> Article 1. 1/ All peoples have the right of self-determination. By virtue of that right they freely determine their political status and freely pursue their economic, social and cultural development.

68 Lebanon, 8 Comm.HR (1952), 258th mtg., (E/CN.4/SR.258) p. 6.

69 US, 6 GAOR (1951), 3rd Cmttee., 364th mtg., (A/C.3/SR.364) para. 19; Byelorussian SSR, 7 GAOR (1952),3rd Cmttee., 444th mtg., (A/C.3/SR.444) para. 4. Venezuala, ibid. 451st mtg., (A/C.3/SR.451) para. 31.

70 Syria, 9 GAOR (1954), 3rd Cmttee., 572nd mtg., (A/C.3/SR.572) para. 7; Iraq, 10 GAOR (1955), 3rd Cmttee., 643rd mtg., (A/C.3/SR.643) para. 4.

71 Pakistan, 7 GAOR (1952), 3rd Cmttee., 448th mtg., (A/C.3/SR.448) para. 17.

72 Belgium, 8 Comm.HR (1952), 254th mtg., (E/CN.4/SR.254) p. 6; 7 GAOR (1952), 3rd Cmttee., 446th mtg., (A/C.3/SR.446) para. 15; Yugoslavia, 8 Comm.HR (1952), 256th mtg., (E/CN.4/SR.256) p. 7.

73 Philippines, 7 GAOR (1952), 3rd Cmttee., 453rd mtg., (A/C.3/SR.453) para. 28.

74 *Ibid* para 5.

75 In 1952 Chile introduced a proposal in the Human Rights Commission for the inclusion of a right of "permanent sovereignty," or economic self-determination into the draft Covenant, Chilean Draft, (E/CN.4/L.24) Comm.HR, Report 8th Session, 14 ESCOR (1952) Supplement No. 4, p. 8, para. 67; see commentary by Chile, 8 Comm.HR (1952) 256th mtg., (E/CN.4/SR.256) p. 10; See Christian Reus-Smit "Post-1945 Decolonisation" in Individual Rights and the Making of the International System (Cambridge: CUP 2013).

> 2/ All peoples may, for their own ends, freely dispose of their natural wealth and resources without prejudice to any obligations arising out of international economic co-operation, based upon the principle of mutual benefit, and international law. In no case may a people be deprived of its own means of subsistence.
>
> 3/ The States Parties to the present Covenant, including those having responsibility for the administration of Non-Self-Governing and Trust Territories, shall promote the realization of the right of self-determination, and shall respect that right, in conformity with the provisions of the Charter of the United Nations.

While most Western powers still opposed a formalized decolonization system, self-determination's inclusion was to provide important early support to ongoing independence conflicts, by providing a powerful counterargument to invocations of Article 2(7). In the case of French North Africa, despite France's objections that the matter was a purely domestic one, the question of Morocco appeared on the agenda of the General Assembly in 1950 and 1951.[76] Arab States proposed a resolution calling on France to recognize:

> The right of the people of Morocco to complete self-determination in conformity with the Charter, [and renewed] its appeal for the reduction of tension in Morocco and [urged] that the right of the people of Morocco to free democratic political institutions be ensured.[77]

Similar demands for independence were raised by Tunisian and Algerian nationalist movements, prompting the Assembly to consider whether France was violating self-determination within Tunisia.[78] As they had done regarding Morocco, the Assembly adopted Resolution 611 (VII) expressing the hope that negotiations would continue "with a view to bringing about self-government for Tunisians."[79] By 1958 Afro-Asian States were demanding the right of independence for the people of Algeria. While a resolution to this effect was not passed, according to Rosalyn Higgins, "the voting records show that not only was the cause of Algeria gaining support, but that so was the idea that there might be a legal right to self-determination in these circumstances even

76 Wilson (1988: 63).

77 UN Draft Res. A/2526, 22 Oct 1953.

78 Wilson (1988: 65).

79 UNGA Res 611 (VII) 17 Dec 1952.

in spite of objections based on domestic jurisdiction."[80] Despite attempts to resolve the conflict through the granting of limited autonomy, by 1959 President De Gaulle had announced proposals for self-determination for Algeria, submitting a resolution to the Assembly which called for "a peaceful solution on the basis of the right to self-determination."[81] The following year – the year of the Colonial Declaration – the Assembly passed a resolution recognizing the right of self-determination for the people of Algeria. The basis of which, as Higgins notes "lies squarely on the international legal right to self-determination, and, by implication, the inapplicability of Article 2(7) in any situation concerning this right."[82] Unable to prevent colonial issues being placed on the General Assembly agenda by arguing for their protection under domestic jurisdiction, colonial powers began to change tactics.[83] As Georges Abi-Saab explains, they began walking out of the General Assembly or emphasized the inability of the UN to effectively force their hands.[84]

## 3 Anti-Colonial Activism

Against this backdrop, the Asian-African Conference held in Bandung, Indonesia in 1955 was to crystallize not only anti-colonial agenda but the broader anti-imperialist framings of self-determination.[85] Von Bernstorff and Dann argue that Bandung marked the first culmination of the Third World's "conscious and concerted 'trans-civilizational' movement" in their quest for formal independence for all colonial territories in international law.[86] Eslava, Fakhri and Nesiah describe the conference as the Third World's "awakening," and

80 Higgins (1963: 96).

81 Draft Res A/L276, GAOR: 14th session, 856th mtg quote in Higgins (1963: 96).

82 Higgins (1963: 97).

83 See Georges Abi-Saab, "The Newly Independent States and the Scope of Domestic Jurisdiction," *Proceedings of the American Society of International Law at Its Annual Meeting* (1921–1969), Vol. 54 (1960) 88.

84 Speech of French delegate, General Assembly, 6th Sess., Official Records, Plenary Meetings, p. 98; also the British delegate made a similar argument during the discussion of the Cyprus question, ibid., 9th Sess., Plenary Meetings, 53. Quoted in *Ibid.*

85 Roland Burke argues that Bandung was also a key development in the 'birth of the Third World' and the non-aligned movement. See Burke (2010: 15).

86 Jochen von Bernstorff and Philipp Dann, 'The Battle for International Law: An Introduction' in Jochen von Bernstorff and Philipp Dann, *The Battle for International Law: South-North Perspectives on the Decolonization Era* (Oxford: OUP, 2019) 4.

represented a key shift towards a common framework for realizing decolonial and post-colonial interests amongst non-western states and peoples.[87]

Leaders from the six independent states of Africa, along with virtually all of Asia – representing nearly 1.5 billion people - met to discuss issues of decolonization, sovereignty and human rights. These concerns were articulated around a common "Third World" identity, in which self-determination was to play a central role.[88] The Pakistani Prime Minister Mohammed Ali summed up the spirit of the conference, and indeed Asian-African attitude toward world affairs when he declared that "the peoples of Asia and Africa ... stand for the fundamental principles of human rights and self-determination."[89] In framing self-determination most delegates made repeated references to human rights and individual freedoms in the context of self-determination, as well as non-interference and respect for state sovereignty, with so many states having been for so long, in President Sukarno's phrase, "the peoples for whom decisions were made by others ... the tools of others, the playthings of forces they cannot influence."[90] The importance of self-determination and (equal) exercise of political rights was also reiterated. As Lebanese diplomat and academic Charles Malik stated:

> What are the ultimate fundamental human rights? For the Communists, these rights are for the most part social and economic rights. But for some of the rest of us the ultimate human rights that should now be guaranteed by the world and by the diverse nations are the personal, legal, political rights to freedom – to freedom of thought, to freedom of expression and certainly of free elections (my emphasis). [...] To the communists, in the present context of this conference freedom meant the liberation of the various nations and peoples of Asia and Africa from foreign Western rule. But to some of us – while this certainly belongs to the notion of freedom, freedom was much larger and deeper than liberation from foreign rule. To us freedom meant freedom of mind, freedom of thought, freedom of

87 Luis Eslava, Michael Fakhri and Vasuki Nesiah (eds), *Bandung, Global History, and International Law: Critical Pasts and Pending Futures* (Cambridge: CUP 2017).

88 Burke (2010: 26).

89 *Ibid* 29.

90 Ahmed Sukarno, Conference Opening Address, as reproduced in Hassan, *Collected Documents from the Asian-African Conference*, (Agency for Research and Development, Department of Foreign Affairs, 1983) 4–5.

> press, freedom to criticise, to judge for yourself, freedom in short, to be the full human being[91]

In keeping with their expanded definition of self-determination, the delegates did not just limit its ambit to the colonial context, but also directed it towards new forms of interventionism. The conference agreed to condemn colonialism "in all its manifestations," declaring it "an evil which should speedily be brought to an end."[92] Indeed, emerging Cold War activities in Asia with the US creation of the Southeast Asia Treaty Organisation in 1954 had been one of the key motivations for the conference. The Iranian delegate warned of "new forms" of colonialism which attempted to subvert the "sovereignty and freedom of peoples."[93] This new colonialism practiced by the "more subtle aggressors of our times" used "various invisible and deceiving weapons" and aimed at "re-inventing colonialism under new forms." "We must be very careful," said the Pakistani Prime Minister, "that we are not misled into opening our doors to a new and more insidious form of imperialism that masquerades in the guise of liberation."[94] The final communiqué declared that "the subjection of peoples to alien subjugation, domination and exploitation represents a denial of fundamental human rights" and called upon the powers concerned to grant freedom and independence to such peoples.

The link between self-determination and human rights was also stressed. Many delegates underlined that the rights of the nation were interdependent with those of the individual. Warning of the dangers of national independence, which could degenerate into "an instrument for a new and different kind of subjection" the Phillipino delegate, President Romulo, argued that freedom was not merely achieved by casting-off of alien rule, and promoted the necessity of a pluralistic, democratic state.[95] This position echoed Malik's position that self-determination and political freedom were mutually dependent. "Our conception of independence is not different in any respect from our conception of the observance of fundamental human rights, especially the right of peoples and nations to self-determination," remarked the Afghani delegate.[96]

91 Talk given by Dr Malik at Luncheon," Canberra 28th April 1955. Department of External Affairs, Australia. Available online, National Archives of Australia A 1838 / 278, 3002/1 Pr 5, File No. 156/3/3.

92 Final Communiqué of the Bandung Conference, April 24, 1955, N. Frankland (ed.), *Documents on International Affairs 1955* (Oxford: OUP, 1958), 433.

93 Opening address of Iran, quoted in Burke (2010: 27).

94 Opening Address of Pakistan, quoted in Burke (2010: 28).

95 Opening Address of Phillipines in Burke (2010: 29).

96 Opening Address of Afghanistan in Burke (2010: 27).

Over the next five years, the anti-colonial lobby continued to use its lobbying power in the Third Committee and the Commission on Human Rights to elevate self-determination and colonial independence. The 1958 and 1960 Conferences of African Independent States, and the 1959 Monrovia meeting for Foreign Ministers, also laid much of the groundwork for the 1960 Colonial Declaration. These efforts were galvanized, Maja Spanu argues, by a number of popular liberation causes which had emerged from incidents of colonial repression: the Viet Minh in Indochina, the Mau-Mau in Kenya and the Armée de Libération Nationale (ALN) – Front de Libération Nationale (FLN) in Algeria.[97] The viciousness with which these movements were suppressed by colonial powers drew widespread condemnation, and solidified public support. However, it was to be the attempted secession of Katanga in early 1960 that was to amplify the anti-colonialist cause, as it became clear that both imperial powers and Cold War powers, would seek by any means to derail independence movements that threatened their political and economic interests.

Just weeks after the Republic of Congo declared its independence in 1960, and the election of prime minister Patrice Lumumba, the southern province of Katanga sought to secede from the newly independent nation.[98] Katangan independence leader Moshe Tshombe, who was closely associated with Belgian settler and international mining interests, immediately appealed to the international community to recognize Katangan independence and sought the admission of Katanga into the United Nations, warning that Katanga was threatened by a communist insurgency.[99] Now fearing that Belgium was attempting to recolonize the country, Lumumba appealed for UN intervention.[100] While recognition was never achieved by the Katangese secessionist movement, the five year long crisis that followed saw the assassination of Lumumba by Katangese soldiers overseen by Belgian advisors, as well as the death of the UN secretary general Dag Hammarskjöld, killed when his plane over Congo mysteriously crashed.[101] Several states, including the US, which

97 Spanu (2014: 134).

98 E. Schmidt, *Foreign Intervention in Africa: From the Cold War to the War on Terror*, (Cambridge: CUP, 2013).

99 Catherine Hoskyns, *The Congo since Independence: January 1960 to December 1961*. (Oxford: OUP 1965) 146.

100 *Ibid* 2–3.

101 See Emmanuel Gerard and Bruce Kuklic, *Death in the Congo: Murdering Patrice Lumumba* (Cambridge, MA: Harvard UniversityPress, 2015). William Mountz, "The Congo Crisis: A Reexamintion," *The Journal of the Middle East and Africa* 5(2) (2014): 151–165. Alanna O'Malley,"Ghana, India and the Transnational Dynamics of the Congo Crisis at the United Nations, 1960–1," *The International History Review* 37(5) (2015): 984. Alanna

was deeply concerned about the threat of Soviet domination in the Congo, made no secret of their sympathy for the secessionists.[102] The Katanga army was bolstered by white mercenaries recruited from Belgium, South Africa, Southern Rhodesia, and France.[103] Belgium claimed it was merely providing "technical assistance" to any part of the Congo that desired 'to escape the grip of the Lumumba movement', a claim which garnered the support of the NATO member states in 1960. France provided Katanga with arms, and was apparently involved in mercenary recruitment, fueled by De Gaulle's "unrelieved hostility" towards the UN, and the situation in Algeria.[104]

For the anti-colonial lobby, the situation in Katanga highlighted the politicized nature of decolonization practice and the toxic combination of legal ambiguity, Cold War politics and neo-colonial financial and mercenary interests that dominated its development. This led to greater demands for a more regulated and UN supervised decolonization process that would curb foreign interest and control. As the events of Katanga underlined, colonial powers would not give up their profitable dependencies without a fight. Ghanaian leader Kwame Nkrumah argued that Katanga was an example of how neo-colonialism could disrupt the independence of colonial states, and highlighted the consequences of "clientele-sovereignty, or fake independence, namely the practice of granting a sort of independence by the metropolitan power, with the concealed intention of making the liberate country a client-state and controlling it effectively by means other than political ones."[105] If self-determination was to truly facilitate the move away from imperialism and towards real and lasting independence, than it needed a clear and binding legal basis.

## 4 The Colonial Declaration

The fifteenth session of the General Assembly of the United Nations which convened in New York in September 1960 was to realise the dream of colonial

O'Malley, "'What an Awful Body the UN Have Become!!' Anglo-American–UN Relations during the Congo crisis, February–December 1961," *Journal of Transatlantic Studies* 14, 1 (2016): 26–46.

102 Hoskyns (1965: 148).

103 *Ibid.*

104 Rosalyn Higgins, "United Nations Peacekeeping 1964–67: Documents and Commentary." *The United Nations Operation in the Congo* (ONUC) 1960–1964 (London, 1980) p. 270.

105 Kwame Nkrumah, "Osagyefo at the United Nations," (Accra: Government Printers, 1960). 8; Kwame Nkrumah, *Neo-Colonialism: The Last Stage of Imperialism* (Thomas Nelson & Sons, 1965).

emancipation – in legal terms at least. The recent admission of seventeen newly independent States sealed the emergence of a voting majority. Taking advantage of the opportunity presented by this numerical advantage, 25 states presented the so-called Colonial Resolution, which was passed without a single dissent and nine abstentions (Australia, Belgium, Dominican Republic, France, Portugal, Spain, Union of South Africa, United Kingdom, United States).[106]

The "subjection of peoples to alien subjugation, domination and exploitation," it declared, constituted "a denial of fundamental human rights (...) and an impediment to the promotion of world peace and cooperation." The Bandung Conference was invoked as the guiding precedent for the declaration by a multitude of delegates.[107] The resolution, noted the Ethiopian delegate, was "a consolidation of the ideals and principles which the African-Asian countries have proclaimed and supported ever since 1955."[108] In line with anti-colonial framings of self-determination, the right to self-determination was articulated as a demand for "an inalienable right to complete freedom, the exercise of their sovereignty and the integrity of their national territory." Moreover, it affirmed that colonialism denied fundamental human rights, that it was contrary to the Charter, and that it impeded the promotion of world peace.[109]

In a last desperate attempt to stave off the inevitable adoption of the Declaration, Western states sought during the debates on the draft resolutions to depict the positive aspects of colonialism, appealing to the Afro-Asian states to take a more balanced account of their colonial past. These attempts were roundly rejected. As the delegate from Mali said:

---

106 The *Colonial Independence Declaration*, GA Res. 1514(XV), 15 GAOR (1960) Supplement No. 16, (A/4684).

107 States referring to Bandung included Cambodia, Iran, Ceylon, Ghana, Ethiopia, Libya, Burma, Liberia, Guatemala, Laos, Sudan, Nepal, Indonesia, Togo, Congo (Brazzaville), Morocco, and Cyprus. African regional conferences in Accra, Monrovia, and Addis Ababa, which endorsed the Bandung decisions, also received prominent mention. In addition to the African and Asian countries, Soviet bloc representatives were also enthusiastic proponents of the Bandung Conference. Of the communist countries, USSR, Poland, and Ukrainian Soviet Socialist Republic referred to Bandung in the general debate, and attempted to position themselves as bearers of the imprecisely defined Bandung Spirit—a difficult task given that representatives from states that attended the conference were pushing a rival text.

108 Verbatim Records of the General Assembly Plenary Meeting, 935th session, 30 November 1960, A/PV. 928, paras. 17.

109 This point was underlined by Emerson (1965: 489).

> The delegations which speak in this Assembly of their colonial experience or proclaim the benefits of colonialism can unfortunately only speak of the empire of their fathers' day; they speak of it as a heritage. If their countries were colonized at some time in history, they know it only from history books. Therein lies the fundamental difference between those delegations and ours, who have personal experience of colonial rule. Our knowledge is not based on hearsay or on what we learnt in school; we were for decades the living embodiment of that system[110]

The earlier position that the fate of colonial peoples lay within the domestic competence of their respective administrators, who could at their own pace and discretion oversee the transition to self-government was replaced by an enforceable right of self-determination for colonial peoples. The prohibition of armed action or repressive measures to prevent colonial peoples from exercising "peacefully and freely their right to complete independence" made this point explicit. Sweeping aside the discourse of guidance by an "advanced nation" – so that after an indeterminate period the "backward" territory in question could become a full member of the international community, the General Assembly declared that lack of preparation should never serve as a pretext for delaying the exercise of self-determination. The very title of Resolution 1514 – "Declaration on the Granting of Independence" – sought to bar any delay in the grant of independence, although in the accompanying resolution 1541 – passed the following day - "free association and integration" were also listed as means of attaining "self-determination" – although these options, as Pomerance notes were viewed with a "jaundiced eye."[111] It became impossible to insist, as Plamenatz puts it, that some countries "ought to be deprived of their independence in order to be made capable of freedom."[112]

Self-determination was no longer something to be 'earned' but a right that could not be denied, regardless of political preparedness; a freedom from foreign rule and intervention that guaranteed equal membership in the society of states. This approach drew immediate criticism for "putting the empirical horse before the juridical cart"[113] and creating states which, in the words of Rupert Emerson, "had little hope of strength of vitality."[114] Similarly, US

110 General Assembly Official Records (15th session), 931st plenary meeting, December 1, 1960, 1065. 16 General Assembly Official Records (15th session), 947th.

111 Pomerance (1982: 25).

112 John Plamenatz, *On Alien Rule and Self-Government,* (Michigan: Longmans, 1960) 22–3.

113 *Ibid* 23.

114 Emerson (1971: 494).

Secretary of State Dean Acheson, writing in 1961 declared that "No sensible person can believe that African peoples can find their way toward a stabilized and civilized life without the help of the Europeans who know them best."[115] Vice President Richard Nixon was even blunter in his judgement "The peoples of Africa have been out of the trees only for about fifty years."[116]

One of the most contentious aspects of the debates leading up to the adoption of the Declaration was that of how colonialism was to be defined in the resolution – a question raised during the Bandung Conference and now debated throughout the Third World. The accompanying resolution, Resolution 1541 adopted a definition of Non-Self-Governing Territories which was to severely limit the Declaration's broader application. The category included any "territory which is geographically separate and is distinct ethnically and/or culturally from the country administering it" and which is subject to "administrative, political, juridical, economic, or historical" factors that "arbitrarily place it in a position or status of subordination." Moreover, the resolution noted that the obligation applies to territories "then known to be of the colonial type," at the time of the Charter, seemingly excluding territories that had become non-self-governing since the time of the Charter. This seemed to indicate a shift away from the condemnation of colonialism in "all its forms and manifestations", expressed by Third World states during the Bandung Conference to a more limited interpretation.[117]

## 5 The Boundaries of Independence

The Colonial Declaration undoubtedly marked a turning point in the UN's approach to self-determination, but the crisis in Portuguese Goa the following year was perhaps the real landmark, when the abstractions of the Resolution were put to the test.[118] Here the growing demand to navigate the practical tensions between self-determination's application began to be stressed through

115 Quoted in Burke, "From Individual Rights to National Development: The First UN International Conference on Human Rights," Tehran, 1968', 19 *Journal of World History* 3 (2008) 288.

116 Quoted in *Ibid.*

117 See Georges Abi-Saab, "The Newly Independent States and the Scope of Domestic Jurisdiction," *Proceedings of the American Society of International Law at Its Annual Meeting* (1921–1969), Vol. 54 (April 28–30, 1960) 87.

118 Wilson (1988: 70–71).

the emphasis on the defined units of political authority.[119] The arguments articulated during the debates moreover underscored a key ideological battle over the legal status of remaining colonial territories and the transferal of sovereignty taking place at this time, as well as the best approach for dealing with the practical remnants of colonialism. To support their claim to immediate independence of colonial territories, the Afro-Asian bloc moved towards a reframing of colonial rule not only as a form of foreign bondage, but as a form of "permanent aggression."[120] In the rhetoric of many of the anti-colonial lobbyists, self-determination became firmly articulated as a disruption of the European nature and structure of international law, which had supported the colonial regimes. As the Indian delegate to the Security Council argued: "[The invasion of Goa] is a question of getting rid of the last vestiges of colonialism in India. That is a matter of faith with us. Whatever anyone else may think, Charter or no Charter, Council or no Council, that is our basic faith which we cannot afford to give up at any cost."[121]

Despite the adoption of Resolution 1542 immediately after the Declaration on Colonialism declaring Portuguese territories non-self-governing within the meaning of Chapter XI of the Charter,[122] there was little indication that Portugal was willing to acknowledge that their dependencies had a right to self-determination. While India had sought to pressure Portugal to withdraw from Goa, Lisbon had, in 1951, incorporated its colonies into the Portuguese state, and from then on regarded any issue relating to its colonies as an "internal" affair, not subject to any external interference.[123] When India invaded Goa in December of 1961 Portugal immediately brought a complaint to the Security Council accusing India of aggression in Portugal's colonial territories of Goa,

119 For a longer discussion of the Goa incident see Quincy Wright, "The Goa Incident", *American Journal of International Law*, 56 (1962) 617–632 and R. P. Anand, "Attitude of the Asian-African States Toward Certain Problems of International Law," *International Comparative Law Quarterly* 15 (1966): 55–75.

120 See statement by VK Krishma Menon, former Defence Minister of India, *Times of India*, January 1, 1962, 1.

121 U.N. SCOR, 16th Sess., 987th mtg., at 9, 40, U.N. Doc. S/PV. 987 (1961).

122 GA Res. 1542 (XV), Dee. 15, 1960. General Assembly, 15th Sess., Official Records, Supp. No. 16 (Doe. A/4684), 30.

123 Caio Simões de Araújo, "A Crisis of Confidence: The postcolonial moment and the diplomacy of decolonization at the United Nations, ca. 1961" in Nicole Eggers, Jessica Lynne Pearson, Aurora Almada e Santos (eds.) *The United Nations and Decolonization* (London: Routledge, 2020) 109.

Damao and Diu.[124] The Soviet delegate, who was the first to intervene in the Security Council debate, argued that:

> Goa and the other Portuguese colonies in Indian territory cannot be regarded as other than temporarily under the colonial domination of Portugal. These territories are linked with the Indian Union both by reason of their geographical position and their history, culture, language and traditions. They were wrested from the Indian State at the time when the countries were establishing their colonial empires[125]

The depiction of the invasion as a sort of wresting away of colonial rule and indeed international law from domination by the West was made explicit by India during the debates over its invasion of Goa. Declaring that Goa was "an integral part of India" the Indian delegate declared that the question of Goa was:

> [a] colonial question, in the sense that part of our country is illegally occupied by right of conquest by the Portuguese. The fact that they have occupied it for 450 years is of no consequence because, during nearly 425 or 430 years of that period we really had no chance to do anything because we were under colonial domination ourselves. But during the last fourteen years from the very day when we came independent, we have not ceased to demand the return of the peoples under illegal domination to their own countrymen to share their independence....[126]

To "throw off the colonial yoke" therefore, even by force, was more or less an act of "self-defence."[127]

India's historic claim to sovereignty raised a particular query regarding the nature of paragraph 6 of the Colonial Declaration. During the drafting of the Declaration, a number of states had sought to link the paragraph to the

124 Ministério dos Negócios Estrangeiros, Vinte Anos de Defesa do Estado Portuguêsda Índia (1947–1967), vol. IV (Lisboa: Imprensa Nacional, 1968), 229.

125 Deora, M. S., *Documents on India's Role in Afro-Asian Liberation Movements,* Vol. 6, Goa, Daman and Diu (New Delhi: Discovery Publishing House, 1994), 304.

126 *Ibid* para 46.

127 S Prakash Sinha, "Perspectives of the Newly Independent States on the Binding Quality of International Law" in F.E. Snyder & S. Sathirathai, (eds.) *Third World Attitudes Towards International Law: An Introduction* (Dordrecht: Martinus Nijhoff, 1987) 13.

re-integration of territory lost during decolonization.[128] The Indonesian delegate had argued that: "My delegation was one of the sponsors of paragraph 6 and in bringing it into the draft resolution we had in mind that the continuation of Dutch colonialism in West Irian is a partial disruption of the national unity and territorial integrity of our country." Guatemala, who sought the reintegration of Belize, sought an amendment to paragraph 6 that stated that "[t]he principle of the self-determination of peoples may in no case impair the right of territorial integrity of any State or its right to the recovery of territory."[129] Other delegations, many with territorial aspirations of their own had expressed a similar interpretation, although this position was rejected by the majority of states. Nevertheless, it underlined a key question, namely which people the new law of self-determination was to serve, particularly when it affected the allocation and organization of territorial authority as it concerned pre-colonial ties. Ten years later this very question would come before the ICJ in the Western Sahara case, where Morocco and Mauritania sought to argue that their pre-colonial ties to the territory required its return, regardless of the will of the population.[130] The eventual refusal by India to grant the populations of Goa, Damao and Din the opportunity to express their wishes as to the future of the territories was in the eyes of many the substitution of one kind of colonial rule for another,[131] and was criticized by Chile and Ecuador as a breach of self-determination[132]

Deeply concerned by India's reliance upon resolutions 1514(XV), 1542(XV) and 1603(XV) in justifying its intervention, and the potential escalation of anti-colonial activity in their own territories, the US, UK, France, Turkey and China supported Portugal in its claim of aggression, calling for a cease-fire and withdrawal of Indian forces from the territory, and urging the parties to work out a permanent solution by peaceful means.[133] The Indian delegate rejected all contrary legal arguments on the ground that they were based on an illegitimate, European, international legal conceptions:

> If any narrow-minded legalistic consideration – considerations arising from international law by European law writers – should arise, these

128 Cited in Miguel Sanchez, "Self-Determination and the Falkland Islands Dispute" in *Ibid* 108.

129 *Ibid.*

130 *Western Sahara* (Advisory Opinion), ICJ Reports (1975).

131 Pomerance (1982: 17).

132 SCOR 988th mtg para 30

133 Quincy Wright, "The Goa Incident," *American Journal of International Law*, 56 (1962) 617–632 at 617.

> writers were, after all, brought up in the atmosphere of colonialism. I pay respect to Grotius, who is supposed to be the father of international law and we accept many tenets of international law. But the tenet…which is quoted in support of colonial powers having sovereign rights over territories which they won by conquest in Asia and Africa is no longer acceptable. It is the European concept and it must die[134]

The comments expressed by the Indian delegate articulated a key ideological shift in in international law for many states in which self-determination was at the heart. Decolonisation was now "irreversible and irresistible," according to the Indian ambassador. supported by a new sea change in International Law.[135] Colonial states could no longer hide behind an outdated claim to sovereignty to protect their colonial holdings – rather their continued presence in the colonies "created a threat to peace and security in various parts of the world including Goa." The Goan incident argues Caio Simoes de Arajujo, "was a crucialmoment in which a moral and political imperative was transformed intoa sanctioned action."[136] Rupert Emerson, writing shortly after the invasion argued that: "The case of Goa is a peculiarly striking illustration of the proposition generally accepted by the UN majority that all colonialism is illegitimate and that the use of force to overthrow it is therefore justified."[137] However, for some it also seemed to underline a problematic double standard in self-determination's application in colonial transfers, given the failure to uphold the rights of the population of Goa to determine its fate. The impact of the Goan incident was swift. Dahomey annexed the Portuguese enclave of Sao Joao Batista de Ajuda in 1962, and Indonesia disembarked its troops in West Irian, despite the protests of the Dutch, and Western Sahara was annexed by Morocco.[138]

The thorny question that had been raised during the Katanga secession and remained unresolved by the Goa crisis was how best to navigate the aftermath of colonial occupation – particularly when it concerned that "quintessentially postcolonial problem: the relationship between people and borders."[139] It was

---

134 Deora, M. S., *Documents on India's Role in Afro-Asian Liberation Movements,* Vol. 6, Goa, Daman and Diu (New Delhi: Discovery Publishing House, 1994), 306.

135 *Ibid.* 319.

136 de Araújo (2020: 118).

137 Emerson (1965).

138 Pomerance (1982: 20).

139 Ryan M Irwin, "Sovereignty in the Congo Crisis" in *Decolonisation and the Cold War: Negotiating Independence*, Leslie James and Elizabeth Leake (eds.) (New York: Bloomsbury, 2015) 205.

becoming evident that despite the professed universality of self-determination, and the devastating effects of colonialism, the transition to independence required practical limits – particularly if it was to ensure the strength and stability of the post-colonial state.

The question of territorial boundaries in particular was to emerge as the most divisive issue amongst the anti-colonial lobby, particularly in Africa. Throughout the 1940s and 50s, as Saadia Touval notes, "an aversion to international borders drawn by the colonial powers, if not their complete rejection had been a consistent theme of anti-colonial nationalism in Africa."[140] The boldest call for boundary revisions occurred at the first All-African Peoples conference held in Accra in December 1958 which denounced "artificial frontiers drawn by imperialist Powers to divide the peoples of Africa, particularly those which cut across ethnic groups and divide people of the same stock; calls for the abolition or adjustment of such frontiers at an early date; [and] calls upon the independent states of Africa to support a permanent solution to this problem founded upon the wishes of the people."[141] Nkrumah was the leading advocate of this cause and in 1959 called for the eradication of "the artificial divisions and boundaries which are responsible for the Balkanization of our continent."[142]

However, following the Katanga crisis, these attitudes were beginning to wane. At the 1963 Conference of the Independent African States, several events served to underline the growing concern over the territorial aspect of self-determination.[143] King Hassan of Morocco had boycotted the conference on the grounds that Mauritania, which was claimed as Moroccan territory, was in attendance.[144] The other major dispute was that of Somalia with Ethiopia and Kenya, which stemmed from the Somali assertion of the need to establish a greater Somali nation-state, which would encompass within its borders all the

140 Saadia Touval, 'The Organisation of African Unity and African Borders," 21 *International Organization 1* (1967) 102.

141 First All African Peoples' Conference, Accra, 5–13 December 1958, cited in Makonnen, Yilma, *International Law and the New States of Africa*, (UNESCO, 1983) 458–59.

142 K, Nkrumah, address, Proceeding at Sanniquellic Conference, 1959, cited in Suzanna Lalonde, *Determining Boundaries in a Conflicted World: The role of uti possedetis juris*, (Montreal: McGill-Queen's University Press, 2002.) 71. See also a similar address: K, Nkrumah, 'United We Stand', address, Proceedings of the Summit Conference of Independent African States, Addis Ababa, vol. 1, section 2, Summit CIAS/GEN/INF/36, May 1963 at 7.

143 Thirty independent African states participated in the conference. Only Morocco because of the presence of Mauritania and Togo because of the reluctance of many states to recognize the new government following the assassination of President Olympio, See Touvall (1972: 111).

144 *Ibid.*

Somali people, based upon a claim of self-determination. "It is no longer possible, nor desirable," argued President Tsiranana of Madagascar, "to modify the boundaries of Nations, on the pretext of racial, religious or linguistic criteria."[145] Most states argued that existing borders should be maintained. In the words of Modibo Keita, the President of Mali: "We must take Africa as it is, and we must renounce any territorial claims, if we do not wish to introduce what we might call black imperialism in Africa.... African unity demands of each one of us complete respect for the legacy that we have received from the colonial system, that is to say: maintenance of the present frontiers of our respective states."[146]

In the Organisation of African Unity's 'Articles of Faith,'[147] it was emphasised that States should respect one another's sovereignty and territorial integrity. The notable lack of any reference to self-determination in the document was telling and seemed to support the position expressed by the Kenyan delegate at the Addis Abada Summit that "the principle of self-determination has relevance where foreign domination is the issue. It has no relevance where the issue is territorial disintegration by dissident citizens."[148] Indeed, the notable lack of support for the Somali and Sudanese secessionist bids suggested that most African states by this stage regarded claims for self-determination by groups within independent states as unacceptable. Two years later the US Assistant Secretary for African Affairs expressed the same view.[149] "Like the question of what constitutes a bargaining gun it in labor relations," he said, "the right of self-determination has to be based on a practical historical unit in order to permit fast and sensible results." And citing African attitudes, he described respect for historical frontiers as a "useful and important base and adjunct for our policy of self-determination."[150] Nevertheless, a number of African commentators drew attention to the "apparent contradiction between

145 *Proceedings of the Summit Conference of Independent African States*, Addis Ababa, May 1963, Vol. 1, section i, Document AGENDA/CONF/5, May 15, 1963. (Document AGENDA/12, May 17, 1963

146 *Ibid* CIAS/GEN/INF/33.

147 They were dubbed the organization's 'articles of faith' by Nigeria's Attorney General at the time. See T.O. Elias, 'The Charter of the Organization of African Unity', *American Journal of International Law*, 59, 2 (1965), 248.

148 Emerson (1971: 35).

149 G. M. Williams, "United States Policy in Africa," Departmentof State Bulletin, 52 (April 12, 1965), 545. G. M. Williams, "Congo Realities and United States Policy," Department of State Bulletin, 52 (May 24, 1965), 798.

150 *Ibid.*

African support for self-determination under colonialism, and opposition to the application of the same principle in a post-colonial setting."[151]

Incidents of groups seeking to establish their own independent states had begun to increase by the late 1960s, particularly in Africa.[152] The decision to preserve existing administrative boundaries sought to ensure the stability of newly emergent States once they had become established. However, it did not engage with the troubling question of the deep divisions wrought by colonial era boundaries.[153] The cracks were beginning to show in the legal logic underlining self-determination's characterization as a legal right, and as secessionist claims grew in number the international community began to depart from self-determination's universalist characterization. For many commentators, including Leo Strauss, it was a great irony that at the moment of self-determination's elevation to law, the chances of it facilitating the independence of other peoples seemed to recede entirely.[154]

Such attitudes were nowhere more prominently aired than in the international response to the Biafran bit for independence in 1967, and the ensuing war with Nigeria between 1967 and 1970, involving the death and displacement of millions. The dispute stemmed from long running tensions in Nigeria's federal structure, that had sparked a series of violent coups, leading to a declaration of independence by the Igbo people.[155] While the conflict saw widespread massacres and various human rights abuses of Biafrans at the hands of the Nigerian Government, the majority of the international community were unwavering in their refusal to recognise the Biafran claim to independence.[156] Most states as well as the OAU, strongly upheld Nigeria's right to defend its territorial integrity, and the primacy of existing states and their borders, insisting that the conflict was an internal matter.

151 O. Kamanu, "Secession and the Right of Self-Determination: An OAU Dilemma" 12 *The Journal of Modern African Studies* 3 (1974), 355.

152 This included groups in Algeria, Angola, Burma, Cameroon, Chad, the Comoros, the Democratic Republic of Congo, Cyprus, Ethiopia, Ghana, Guinea, India, Indonesia, Ivory Coast, Kenya, Laos, Mali, Mozambique, Namibia, Niger, Nigeria, Oman, Pakistan, Papua New Guinea, the Philippines, Saint Kitts and Nevis, Saint Vincent and the Grenadines, Senegal, the Solomon Islands, Somalia, Sri Lanka, Sudan, Tanzania, Uganda, Vanuatu, and Zambia.

153 Mathhew Craven, "Statehood, Self-Determination and Recognition" in Malcolm Evans (ed) *International Law* (Oxford: OUP, 2010) 233.

154 Leo Strauss, *The City and Man*, (Chicago: University of Chicago, 1978) 6.

155 Getachew (2019: 103).

156 Proclamation of the Republic of Biafra 9, *reprinted in* 6 Int'L Legal Materials 673 (1967) Int'l Herald Tribune (Paris), Jan. 19, 1970, at p. 6. Ojukwu and other Biafran officials' statements in DS (vol I pp. 427–44, vol II pp. 247–272).

The Biafran claim was based on an extension and expansion of self-determination, and centered on several aspects, including an appeal to the normative core of self-determination which they claimed paralleled their own political grievances, the retention of an inherited colonial framework in which they could not live peacefully, and a reinterpretation of *uti possedetis*.[157] The most central element of their claim was that their treatment at the hands of other Nigerian groups amounted to exploitation, that it was impossible due to the actions of the central government to reestablish political relations between the Eastern Region and the rest of the country, and that genocide was inevitable, giving rise to a legitimate cause for secession.[158] The widespread human rights violations they had experienced at the hands of the Nigerian state, they argued, triggered the application of self-determination, necessitating a reorganization of territorial boundaries to ensure their protection.

This was accepted by just five states: Tanzania, Gabon, the Ivory Coast, Zambia, and Haiti.[159] Among them it was argued that the massive violations of human rights of its population dealt an irreparable blow to Nigerian unity,[160] with some states drawing parallels between the Biafran suffering and the fate of the Jews in Germany.[161] The more dominant view was encapsulated by the British position (who had incidentally kept up the arms supply to the Nigerian central government) that the Biafrans, "whatever their grievances, at rebellion and secession…was a tragic and disastrous error and therefore the Nigerian government were right to resist it."[162] Tanzanian President Julius Nyerere circulated a memorandum to his fellow African Heads of State during a 1969 OAU conference, arguing that, in this case they should abandon the commitment to territorial integrity given the humanitarian nature of the crisis. While colonial borders were a practical necessity to facilitate inter-state cooperation and minimize conflict, he argued, the right of governments to rule nevertheless rested on their ability to serve the population as a whole.[163] In situations such as Biafra, "where a government could no longer protect the lives of all of its

---

157 Brad Simpson, "The Biafran Secession and the Limits of Self-Determination," *Journal of Genocide Research* 16 (August 2014): 337–54, 343.

158 A. Pavkovic and P. Radan, *The Ashgate Research Companion to Secession*, (London: Ashgate, 2011), 100.

159 Fabry (2010: 166).

160 D. A. Ijalaye, "Was 'Biafra' at Any Time a State in International Law?," *The American Journal of International Law*, 65 (1971), 553–4.

161 Nyere in "Why We Recognised Biafra" in *The Observer*, 28 April 1968.

162 Quoted in Fabry (2010: 166).

163 James Mayall *World Politics: Progress and its Limits* (Cambridge: Polity Press, 2013) 56.

citizens, and when a particular group believed itself to be threatened by genocide, it forfeited its legitimacy."[164]

The OAU and UN were unwavering in their insistence that the matter was an internal one.[165] The Biafra case had "raised the specter many have feared:" that the concept of self-determination may be attached to new contexts and would inevitably spark secessionist events;[166] a fear that was compounded by the ultimately successful secession of Bangladesh in 1971. Nyerere, who condemned the hypocrisy on self-determination, lamented that "we will soon be tolerating fascism in Africa as long as it is practiced by African governments against African peoples."[167] After all, "these [Biafran] people are still dead; the colour of those who killed them is irrelevant."[168]

---

164 Julius Nyerere, "Biafra, Human Rights and Self-Determination in Africa," April 13, 1968.

165 O. Schacter, 'The United Nations and Internal Conflict', in J.N. Moore, *Law and Civil War in the Modern World*, (London: The Lawbook Exchange, 1974) 419.

166 Charles R. Nixon, "Self-Determination: The Nigeria/Biafra Case" 24 *World Politics* (1972) 473–497.

167 Pomerance (1982: 47).

168 Quoted in Burke (2010: 57).

CHAPTER 4

# Remaking the World after Empire

Having been formally established as the legal standard for colonial independence, the debate over self-determination's ongoing articulation beginning in the mid-1960s was to give rise to increasingly divergent ideological positions.[1,2] The independence of former colonies seemed to support the claim that for the first time international law had become universal and that a true "community of nations" had emerged.[3] Given the centrality of the decolonisation period to the development of self-determination as a legal norm, it may be tempting to view the significance of self-determination in international legal terms as lying primarily in this era. Indeed, for many scholars the historical legacy of self-determination is tied almost exclusively to elevation of the right to independence of colonial peoples in the 1960s.[4] At this point it is often claimed that the progressive unfolding of self-determination secured the successful diffusion of the model of the nation-state, replacing vertical sovereign hierarchies with

---

1 The title is inspired by Nathaniel Berman, 'In the Wake of Empire', 14 *American University International Law Review* (1999) 1521–1554.

2 See Brad Simpson 'Self-Determination, Human Rights, and the End of Empire in the 1970s', 4:2 *Humanity* (2013) 239–260 and Getachew (2019: Chapter 5).

3 See Anghie who notes that the existence of such a universal community is assumed in much contemporary theorizing. Anghie (2005); See also Haskell Fain, Normative Politics and the Community of Nations (Philadelphia, PA: Temple University Press, 1987); James Mayall (ed.), *The Community of States* (London: Allen & Unwin, 1982).

4 For an example of the literature emanating from the period see M. Cherif Bassiouni, "Self-Determination and the Palestinians," *Proceedings of the American Society International Law* (1971) p. 31; Yoram Dinstein, "Collective Human Rights of peoples and Minorities," 25 *International & Comparative Law Quarterly* 102 (1976); Rupert Emerson, "Self-Determination," *Proceedings of the American Society International Law* (1966) 135; Robert Friedlander, "Self-Determination: A Legal-Political Inquiry," *1 DET. C.L. REV.* 71 (1975); Leslie C. Green, "Self-Determination and Settlement of the Arab-Israeli Conflict," *Proceedings of the American Society International Law.* (1971) 40; Chen, Lung-Chu, "Self-Determination as a Human Right," in *Towards World Order and Human Dignity*, W Michael Reisman and Burns H Weston eds. (New York: The Free Press, 1976); John Murphy, "Self-Determination: United States Perspectives" in *Self-Determination: National, Regional and Global Dimensions,* Y. Alexander & R. Friedlander eds., (Boulder: Westview Press, 1978); Zubeida Mustafa, "The Principle of Self-Determination in International Law," 5 *International Law*, 479 (1971); Ved P Nanda, "Self-Determination Outside the Colonial Context: The Birth of Bangladesh," 1 *Hous J Int'l L* 71 (1978–1979) pp. 71–93; M.G Kaladharan Nayar, "Self-Determination Beyond the Colonial Context: Biafra in Retrospect," 10 *Texas International Law Journal* (1975) 321–345.

 | DOI:10.1163/9789004479197_006

the horizontal logic of sovereign equality.[5] The gap in the ordinary functions of international law which proceeded the entry into statehood of the former colonies was then closed as it resumed its normal framework, largely rendering self-determination redundant in the post-imperial period.

Nevertheless, as this chapter argues, contestations over the reconstruction of the post-colonial world, particularly expectations of sovereignty continued to be framed around self-determination. In the case of states of the global South, it had become increasingly evident that the removal of imperial hierarchies had not brought a complete end to international differentiation or stratification. “The UN resolution on decolonization has created a new situation for our struggle,” argued Amilcar Cabral, leader of the Guinea-Bissau liberation movement, where the anti-colonial struggle had moved beyond its national character and onto “an international level.”[6] Formal post-colonial sovereignty did not necessarily translate to freedom and independence in an international system that was still broadly structured around imperial hierarchies. Political, economic and legal impediments still existed, particularly at the international level. Issues of economic inequality and patterns of political intervention in particular provoked acute concern.

Therefore, states in the global South increasingly turned to self-determination to assert their demands for national sovereignty, non-intervention and the ‘economic development and collective rights of the nation’[7] as a “means of clearing away the last traces of bondage and preventing any further bondage.”[8] These efforts were to culminate in the grafting of self-determination onto demands for a New International Economic Order, in a dramatic attempt to transform the world economy on the basis of global redistribution as a matter of right and to redress the broader structural system which had underpinned empire.

Simultaneously, another group of actors was trying to reshape the discourse of self-determination in pursuit of a new model of sovereign responsibility;

5 As James Mayall argues, with decolonization “the naturalness of hierarchy was replaced by the naturalness of equality.” James Mayall, *Nationalism and International Society*, (Cambridge: CUP, 1990) 33.

6 Amilcar Cabral, “Anonymous Soldiers for the United Nations,” in *Revolution in Guinea: An African People's Struggle* (London: Love and Malcomson, 1969) 40–41.

7 Roland Burke, ‘From Individual Rights to National Development: The First UN International Conference on Human Rights, Tehran, 1968’, 19:3 *Journal of World History* (2008) 275–296, 276.

8 As Sinha argues: ‘Sovereignty is the most treasured possession of the newly independent States. On the one hand, it makes them the master of their own house, and on the other hand, it provides them with a legal shield against foreign incursions or attempts thereat by stronger States.’ S. Prakash Sinha, “Perspective of the Newly Independent States on the Binding Quality of International Law,” (1965) 14 *International and Comparative Law Quarterly* 127.

one enmeshed with the project of promoting a liberal human rights discourse, democratic politics and individual-based human rights activism. While recent years have seen a renewed interest in the relationship between human rights and decolonisation, very little attention has been paid to interrogating the role of self-determination in this process. Some scholars, including Kenneth Cmiel have argued that this is because self-determination was "off the radar" during human rights debates,[9] while Samuel Moyn notes that "human rights entered global rhetoric in a kind of hydraulic relationship with self-determination: to the extent the one appeared, and progressed, the other declined, or even disappeared."[10] However, as the chapter will explore, self-determination was not an absent norm in the human rights revolution, but was a central tool, used to promote new understandings of state authority and domestic behaviour from within the human rights movement. Western states continued to support the notion of non-intervention as a concomitant of self-determination; however they largely sought to adapt or rather confine the notion of self-determination to one more in keeping with their democratising and human rights oriented vision of world politics.[11] Seeking to limit the fall-out from demands for economic redistribution and strict non-interference professed by post-colonial and non-aligned states, self-determination was instead articulated as necessitating the exercise of civil, political and social rights, and particularly democratic rights, within the framework of the state.[12] The denial of those rights, in this conception, implicate issues of self-determination and justify international interest and concern, as the debate of humanitarian intervention began to address. Legal commentators in particular played a key role in this development, as they increasingly called for self-determination to reflect a growing human rights consciousness, and as encompassing duties states

---

9 Kenneth Cmiel, 'The Recent History of Human Rights', 109 *American Historical Review* (2004) 117–136.

10 Samuel Moyn, The Last Utopia (Cambridge MA: Harvard University Press 2010) 88. Daniel Sargent meanwhile argues 'Defenders of human rights in the West paid little attention to collectivist concepts of rights, such as the right to national self-determination' in Daniel Sargent, *'Oasis in the Desert? America's Human Rights Rediscovery', in* Jan Eckel and Samuel Moyn (eds.) *The Breakthrough: Human Rights in the 1970s* (Philadelphia: University of Pennsylvania Press, 2014) 137.

11 See Edward Morgan, 'The Imagery and Meaning of Self-Determination', 20 *International Law and Policy* (1988) 357–358.

12 Brad Simpson notes that "the end of formal European colonialism, by delivering the "first right" to the vast majority of the world's peoples, made possible the strategic embrace by the West of individual human rights and facilitated the explosion of rights activism." Brad Simpson 'Self-Determination, Human Rights, and the End of Empire in the 1970s', 4:2 *Humanity* (2013) 239–260 at 240.

had towards peoples within their jurisdictions, which would have a continuing character. Thus, the emergence of the sovereignty of colonial people was simultaneous with the creation of international human rights law which sought to condition the character of that sovereignty.[13]

## 1 A New International Law

By 1970 there was little remaining opposition to decolonisation in either the UN or in the international community more generally. However, there was still considerable debate about the legal status of self-determination – namely whether it had emerged as a legal right or remained a general principle of international law. After 1960, references to self-determination continued to appear in international documents, most prominently in the Covenants on Human Rights, seeming to confirm self-determination's application beyond the colonial context. To Rosalyn Higgins, the general practice of States as illustrated by a series of General Assembly resolutions indicated the "inescapable" conclusion that self-determination had developed into an international legal right by this time, although one whose extent and scope was still open to considerable debate.[14] Leo Gross countered that it was political expediency, not legal obligation, which had prompted states to award independence to their colonies, and that no legal right of self-determination had emerged.[15] Writing in 1968 J H W Verzijl assumed an even more cynical stance, writing':

> The "right of self-determination"...has never been recognized as a genuine or positive right of "peoples" of universal and impartial application, and it never will, nor can be so recognized in the future. It would indeed in its general implementation prove a constant source of disruption and subversion, and the international legal order of established States will never be prepared to acknowledge with sincerity its universal existence as a matter of law or right[16]

---

13 Christian Reus-Smit, "Human Rights and the Social Construction of Sovereignty." *Review of International Studies* 27, no. 4 (2001): 519–38.

14 Rosalyn Higgins, "The United Nations and Law Making: The Political Organs," 64 *AJIL* 43 (1970).

15 Leo Gross, "The Right of Self-Determination in International Law," in *New States in the Modern World*, Martin Kilson (ed.) (Cambridge MA: Harvard University Press, 1975).

16 JHW Verzijl, *International Law in Historical Perspective* (Leiden: Brill, 1968) 324–25, 558.

Sir Gerald Fitzmaurice asserted that the concept of self-determination was incompatible with international law. He acknowledged some "sympathy" with the "principle ... politically considered" "[J]uridically," however, he concluded that "the notion of a 'legal right' of self-determination is nonsense."[17]

The 1971 *Namibia* Advisory Opinion was a milestone in this debate, as the ICJ affirmed for the first time the validity of self-determination as a legal principle with corresponding duties.[18] Whilst shying away from the acknowledgement of self-determination as a legal right, the 1971 Opinion marked the Court's first explicit recognition[19] of self-determination as an overarching principle of the international community as enshrined in the Charter and its further development in the Colonial Declaration.[20] The Opinion, along with the separate judgement offered by Judge Ammoun is also an excellent illustration of the deepening rifts in North/South interpretations of self-determination, and the continuing importance of self-determination as a means to challenge dominant normative and even historical accounts of international law which became prominent in the post-colonial period.[21]

The Advisory Opinion followed a request by the Security Council, in which it for the first time exercised its rights under Article 96(1) of the Charter to determine the legal consequences of South Africa's continued presence in Namibia

17 Gerald Fitzmaurice, "The Future of Public International Law and the International Legal System in the Circumstances of Today," in *Institute de Droit International, Evolution et perspectives du droit international*, (1973) 233 cited in Berman (1988: 60).

18 The Advisory Opinion followed a request by the Security Council, in which it for the first time exercised its rights under Article 96(1) of the Charter to determine the legal consequences of South Africa's continued presence in Namibia despite SC Res. 276 of 1970, which declared this presence illegal. See. John Dugard, "The South West Africa Cases, Second Phase, 1966" 83 *African L.J.* (1966) 429; Richard Falk, "The South West Africa Cases: An Appraisal" 21 Int'l Org. 1 (1967); W.G. Friedmann, "The Jurisprudential Implications of the South West Africa Case" 6 Col. J. Transnational. Law 1. (1967).

19 This was not for lack of opportunity. In the *Right of Passage* (*Portugal v. India*) (1960) and the *South West Africa* cases 1962 and 1966 both sides in the dispute submitted arguments involving self-determination. The principle also seemed particularly relevant to the *Northern Cameroons* case 1963, which involved a disagreement over a plebiscite in a trust territory.

20 In Namibia the Court called self-determination a principle (in one of two references), but later on referred to the "rights of the people of Namibia." *Namibia* (Advisory Opinion), ICJ Reports (1971) p. 31, paras. 52–3, and p. 54, para. 118.

21 The depiction of self-determination at the core of a corrective and refashioned international law, was also prominently seen in submissions to the *Western Sahara* case. For Mohammed Bedjaoui, representing Algeria, the doctrine of colonial terra nullius signified the exclusion of non-European peoples from classical international law. The remedy for this protracted injustice, he argued, was found in the development and application of a new international law, and the inclusionary logic of self-determination.

despite SC Res. 276 of 1970, which declared this presence illegal.[22] However, SC Res. 276 was only an enforcement measure for a previous decision by the General Assembly, GA Res. 2145 (XXI) of 1966, which terminated South Africa's mandate over the territory. The legality of this termination was, therefore, an important element in assessing the legality of the South African presence in Namibia. A previous case on the matter, brought by Liberia and Ethiopia, which had denied these states' standing, had been greeted with outrage.[23] The decision, reached by the tiebreaking double vote of Percy Spender,[24] was later credited by James Crawford as instigating a move towards "decolonizing the Court."[25] The new makeup of the bench abandoned the previous decision in it its avoidance of self-determination. It went on to affirm self-determination's role in the decolonisation process, as well as affirming the elevation of colonial peoples to the status of rights holders. In upholding the legality of the General Assembly's revocation of South Africa's mandate over Namibia, and the duty of South Africa to withdraw its occupation, the majority opinion affirmed that the emergence of self-determination as an international legal principle had impacted the original C mandate agreement conferred on South Africa – a status conferred on territories least likely to stand alone under the "strenuous conditions of the modern world." Citing the shifts that had occurred in international law and practice in the intervening decades, the Court concluded that "these developments leave little doubt that the ultimate objective of the sacred trust was the self-determination and independence of the peoples concerned."[26] Self-determination, it was held, must of necessity apply not only to current and future international relations, but to pre-existing legal institutions as well. In this regard, as Cassese notes, self-determination "constitutes a fundamental standard of behaviour which, in a way, projects itself into the past."[27]

---

22 See Berman (1988: 96–103).

23 Knop (2002: 113).

24 This occurred because of the absence of three liberal judges from so-called Third World countries. The need for Spender's tie-breaking vote arose from the death of Judge Badawi of Egypt and the absence of Judge Bustamante of Peru who had both voted in favor of the plaintiffs in 1962. In the 1966 case Judge Spender, without the consent of the rest of the ICJ, also disqualified Judge Zafrulah Khan of Pakistan on the ground that the plaintiffs had asked him to be their judge ad hoc even though he had not accepted the invitation.

25 James Crawford, "The General Assembly, the International Court and self-determination" in V. Lowe & M. Fitzmaurice, eds., *Fifty Years of the International Court of Justice: Essays in Honour of Sir Robert Jennings* (Cambridge: Grotius Publications, 1996) 587, quoted in Knop (2002: 113).

26 *Namibia* (Advisory Opinion), 31–32 para 53.

27 Antonio Cassese, "The ICJ and Self-Determination," in V. Lowe & M. Fitzmaurice, eds., *Fifty Years of the International Court of Justice: Essays in Honour of Sir Robert Jennings* (Cambridge: Grotius Publications, 1996) 354.

While the majority opinion centred upon the notion of the 'sacred trust' as a prior legal obligation of the mandate holders towards the peoples of the territories – thus framing self-determination as the natural final step in the civilizing mission of colonial territories begun centuries before, Judge Ammoun sought to construct a different account of self-determination in international law, with which to reconstruct the nature of African sovereignty. The case, he argued, raised a swathe of issues:

> These are, in particular, the sovereignty of dependent peoples, the mandate institution, its nature and its objects, the right of peoples to self-determination and decolonization, equality between nations and between individuals, racial discrimination as expressed in the doctrine of apartheid in South Africa and in Namibia and, in sum, the whole body of human rights and their imperative universal character.[28]

These questions, he posited, were part of ongoing struggles between European and non-European legal traditions, in which self-determination formed part of "the fight of the peoples for freedom and independence, which has been going on ever since there have been conquering and dominating peoples."[29] The right of self-determination "before being written into charters that were not granted but won in bitter struggle, had first been written painfully, with the blood of peoples, in the finally awakened conscience of humanity."[30] Ammoun posits a different historical account of self-determination, tracing it from the philosopher Zeno to its circulation in the Age of Reason through the influence of Stoicism on Papinius and Ulpian, "the greatest of the Roman juriconsults, who were of Phoenician origin."[31] In Ammoun's eyes, self-determination's legal crystallisation did not form part of a Western narrative of progress, but rather was symbolic of the triumph of the non-European tradition. It was "the outward expression of a new body of international law, the consequence of an irreversible social and political evolution of the modern world."[32]

The depiction of sovereignty as a concept not necessarily rooted in classical European law, but as a broader, more universal concept that extends back into the past, centres upon Ammoun's depiction of the Namibian 'people':

28 Separate opinion of Judge Ammoun, page 16 para 72–73.
29 *Ibid* para 74.
30 *Ibid.*
31 *Ibid* para 78.
32 Ibid para 55.

> Namibia, even at the periods when it had been reduced to the status of a German colony or was subject to the South African Mandate, possessed a legal personality which was denied to it only by the law now obsolete. It was considered by the Powers of the day as a merely geographical concept taking its name from its location in the South-West of the African Continent. It nevertheless constituted a subject of law that was distinct from the German State, possessing national sovereignty but lacking the exercise thereof. Sovereignty, which is inherent in every people, just as liberty is inherent in every human being, therefore did not cease to belong to the people subject to mandate. It had simply, for a time, been rendered inarticulate and deprived of freedom of expression.

Indeed, Ammoun's description of an African sovereignty predating European colonialism is central to his claim of self-determination's retroactive character. Ghana, he notes was an empire, "the power and wealth of which was unequalled in Western Europe after the fall of the Roman Empire."[33] The Empire of Mali, "covered territories more vast than Europe at a time when a considerable part of the latter was a feudal and often feuding patchwork."[34] The state of Bornu, he notes, was so prosperous that a nineteenth century English traveler claimed that, "even the most humble citizen appeared… happy and comfortable."[35] The disruption of African sovereignty by the introduction of colonialism, culminating in the Conference of Berlin, where "a monstrous blunder and a flagrant injustice" and "one of fate's ironies"[36] Western Powers had declared Africa south of the Sahara *terrae nullius* and divided it amongst themselves, had now been succeeded by a period of national awakening and the struggle for independence: "the people of Namibia, which always used to be the master of the country, is nowadays united by common aspirations, the legal foundation of nationhood, towards a life of independence and freedom, whatever may be the political régime which it will select after obtaining independence".[37]

In keeping with this expanded depiction of self-determination's corrective ongoing value in international law, Ammoun also utilized the discourse of self-determination to decry the policies of apartheid, rebuking the majority opinion for evading this key question. He also articulated the growing impetus of the Afro-Asia bloc in construing the frustration of self-determination through

33 *Ibid* para 85.

34 *Ibid.*

35 *Ibid.*

36 *Ibid* para 86.

37 *Ibid* para 86.

continued colonial rule as an act of aggression: "In law, the legitimacy of the peoples' struggle cannot be in any doubt, for it follows from the right of self-defense, inherent in human nature, which is confirmed by Article 51 of the United Nations Charter." This point was to increasingly drive a wedge between North and South in understandings of self-determination in the coming years, particularly after the 1970 Friendly Relations Declaration which had declared that 'the continuation of colonialism in all its forms and manifestations is a crime' and upheld 'the inherent right of colonial peoples to struggle by all necessary means at their disposal against colonial powers which suppress their aspirations for freedom and independence'.[38] A normative and legal shift had undoubtedly occurred surrounding self-determination's presence in international law, however as the following decades would indicate, just what this would mean in the future would give rise to fierce debate.

## 2 Strengthening the Post-Colonial State

While the independence of former colonies seemed to support the claim that a true "community of nations" had emerged, newly independent states, as Makau Mutua has noted, "quickly realised that political independence was largely illusory…although now formally free, Third World states were still bonded—politically, legally, and economically—to the West."[39] While in 1950 Europe's GDP was five times greater than that of Africa and Asia, by 1970 – this gap had grown to about 8:1 for Africa and 8.5:1 for Asia.[40] This ongoing "material subordination" as Susan Marks explains, had been caused by the structural inequalities of colonialism, but were not remedied by the formal process of decolonisation.[41]

As a wealth of critical scholarship has shown, the trajectory from decolonisation to nation state was to be a lengthy and fraught process, and further

38 The *Friendly Relations Declaration*, GA Res. 2625(XXV), 25 GAOR (1970) Supplement No. 28, (A/8028) at 1214. As Principle VIII (Equal Rights and Self-Determination of Peoples) stated: *By virtue of the principle of equal rights and self-determination of peoples, all peoples always have the right, in full freedom, to determine, when and as they wish, their internal and external political status, without external interference, and to pursue as they wish their political, economic, social and cultural development.*

39 M.W. Makau, 'What is TWAIL?' *ASIL, Proceedings of the 94th Annual Meeting* (2000).

40 Quoted in Arne Westad, *The Global Cold War: Third World Interventions and the Making of Our Times* (New York: CUP, 2007) 90.

41 Susan Marks, 'Empire's Law', 10 *Indiana Journal Global Legal Studies* (2003) 449–466, 451.

complicated by the complex geopolitical conflicts that intensified during this time.[42] The spectre of neo-colonialism had been ever present since the Katanga crisis in 1960, underpinned by an existing economic structure which allowed powerful states to exert economic pressure on weaker economies.[43] "We are not the prime movers of our destiny," declared Nyerere in 1979, "we are ashamed to admit it; but economically we are dependencies – at best semi colonies – and not sovereign States."[44] The United States and the Soviet Union had by this time established an interventionist policy with a global reach, and patterns of transnational political influence cut across every ideological, economic and regional grouping of states.[45] These conditions meant that the chief concern for newly independent states was centred upon regaining control over their own economic and political affairs, and, as Anthony Anghie argues, to separate international law from its colonial past by restructuring the international legal regime to serve the interests of the entire international community.[46]

With the formal retreat of empire, the Afro-Asian bloc increasingly turned its attention to the remnants of the ideological racism that had accompanied colonial expansionism in the nineteenth century, and which remained embedded in the domestic and international structures of the international community.[47] Self-determination, and the legal and ideological links that had been forged between racism and colonialism in the Third Committee was extended to new situations in which colonial rule persisted. The situations in South Africa and Rhodesia – dubbed "the great shame of our continent" by Cote d'Ivoire's

42 See eg. Sundyha Pahuja, *Decolonising International Law* (Cambridge: CUP, 2011) 44–94; see also Sundyha Pahuja, 'Global Poverty and the Politics of Good Intentions', in Ruth Buchanan and Peer Zumbansen (eds.), *Law in Translation: Human Rights, Development and Transitional Justice* (London: Hart, 2014); R. W. Tucker, *The Inequality of Nations* (London: Martin Robertson, 1977).

43 Antionio Cassese, *International Law* (Oxford: OUP, 2005) 100.

44 Address by Julius Nyerere, President of the United Republic of Tanzania, to the Fourth Minister Meeting of the Group of 77, Arusha, 12–16 February 1979.

45 L.F. Damrosch, 'Politics Across Borders: Non-intervention and Non-Forcible Influence over Domestic Affairs', 83 *American Journal of International Law* (1989) 1–50.

46 See Anthony Anghie, *Imperialism, Sovereignty and the Making of International Law* (CUP, Cambridge, 2005) and F.E. Snyder & S. Sathirathai, (eds.) *Third World Attitudes Towards International Law: An Introduction* (Dordrecht: Martinus Nijhoff, 1987).

47 The US was fighting its only internal race war, and many states retained racist policies of their own. In the case of Australia, prior to a 1967 constitutional referendum in which indigenous Australians were finally granted citizenship and corresponding rights, the "Flora and Fauna Act," had mandated that indigenous Australians were to be governed and managed under the same portfolio as Australian wildlife.

President Felix Houphouet-Boigny,[48] and their policies of racial exclusion, and the obstinacy of the Portuguese empire,[49] gave rise to an innovative application of self-determination in order to challenge the insulated domestic political order in each state – even when the states in question were also trying to harness the rhetoric of self-determination to resist external challenges.[50]

Capitalising on their newfound majority within the UN, states of the global South began to recast self-determination as a corollary of non-interference and sovereign equality.[51] Self-determination had been the fundamental tool by which the new sovereignty regime was established, the moral imperative in decolonisation, which had underwritten the independence and territorial integrity of the former colonial territories. It was therefore logical, as Benjamin Rivlin suggests, "that both the attainment of independence and its maintenance and preservation, are part of the idea of self-determination."[52] This articulation of anti-imperial self-determination, was joined by new elements of sovereign consolidation, such as economic rights and permanent sovereignty over natural resources, which had been proposed during the Covenant debates in 1952.[53]

From the mid-1960s onwards concerns over neo-colonial and Cold War intervention were expressed in a series of General Assembly resolutions, in which self-determination was increasingly cast as a principle linked to non-intervention and sovereign consolidation, and the protection of their political, social and economic choices.[54] During the drafting of the Human Rights

---

48 Quoted in C.O.C Amate, Inside the OAU: Pan-Africanism in Practice (St Martin's Press, 1986) 212.

49 The war for independence in Angola for example lasted 13 years and was essentially a global proxy war. The FNLA forces being supported by the US, China, Israel and South Africa while the Soviets armed the MPLA forces and large force of Cuban troops fought with it for several years. When Anglo finally achieved independence in 1975 nearly a million Angolans fled to neighbouring lands.

50 According to the official position in South Africa, the whites themselves constituted a distinct nation "entitled to insist upon our right to self-determination" Cited in Vernon Van Dyke, "Self-Determination and Minority Rights" *International Studies Quarterly* 13(3) (1969) 223–53.

51 For a discussion of Third World attitudes to self-determination *see* Subrata Roy Chowdury 'The Status and Norms of Self-Determination in Contemporary International Law', 24 *Netherlands International Law Review* (1977) 72–84.

52 Benjamin Rivlin, *Self-Determination and Dependent Areas: International Conciliation* (Washington, DC: Carnegie Endowment for International Peace, 1955), 200.

53 See Christian Tomuschat, *Human Rights: Between Idealism and Realism* (Oxford: OUP, 2003) 48–49.

54 See for example General Assembly resolutions 2649 (XXV) of 30 November 1970, 2955 (XXVII) of 12 December 1972, 3070 (XXVIII) of 30 November 1973, 3236 (XXIX) of 22

Covenants, a number of state representatives expressed the view that self-determination involved safeguarding and strengthening the independence of those peoples, especially in the economic field.[55]

The 1965 Declaration on the Inadmissibility of Intervention in the Domestic Affairs of States, solidified a sovereignty-based notion of self-determination as a buffer against interference and "foreign pressure." "Every state," it affirms, "has an inalienable right to choose its political, economic, social and cultural systems, without interference in any form." During the preceding debates, many states stressed this interpretation. The United Arab Republic argued that the two principles were "inseparable,"[56] a position supported by a number of other states.[57] Honduras declared that "for Latin America, non-intervention represented not merely a principle but also an indispensable basis for ensuring independence and territorial integrity and for guaranteeing the legitimate and permanent self-determination of peoples."[58] The delegate from Liberia stated "intervention was... more than a violation of the rules governing the relations of States; what it amounted to was the domination of one people by another."[59]

In the following years, Third World and Socialist states sought to further strengthen the legal nexus between self-determination, non-intervention, and political and economic independence. During the drafting of the Friendly Relations Declaration, a clear line emerged that the promotion and implementation of self-determination and equal rights were among the most important measures of the international order to ensure universal peace. As these debates inevitably turned to the question of particular forms of government and human rights concerns,[60] Third World and Socialist states railed against the imposition that self-determination embodied imposed ideas of

---

November 1974, 3246 (XXIX) of 29 November 1974, 3382 (XXX) of 10 November 1975, 33/24 of 29 November 1978, 35/35 of 14 November 1980, 36/68 of 1 December 1981, 36/76 of 4 December 1981 and 37/35 of 23 November 1982.

55 See Chile, 8 Comm.HR (1952) 253rd mtg., (E/CN.4/SR.253) p. 6; Uruguay, 7 GAOR (1952) 3rd Cmttee., 452nd mtg., (A/C.3/SR.452) para. 13; Afghanistan, *ibid.* 454th mtg., (A/C.3/SR.454) para. 54; Poland, 10 GAOR (1955) 3rd Cmttee., 643rd mtg., (A/C.3/SR.643) para. 36; Bolivia, *ibid.* 654th mtg., (A/C.3/SR.654) para. 31.

56 UAR, 20 GAOR (1965) 1st Cmttee., 1403rd mtg., (A/C.1/SR.1403) para. 3.

57 The delegate from Chile argued, 'intervention destroyed the very foundations of international coexistence, such as the principles of sovereign equality of States and the right of peoples to self-determination' Chile, 20 GAOR (1965) 1st Cmttee., 1402nd mtg., (A/C.1/SR.1402) para. 44.

58 Honduras, 20 GAOR (1965) 1st Cmttee., 1400th mtg., (A/C.1/SR.1400) para. 27.

59 Liberia, 20 GAOR (1965) 1st Cmttee., 1401st mtg., (A/C.1/SR.1401) para. 42.

60 US, A/AC.125/SR.68 (1967) para 4.

governance.[61] Burma called the UK draft, with its emphasis on representative government, "a mild attempt to impose certain of its own political persuasions on the constitutional law and practice of other States."[62] Against the backdrop of a general consensus that colonialism was to be, "liquidated completely and without delay," Article 1 proclaimed that "by virtue of the principle of equal rights and self-determination of peoples enshrined in the Charter of the United Nations, all peoples have the right freely to determine, without external interference, their political status and to pursue their economic, social and cultural development."

Against the backdrop of the situations in the Portuguese territories and South Africa, Third World and Socialist also began to pursue the argument that the use of force was warranted as a form of self-defence against continued colonial domination.[63] The question of the relationship between anti-colonial struggles with the Charter prohibition against the use of force had been raised throughout the decolonization process.[64] The Colonial Declaration, while not sanctioning the use of force by national liberation movements, had invalidated the use of force by the colonial administration to repress the exercise of self-determination.[65] Thus both the Security Council and the General Assembly repeatedly condemned the "acts of repression" in the Portuguese territories.

---

61 Ukrainian SSR, 21 GAOR (1966) 6th Cmttee., 928 mtg., (A/C.6/SR.928) para. 16, Guatemala, 23 GAOR (1968) 6th Cmttee., 1086mtg., (A/C.6/SR.1086) para. 52.

62 Burma, A/AC.125/SR.68 (1967) p. 9.

63 Cassese (1996: 151). A resolution adopted by the Conference of Jurists of Afro-Asian Counties in 1964 claimed 'all struggles undertaken by the peoples for their national independence of the restitution of the territories or occupied parts thereof, including armed struggle, are entirely legal'. The 1964 Conference of Non-aligned Countries declared that 'colonised peoples may legitimately resort to arms to secure the full exercise of their right to self-determination'.

64 In 1965 General Assembly Resolution 2105 was passed in response to the continuation of colonialism by Portugal, South Africa and Rhodesia. This resolution "recognizes the legitimacy of the struggle by the peoples under colonial rule to exercise their right to self-determination and independence and invites all states to provide material and moral assistance to the national liberation movements in colonial territories." Resolutions affirming UNGA Res. 2105 (XX) using similar language were adopted in the next four years. See UNGA Res 2189 (XXI), 13 Dec, 1966; UNGA Res 2326 (VVII), 16 Dec 1967; UNGA Res 2446 (XXIII), 19 Dec, 1968; UNGA Res2465 (XXIII) 20 Dec 1968; UNGA Res 2548 (XXIV) 11 Dec 1969.

65 In Resolution 1514 paragraph 4 focuses on the means whereby the right to self-determination can be realised. This states that "[a]ll armed action or repressive measures of all kinds directed against dependent peoples shall cease in order to enable them to exercise peacefully and freely their right to complete independence, and the integrity of their national territory shall be respected."

The Security Council requested that "all States refrain forthwith" from the sale or supply to Portugal of military equipment to be used "to continue its repression of the peoples of the Territories,"[66] a call later simplified to encompass all such equipment "to be used in the Territories."[67] By 1972 the Security Council went so far as to endorse, in Resolutions 312 and 322, the legitimacy of the struggle by the liberation movements of the four territories under Portuguese rule.[68]

Western states sought to prevent any acknowledgement of the legitimacy of armed struggle, on the grounds that the use of force for any other purpose than self-defense was contrary to the Charter.[69] This was countered by Third World states on the grounds that colonial domination itself was a form of armed aggression warranting self-defense.[70] The 1970 Friendly Relations Declaration had seemed to offer an implicit acceptance of the use of force:

> Any groups engaged in the struggle to assert this right of self-determination, and free themselves from colonial domination, a racist regime, or alien occupation, were not to be hindered by any State in their efforts to assert this right.[71]

This position was confirmed by scholars of the period, including Georges Abi-Saab, who concluded that "armed resistance to forcible self-determination – by imposing or maintaining by force colonial or alien domination – is legitimate according to the Declaration…in other words, liberation movements have a jus ad bellum under the Charter."[72] Rendering assistance to anti-colonial armed

66 *Ibid* para 6.

67 S.C. Res. 312 (1972) (9-0-6).

68 See Pomerance (1982: 54).

69 Cassese (1996: 151).

70 Cassese (1996: 151). A resolution adopted by the Conference of Jurists of Afro-Asian Counties in 1964 claimed 'all struggles undertaken by the peoples for their national independence of the restitution of the territories or occupied parts thereof, including armed struggle, are entirely legal'. The 1964 Conference of Non-aligned Countries declared that 'colonised peoples may legitimately resort to arms to secure the full exercise of their right to self-determination'.

71 The 1970 Friendly Relations Declaration also affirmed that: *A Every State has the duty to refrain from any forcible action which deprives peoples … of their right to self-determination and freedom and independence. In their action against, and resistance to, such forcible action in pursuit of the exercise of their right to self-determination, such peoples are entitled to seek and receive support in accordance with the purposes and principles of the Charter.*

72 Georges Abi-Saab, "Wars of National Liberation and the Laws of War" 3 *Annale d'Etudes Internationales* (1972) 100.

resistance was also endorsed by Resolution 2621 (XXV) in 1970 which stated that "Member States shall render all necessary moral and material assistance to the peoples of colonial territories in their struggle to attain freedom and independence."[73] It also reaffirmed that "the further continuation of colonialism in all its forms and manifestations is a crime," and affirmed "the inherent right of colonial peoples to struggle by all necessary means at their disposal."[74] In 1973 Resolution 3070 (XXVIII) also reaffirmed the legitimacy of "all available means, including armed struggle," and called for "moral, material and any other assistance to all peoples struggling" for self-determination. This was joined by resolutions declaring support for "the armed struggle of the Namibian people," and calling for "increased and sustained support and material, financial, *military* and other assistance to the South West Africa People's Organization."[75]

States also began to express support for and recognition of liberation movements as the legitimate representatives of their people and include them as observers, associate members, and members of international organisations.[76] The Economic Commission for Africa expelled Portugal and South Africa, which opened the way for the inclusion of representatives from their respective liberation movements.[77] In 1971, the General Assembly voted to include representatives from the Commission officials of the National Front for the Liberation of Angola (FNLA) and Popular Movement for the Liberation of Angola (MPLA), the Mozambique Liberation Front (FRELIMO), the African Party for the Independence of Guinea and Cape Verde (PAIGC), and the South West Africa People's Organization (SWAPO), and they later gained observer status in eight additional U.N. bodies.[78] The General Assembly and Security also moved to deprive Rhodesia of international personality, with Security Council Resolution 277 calling for states to "ensure that any act performed by officials and institutions of the illegal regime in Southern Rhodesia shall not be accorded any recognition, official or otherwise, including judicial notice, by the

---

73 UNGA Res 2621 (XXV) (1970).
74 See 28 GAOR, 1862d plen mtg para 98–9.
75 UNGA Res 35/277 A (1981).
76 See Heather A. Wilson, *International Law and the Use of Force by National Liberation Movements* (Oxford: OUP 1988) 117–18 and Simpson (2013: 244).
77 *Ibid.*
78 These were: the Special Committee on the Implementation of the Declaration on Colonialism; the Fourth Committee of the General Assembly; the U.N. Council on Namibia; the U.N. Educational, Scientific and Cultural Organization; the International Labor Organization; the International Telecommunication Union; the Food and Agriculture Organization; and the Inter-governmental Maritime Consultative Organization. Ibid. 118–19.

competent organs of their State."[79] U.N. opposition to apartheid and efforts to deny the South African government's legitimacy also intensified from the 1970s onwards. In 1973 the International Convention on the Suppression and Punishment of the Crime of Apartheid was approved.[80] The Convention purported to criminalize "[a]ny legislative measures and other measures calculated to prevent a racial group or groups from participation in the political, social, economic and cultural life of the country…, in particular by denying to members of a racial group or groups basic human rights and freedoms…" Subsequently, in Resolution 3151 (XXVIII), the General Assembly sought to remove international recognition of South Africa as a representative of the population.[81]

Following on from the Friendly Relations Declaration, a series of General Assembly resolutions began to condemn foreign intervention into the political and economic affairs of states as a breach of the right to self-determination in increasingly hardened terms, and states frequently raised the issue. With interventionist tactics ramping up during the Cold War,[82] the General Assembly in its resolution on the Universal Realisation of Rights of Peoples to Self-Determination requested the Council "to continue to give special attention to the violations of human rights, especially the right to self-determination, resulting from foreign military intervention, aggression or occupation".[83] Economic intervention was of particular concern. As Abi-Saab observed, "[b]oth principles of free choice of the economic system and of permanent sovereignty over natural resources derive from the same premise, sovereign equality, and purport to specify its implications in the economic field".[84] In the 1973 Draft Resolution on Permanent Sovereignty Over Natural Resources, states declared that any efforts to pressure member states over the disposition of their natural resources violated UN principles of self-determination and non-interference in the internal affairs of states.[85]

The General Assembly also frequently condemned the use of mercenaries as a means to violate human rights and to impede the exercise of the right of

79 S.C. Res. 277 (1970) (14-0-1, Spain abstaining).

80 G.A. Res. 3068 (XXVIII) (1973) (91-4-26).

81 G.A. Res 3151 G (XXVIII) (1973) (88-7-28).

82 See Klaus Knorr, 'Is International Coercion Waning or Rising?', 4 *International Security*, (1975) pp. 92–110.

83 General Assembly Resolution 31/91 of 14 December 1976, 32/153 of 19 December 1977, 33/74 of 15 December 1978, 34/101 of 14 December 1979 and 35/159 of 12 December 1980.

84 Georges Abi-Saab, 'Permanent Sovereignty over Natural Resources and Economic Activities', in Mohammed Bedjaoui (ed.), *International Law: Achievements and Prospects* (Dordrecht: M. Nijhoff, 1991) 599.

85 UN Doc. S/10931/Rev.1, 20 March 1973.

peoples to self-determination.[86] In 1974 the Consensus Definition of Aggression affirmed "the duty of States not to use armed force to deprive peoples of their right to self-determination, freedom and independence, or to disrupt territorial integrity." The document also characterised as an act of aggression "the sending by or on behalf of a state of armed bands, groups, irregulars or mercenaries, which carry out acts of armed force against another state." Led by Socialist states, the 1975 Final Helsinki act also reaffirmed the position offered in the Friendly Relations Declaration declaring: "by the principle of equal rights and self-determination of peoples" it stated, "all peoples always have the right, in full freedom, to determine, when and as they wish, their internal and external political status, without external interference, and to pursue as they wish their political, economic, social and cultural development."[87]

The most clearly articulated repudiation of ongoing domination was the emergence of the prohibition of "alien domination and foreign occupation" as a new unit of peoples to which self-determination would apply. At the insistence of Third World States, the Friendly Relations Declaration had expanded self-determination from the colonial context to situations of "subjection of peoples to alien subjugation, domination and exploitation." The situations in Afghanistan, Lebanon,[88] Uganda, Cambodia, Grenada[89] and the situation in Central America dominated UN debates in which self-determination was raised in terms of foreign domination. While this development found wide support amongst States, it still revealed a major ideological split between states. Arab states drew attention to the cause of the Palestinians,[90] while African states were consistent in their attacks on the racist regimes of South Africa

86 General Assembly resolutions 2465 (XXIII) of 20 December 1968, 2548 (XXIV) of 11 December 1969, 2708 (XXV) of 14 December 1970, 3103 (XXVIII) of 12 December 1973 and 3314 (XXIX) Of 14 December 1974.

87 *Helsinki Final Act* 1975, 14 ILM (1975) Principle VII.

88 Singapore: 'The principle of self-determination was also being undermined in the Middle East ... It called for the withdrawal of all forces from Lebanon and for respect for the right of the Lebanese to self-determination. 3rd Cmmtt 15th mtg., (A/C.3/38/SR.15) para. 22.

89 USSR: 'The right to self-determination was currently being violated in Grenada as well. The armed occupation of Grenada was form of military reprisal against any young countries which exercised their right to determine their own social structure'. 39 GAOR (1984) 3rd Cmttee., 11th mtg., (A/C.3/39/SR.11) para. 33; Cuba: 'The United States continued to occupy Grenada, and the population was still being deprived of its right to self- determination'. *Ibid.*, para. 35.

90 Libya: '[S]elf-determination of peoples should be accepted in its widest meaning and applied not only to peoples under alien subjugation but also to peoples under military occupation. It was indeed inconceivable that peoples in that position – the Palestinian Arab people, for instance –could be thought of as enjoying those rights'. 24 GAOR (1969) 6th Cmttee., 1162 mtg., (A/C.6/SR.1162) para. 78.

and Southern Rhodesia.[91] Pakistan argued that subjugation should be, "purged of any racial or continental connotation," and, "a people was dependent when its territory was occupied by another State in contravention of international agreements or Security Council resolutions."[92] The United States was also quick to refer to the recent Soviet invasion of Czechoslovakia as a clear violation of self-determination.[93] In 1977 an Additional Protocol to the Geneva Red Cross Conventions of 1949, included "peoples fighting against colonial domination and alien occupation and against racist regimes in the exercise of their right to self-determination as enshrined in the Charter of the United Nations and the Declaration on… [Friendly Relations]". Similar wording was used in the Definition of Aggression, which referred to, "peoples under colonial and racist regimes or other forms of alien domination". Writing on the then status of self-determination under international law, UN Special Rapporteur Héctor Gros Espiell stated in his 1979 report that: '"colonial and alien domination" means any kind of domination, whatever form it may take, which the people concerned freely regards as such".[94] He noted that: "if the national unity claimed and the territorial integrity invoked are merely legal fictions which cloak real colonial and alien domination, resulting from actual disregard of the principle of self-determination, the subject people or peoples are entitled to exercise, with all the consequences thereof their right to self-determination".

By the 1980s, the international community was becoming increasingly intolerant of patterns of Cold War interventionism, now embodied by the Regan Doctrine which had instigated the 1983 invasion of Grenada, support for Mujahideen forces in Afghanistan, and support for the Contras in Nicaragua. Despite attempts by the US government to frame human rights and democracy as a justification for funding counterrevolutionary insurgents,[95] the International Court of Justice in the 1986 *Nicaragua Opinion* was unequivocal in its endorsement of non-intervention and sovereign equality.[96] The Court refused to

---

91 Kenya, 22 GAOR A/AC.125/SR.69 (1967) p. 22; Columbia, 21 GAOR (1966) 6th Cmttee., 929mtg., (A/C.6/SR.929) para. 15; Congo (Brazzaville), 22 GAOR (1966) 6th Cmttee., 998 mtg., (A/C.6/SR.998) para. 9; Cameroon, 23 GAOR (1968) 6th Cmttee., 1086 mtg., (A/C.6/SR.1096) para. 19.

92 Pakistan, 23 GAOR (1968) 6th Cmttee., 1096mtg., (A/C.6/SR.1096) para. 19.

93 US, 23 GAOR A/AC.125/SR.92 (1968) para. 129.

94 Hector Gros Espiell, 'Self-Determination and Jus Cogens' in Antonio Cassese (ed.), *UN Law/Fundamental Rights: Two Topics in International Law* (Alphen aan den Rijn: Sijthoff & Noordhoff, 1979) 6.

95 See Brad Simpson, "The United States and The Curious History of Self-Determination" *Diplomatic History* 36.4 (2012) 675–694 at 688.

96 *Case Concerning Military and Paramilitary Activities in and against Nicaragua* (Nicaragua v. United States of America) (Merits), ICJ Reports (1986) p. 101, para. 191, and paras 202 to

"contemplate the creation of a new rule opening up a right of intervention by one State against another on the ground that the latter has opted for some particular ideology or political system." The choice of a political, economic, social and cultural system, and the formulation of foreign policy were to be "free choices," unencumbered by intervention and coercion by other states. Although the majority decisions made only implicit references to self-determination, the Separate Opinion of Judge Sette-Camara, drew a direct parallel, arguing: "the non-use of force as well as non-intervention - the latter as a corollary of equality of States and self-determination - are not only cardinal principles of customary international law but could in addition be recognised as peremptory rules of customary international law which impose obligations on all States."[97]

## 3 Economic Self-Determination and the New International Economic Order

By the late 1970s it had become increasingly evident that despite the efforts made during the First Development Decade "the gap between the standards of living in the developed and developing countries has widened instead of narrowing."[98] UN Secretary General U Thant warned of "the growing economic disparity of the nations of the world which faces us with our most serious source of tension and with the direct possibility of future calamity".[99] Against this backdrop, attention began shifting more intensely from the political aspects of self-determination to economic strategies aimed at overcoming inequalities and disrupting western economic hegemony – embodied in demands for a New International Economic Order (NIEO).[100] The theme of exploitation which emerged in Third World rhetoric during this time linked colonial to neo-colonial imperialism embodied in the international economic order. As Algerian diplomat Mohammed Bedjaoui argued:

---

209.

97 ICJ Rep (1986) p. 199 (Sette-Camara, J., sep. op.).

98 GA Resolution 2084 (XX) 'United Nations Development Decade' 1404th plenary meeting, 20 December 1965.

99 UN, OPI, Press Release/SG/SM/488, cited in Moses Moskowitz, *The Politics and Dynamics of Human Rights* (New York: Oceana Publications, Inc, 1968), 192.

100 See Roland Burke, "Competing for the Last Utopia?: The NIEO, Human Rights, and the World Conference for the International Women's Year, Mexico City, June 1975" (2015) 6(1) *Humanity* 47, 57.

> The direct connection between Declaration 1514(XV) of 1960, which confirmed the intrinsic illegality of the "colonialist political order," and the Charter of Economic Rights and Duties of States of 1974, which tolled the bell for the "imperialist economic order," is undeniable… The one is connected to the other by the umbilical cord represented by Declaration 2625 (XXV) on the seven principles of international law, which ratifies the sovereign equality of States, the self-determination of peoples in every field, and international co-operation.[101]

During the early stages of decolonisation, when it became evident that colonial powers would seek to protect their economic interests by whatever means possible – as underlined by the Katanga conflict – anti-colonialists began to link self-determination to economic sovereignty. This included the proposed inclusion of a right of permanent sovereignty over national natural wealth and resources in article 1 of the future Covenants. This was joined by a growing number of resolutions from the 1960s onwards, which stressed the right of States to dispose of their own wealth and natural resources and condemned the activities of foreign economic and other interests which impeded the implementation of decolonisation.[102] Sovereignty over natural resources became a particular point of contestation.[103] El Salvador cited the example of Nauru which had conceded substantial amounts of its main resource, phosphates, under trusteeship to Australia.[104] Western states meanwhile maintained resistance to any link between self-determination and economic activities,[105] however this was not enough to prevent the inclusion of the right to permanent sovereignty over natural resources in common Article 1 (2) of the Covenants which declared "all peoples may, for their own ends, freely dispose of their natural wealth and resources without prejudice." The representative of Poland proclaimed that his delegation "attached the greatest importance to the sovereignty of peoples over their natural resources, believing that it was often a

---

101 Mohammed Bedjaoui, *Towards a New International Economic Order* (UNESCO, Paris, 1979) 184.

102 GA resolutions 48/46, 49/40, 50/33 and 51/140.

103 See Rudolph Dolzer, 'New Foundations of the Law of Expropriation of Alien Property', 75 *American Journal of International Law* (1981) 553–589, 562.

104 El Slavador, 10 GAOR (1955) 3rd Cmttee., 674thmtg., (A/C.3/SR.674) para. 8.

105 See UK, 10 GAOR (1955) 3rd Cmttee., 670th mtg., (A/C.3/SR.670) para. 14; Memorandum from Gordon Chase of the National Security Council Staff to the President's Special Assistant for National Security Affairs, September 13, 1965, *FRUS, 1964–1968*, vol. 33, *Organization and Management of Foreign Policy* (Washington, D.C., 2001).

necessary condition for securing full self-determination and equal rights."[106] In 1970 Resolution 2692 asserting the right of permanent sovereignty over natural resources of developing countries was passed, followed in 1972 by the UN Committee on Trade and Development (UNCTAD) resolution on the 'Charter of the Economic Rights and Duties of States' which affirmed that "the respect for the principle of self-determination of peoples and of the free disposition of their wealth and natural resources."[107]

Sovereignty over natural resources was, however, only one part of, what Howard Tolley described as a "larger campaign for racial and economic equality waged throughout the United Nations system" during this time.[108] Economic self-determination foregrounded a radical plan to dismantle and craft a new international law "that would facilitate resource distribution in a world economy whose regulatory architecture had revealed itself to be fragile, if not obsolete"[109] which had begun to gain traction by the mid-1960s. In his opening speech to the General Assembly in September 1966 Senegalese foreign minister, Doudou Thiam declared that stressed the new to lay the foundations for a new international economic system. "The right of peoples to self-determination," he noted would remain empty phrases "until relations between nations are viewed in the light of economic and social facts."[110] Two years later at the 1968 Human Rights Conference in Tehran, the conference Proclamation highlighted the problem of economic inequality, stating that the closing the development gap between nations was its utmost priority.[111] At the fourth conference of the Non-Aligned Movement (NAM) in Algiers in September 1973, states evoked the language of self-determination in affirming that in order to establish the "conditions for real development" it was necessary to "put an end to all forms of foreign domination and exploitation."[112] Without this commitment, many delegates argued, the formal independence guaranteed by self-determination was essentially meaningless.

106 Poland 23 GAOR, A/AC.125/SR.93, (1968) 142.

107 UNCTAD, Resolution 45(III), 18 May 1972.

108 Howard Tolley, Jr, *The U.N. Commission on Human Rights* (Boulder: Westview Press 1987) 83.

109 Umut Özsu, 'Neoliberalism and the New International Economic Order: A History of Contemporary Legal Thought', in C. Tomlins and J. Desautels-Stein (eds.), *In Search of Contemporary Legal Thought* (Cambridge: CUP, 2016).

110 Cited in Daniel J. Whelan, "Under the Aegis of Man': The Right to Development and the Origins of the New International Economic Order', 6:1, *Humanity* (2015) pp. 93–108, 94.

111 Proclamation of Tehran, Final Act of the International Conference on Human Rights, UN Doc. A/CONF.32/41, Para 12.

112 4th Summit Conference of Heads of State of Government of the Non-Aligned Movement, Algiers, A/9330 (23 November 1973) 18.

With the oil crisis and the collapse of the Bretton Woods agreement the following year, demands for a NIEO[113] were ramped up during a special session of the Economic and Social Council.[114] Prefaced on addressing the legacy of colonial exploitation and its lasting asymmetry for economic growth between nations, the NIEO was, as Umut Őzsu explains "a sustained attempt to craft a new international law that would facilitate resource distribution in a world economy whose regulatory architecture had revealed itself to be fragile, if not obsolete."[115] This argument was advanced by the Algerian President Houari Boumédiène who noted: "in the eyes of the vast majority of humanity it is an (economic) order that is as unjust and as outdated as the colonial order to which it owes its origin and its substance."[116] The accompanying Declaration and the related Program of Action, and later the Charter on Economic Rights and Duties of States, reiterated the link between self-determination, sovereignty over natural resources, economic control and the continuing project of anti-colonialism.[117] The link was made more explicit in the 1976 General Assembly resolution 3398, entitled 'Activities of foreign economic and other interests which are impeding the implementation of the Declaration on the Granting of Independence to Colonial Countries and Peoples in Southern Rhodesia, Namibia and Territories under Portuguese domination and in all other Territories under colonial domination and efforts to eliminate colonialism, apartheid and racial discrimination in southern Africa. In this regard, it was said that neo-colonial activities of transnational corporations now had a similar role to that played in the past by colonialism as a violation of self-determination. Before the Third Committee the representative of Vietnam argued that: "the forces of colonialism had never stopped using any means at hand to preserve their colonial interests…today, economic means were being

113 Its main components were the 1974 Declaration and the related Programme of Action on the Establishment of a New International Economic Order passed at the Sixth Special Session of the General Assembly, as well as the subsequent Charter of Economic Rights and Duties of States.

114 4th Summit Conference of Heads of State or Government of the Non-Aligned Movement, Algiers, Algeria 5–9 September 1973, A/9330 (23 November 1973), 18.

115 Őzsu (2016); *see also* Nils Gilman, 'The New International Economic Order: A Reintroduction', 6:1 *Humanity* (2015) 1–16.

116 Cited in Julia Dehm, 'Highlighting Inequalities in the Histories of Human Rights: Contestations over Justice, Needs and Rights in the 1970s', 31:4 *Leiden Journal of International Law* (2018) 871–895, 880.

117 General Assembly Resolution 3202(S-VI), Programme of Action on the Establishment of a New International Economic Order, A/RES/S-6/3203 (1 May 1974). See also UNCTAD, Resolution 45(III), 18 May 1972.

used more frequently and intensively to exert political pressure and maintain domination."[118]

Attempts to integrate economic self-determination with practical demands were also prominently seen in relation to calls for the right to development.[119] First raised in 1966, it gained traction throughout the decade and into the 1970s.[120] In 1977 the Commission on Human Rights called for a study on "the international dimensions of the right to development as a human right," which was mandated to take into account the need for a New International Economic Order as well as fundamental human needs. The right, Mohammed Bedjaoui argued, was a reflection of the fact that "four fifths of the world's population no longer accept the fact that a fifth of the world's population continues to build its wealth on the basis of the remainders poverty."[121] In 1986 the right to development was formally recognised by the General Assembly in the Declaration on the Right to Development in Article 1 which proclaimed that "[t]he right to development is an inalienable human right by virtue of which every human person and all peoples are entitled to participate in, contribute to, and enjoy economic, social, cultural and political development, in which all human rights and fundamental freedoms can be fully realised," and "[t]he human right to development also implies the full realisation of the right of peoples to self-determination, which includes, subject to the relevant provisions of both International Covenants on Human Rights, the exercise of their inalienable right to full sovereignty over all their natural wealth and resources."[122] "How can," argued Senegal's Ibrahima Boye argued at the Commission on Human Rights "a poor people, physically, morally and intellectually unhealthy, enjoy civil and political rights?"[123] His sentiments were shared by René Maheu, the director of UNESCO, who made a poignant case for the plight of the under-developed world. Maheu's statement on the International Human Rights Year

---

118 Vietnam, 44 GAOR 3rd Cmttee 9th mtg., (A/C.3/44/SR.9) (1989).

119 Roger Normand and Sarah Zaidi, *Human Rights at the UN: The Political History of Universal Justice* (Bloomington: Indiana University Press, 2007).

120 Whelan, (2015: 94). See Susan Marks, 'The Human Right to Development: Between Rhetoric and Reality', 17 *Harvard Human Rights Journal* (2004) pp. 137 – 168, 137.

121 Mohammed Bedjaoui, 'The Right to Development', in Mohammed Bedjaoui (ed) *International Law: Achievements and Prospects* (The Hague: Martinus Nijhoff/UNESCO, 1991), 1177–1204.

122 *Declaration on the Right to Development* GA Res. 41/128 (Dec. 4, 1986).

123 *Statement by Chairman of Commission on Human Rights, Ibrahima Boye, on 20th Anniversary of Declaration of Human Rights*, 9 December 1968, UN Document GA/3845/HRD/50, p. 4 Cited in Roland Burke, 'From Individual Rights to National Development: The First UN Conference on Human Rights, Tehran, 1968' (2008) 19(3) *Journal of World History* 275, 291–2 fn 68.

spoke of those "still in the grip of hunger and malnutrition" and the millions of illiterates "shut out from the world of ideas."[124] For these people, he asserted, "the provisions of the Universal Declaration are still nothing more than empty promises."[125]

## 4 The Human Rights Revolution and Self-Determination

Against this backdrop, Western states had begun to express increasing frustration about the way self-determination had been "hijacked" by the Third World bloc to advance the colonial cause.[126] Efforts to reframe self-determination, particularly as a basis for redistributive justice and equality as embodied in the NIEO, were criticised as a distortion of the "Western tradition of human rights [that] centres on the individual and his need for protection against the society and the state."[127] As British jurist J-E-S Fawcett observed "the UN has appeared to understand and apply the principle of self-determination for the protection of human rights in ways....which have had political effects that are not in the long term in the interest of human rights."[128]

In this context, Western states began to attempt to reclaim the focus of self-determination away from economic and redistributive demands towards human rights.[129] In one of the first commentary pieces to flag a broader shift in US policy concerning human rights, Elizabeth Spiro argued in 1977 that the US would not be able to focus on human rights – what she termed "individual

124 René Maheu, 'Message from René Maheu, Director-General of UNESCO. International Year for Human Rights', *UNESCO Courier*, 21 April 1968, 32.

125 *Ibid.*

126 For a general discussion of these debates see Roland Burke, 'Competing for the Last Utopia?: The NIEO, Human Rights, and the World Conference for the International Women's Year, Mexico City, June 1975' (2015) 6(1) *Humanity: An Interdisciplinary Journal of Human Rights, Humanitarianism, and Development.*

127 John Scali, 'Address by Ambassador John Scali, United States representative to the United Nations, at the Twelfth North American Invitational Model United Nations, Washington DC, 6 March 1975' in Willem Veenhoven (ed.), *Case Studies on Human Rights and Fundamental Freedoms: A World Survey* (Vol V) (Dordecht: Martinus Nijhoff, 1976) 565.

128 J-E-S Fawcett quoted in Moyn (2010: 198).

129 For a discussion of the 'internal' aspect of self-determination developed during this period *see also* Brad Fox, 'Self-Determination in the Post-Cold War Era: A New Internal Focus?', 16 *Michigan Journal of International Law* (1995); Robert McCorquodale, 'Self-Determination: A Human Rights Approach', 43 *International and Comparative Law Quarterly* (1994); Jean Salmon, 'Internal Aspects of the Right to Self-Determination: Towards a Democratic Legitimacy Principle?', in Chistian Tomuschat (ed.), *Modern Law of Self-Determination* (Dordecht: Martinus Nijhoff, 1993) 254–255.

self-determination" until it had severed the false connection between human rights and national self-determination.[130] In the United States' optic self-determination was an element of a proud American tradition established by Wilson of exporting freedom and representative government to the world. In 1974, future US ambassador to the UN Daniel Patrick Moynihan, raised the issue of self-determination, noting that while empire was now fast becoming a thing of the past, this "Wilsonian vision" had not led to the civil liberties and freedom that the former president had envisaged.[131] Moynihan urged greater US engagement with human rights as a tool "in the struggle against totalitarianism," condemning the "perversion of the language of human rights and its transformation into a weapon against democracy."[132]

Recent histories of human rights have identified the 1970s as the 'breakthrough' moment, where "the idea of international human rights achieved a prominence that far outstripped even that of its founding epoch thirty years before."[133] As historians have underlined, during the height of the Cold War in the 1950s and 1960s, Western support for human rights had generally been weak.[134] Mark Mazower notes that the United States, once the champion of individual freedoms, had largely moved towards a conservative policy that favoured stability over morality.[135] The US had supported numerous dictators for strategic reasons, and had largely stressed that it was indifferent to patterns of internal governance.[136] With the beginning of détente, the sentiment of the United States changed, and human rights assumed a new significance. In a moment that has been identified as the turning point for the human rights revolution, the newly elected US President Jimmy Carter in his inaugural address in January 1977 sought to recapture the moral centre of human rights: "Our commitment to human rights must be absolute."[137]

---

130 Elizabeth Spiro, "A Paradigm Shift in U.S. Foreign Policy: From Self-Determination to Human Rights," *Worldview* 20, no. 1/2 (1977): 42–49. Cited in Simpson (2013: 246).

131 Daniel Moynihan, 'Was Woodrow Wilson Right? Morality and American Foreign Policy', 57 *Commentary* (1974) pp. 25–31.

132 *Ibid.*

133 *See* Samuel Moyn, 'The 1970s as a Turning Point in Human Rights History', *in* Jan Eckel and Samuel Moyn (eds.) *The Breakthrough: Human Rights in the 1970s* (Philadelphia: University of Pennsylvania Press, 2014) 2.

134 *Ibid.*

135 Mark Mazower, *Governing the World: The History of an Idea* (London: Penguin, 2012), 379.

136 The process has started with Franco and Peron, and by the 1970s the pantheon included Pinochet, Mobutu, the Shah of Iran, Marcos, Suharto, and Salazar, as well as the military juntas in Greece and Turkey.

137 Moyn (2010: 139).

Much of this new concern for human rights was directed towards the structure of the post-colonial state. By the 1970s, criticisms were directed at the way in which decolonial self-determination had led to what Robert Jackson termed "negative sovereignty" for post-colonial states.[138] This, he argued related to the automatic granting of "juridical" statehood without the accompanying capacity of ability to uphold "empirical" statehood – which he largely identified as "capacity of a government to provide political goods to its citizens."[139] Human rights violations, he argued, were the inevitable result of this discord in "quasi-states." Writing in 1975 Rupert Emerson voiced his concerns that "the wholly legitimate drive against colonialism and apartheid was in some measure called into question when the new countries habitually shrugged off any concern with massive violations of human rights and dignity in their own domain."[140] The problem, he argued, was not only that independence offered no guarantees of human rights but also that self-determination "may serve to bar more tightly the sovereign-gates which exclude intervention of any kind, including intervention aimed at the protection and promotion of rights of individuals."[141]

Despite their earlier reservations towards the inclusion of self-determination into common article 1 of the Covenants most Western states now used the UN human rights forums to counter Third World and Soviet framings of self-determination with their own democratically oriented interpretation. It was argued that post-colonial self-determination should resituate itself, not as a carte blanche for new world sovereigns, but as a corollary to human rights protection and good governance, including the protection of disparate groups within these states. Political participation, democratic government, free and fair elections, and public accountability became increasingly referred to as falling within the rubric of 'internal' self-determination by Western states and scholars. During the drafting of the Friendly Relations Declaration the US, joined by a number of other states, had equated self-determination with the right to democratic and representative government.[142] While, the inclusion of democratic criteria as part of the definition of self-determination ultimately failed, Western states continued to push the democratic interpretation. In 1972 the US delegate to the Third Committee underlined his country's position on self-determination and human rights when he declared "if freedom of choice is to

138 Jackson (1990: 24; 76).

139 *Ibid*, 12.

140 Rupert Emerson, "The Fate of Human Rights in the Third World," *World Politics* 27 (January 1975): 201–26, 223.

141 *Ibid*, 225.

142 US, (A/AC.125/SR.68) (1967) 4; Italy, (A/AC.125/SR.114) (1970) 45; Canada, (A/AC.125/SR.114) (1970) 57.

be meaningful, there must be corresponding freedom of thought, conscience, expression, movement and association… Self-determination entails legitimate lively dissent and testing at the ballot box with frequent regularity."[143]

Although it was not until the late 1980s that Thomas Franck sought to link self-determination to a right of democratic governance,[144] in the drafting of international instruments, and in the practice of the Human Rights Committee states began to support a connection between the two. During the drafting of the 1975 Helsinki accords, the Netherlands, with the situations of Soviet interference in Eastern Europe in mind, referred to self-determination as the "the peoples' democratic rights to adapt its structures."[145] According to Antonio Cassese, writing in 1979, the inclusion of the phrase 'in full freedom' in Principle VIII[146] reflected the Western view that "self-determination cannot be implemented if basic human rights and fundamental freedoms, in particular freedom of expression, association etc., are not ensured to all members of the people concerned."[147] The philosophy behind this conception, he argued, lay in the rejection of authoritarian government, noting the requirement stipulated by the Friendly Relations Declaration of 'representative' government that does not discriminate as to race is no longer enough "the government must also be democratic (i.e. authoritarian) and able to guarantee effectively the free exercise of human rights."[148] It was questionable, the British representative later noted, "whether any system short of election on the basis of the "one person, one vote" principle could be a satisfactory expression of self-determination."[149] The Federal Republic of Germany claimed that: "Where the political will cannot be expressed freely and in a democratic manner, the right of self-determination is a travesty."[150]

---

143 'US Urges Self-Determination for Peoples Everywhere' (1972) *Department of State Bulletin* (25 Dec 1972) p. 741.

144 See Thomas Franck, 'The Emerging Right to Democratic Governance', 86 *American Journal of International Law* (1992) 46–91.

145 The Netherlands (CSCE/I/PV.7) 18.

146 Helsinki Final Act 1975, 14 ILM (1975) Principle VIII (Equal Rights and Self-Determination): 'By virtue of the principle of equal rights and self -determination of peoples, all peoples always have the right, in full freedom, to determine, when and as they wish, their internal and external political status, without external interference, and to pursue as they wish their political, economic, social and cultural development'.

147 Antonio Cassese, 'Political Self-Determination: Old Concepts and New Developments', in Antonio Cassese (ed.), *U.N Law, Fundamental Rights: Two Topics in International Law* (Leiden: Sijthoff & Nordhood, 1979) 152.

148 *Ibid.*, 154.

149 UK YHRC (1985–6) I, SR.604, para. 44.

150 German Federal Republic, (CCPR/C/52/Add.3) 37–9 HRCOR (1989–90) II, 163.

Over the course of the following years the idea of democratic self-determination was promoted in various UN settings, including the Human Rights Committee, which stated in its General Comment No. 12 (21) of 1984 statement in General Comment No. 12 (21) that state parties should describe how in practice their constitutional and political process allowed for exercise of self-determination.[151] Similarly, the United Kingdom appeared before the Third Committee stating that self-determination was not a 'single event' but a 'continuous process'. "If peoples are to freely determine their political status," he stated, "they must have regular opportunities to choose their government and their social systems freely, and to change them when they so wish."[152] The Australian representative also declared: "self-determination implied the continuing right of all peoples and individuals within each nation to participate fully in the political process by various means, including free and fair elections."[153] The link between self-determination and individual human rights was also stressed, particularly by the Human Rights Committee who declared "the right to self-determination could not be freely exercised unless it was also possible to exercise other rights, such as freedom of expression and of opinion."[154] The West German representative linked the interdependence of the two areas:

> The right of self-determination had far broader connotations than simply freedom from colonial rule and foreign domination.... The right of self-determination was indivisible from the right of the individual to take part in the conduct of public affairs, as was very clearly stated in Article 21 of the Universal Declaration of Human Rights. The exercise of the right to self-determination required the democratic process which, in turn was inseparable from the full exercise of such human rights as the right to freedom of thought conscience and religion; the right of freedom of expression; the right of peaceful assembly and of association; the right to take part in cultural life; the right to liberty and security of person; the right to move freely in one's country and to leave any country, including one's own, as well as to return to one's country.[155]

---

151 General Comment No. 12 (21), 39 GAOR (1984), Supplement No. 40, (A/39/40), para. 4.

152 'United Kingdom Materials on International Law', 57 *British Yearbook of International Law* (1986) 516.

153 C. Brown, *Australian Yearbook of International Law* 1984–1984 (1987) 25.

154 17–22 YHRC (1983–4) I, SR.474, para. 51.

155 UN Doc A/C.3/43/SR.7 (13 October 1988), 16, para 76.

This statement was echoed by Australia who noted that it interpreted self-determination as the matrix of civil, political and other rights required for the meaningful participation of citizens in the kind of decision-making that enabled them to have a say in their future. Self-determination, they said, included "participation in free, fair and regular elections and the ability to occupy public office and enjoy freedom of speech and association."[156] The representative of Ireland stressed the continuous nature of self-determination, and that it was intimately connected and dependent upon other human rights.[157]

By the end of the 1980s, Western iterations of self-determination were linked to sovereignty as an increasingly relative concept which limited state action in a range of areas.[158] "Today, for the first time in history" argued Paul Sieghart in 1985, "how a sovereign state treats its own citizens is no longer a matter for its own exclusive determination, but a matter of legitimate concern for all other states, and for their inhabitants."[159] This shift coincided with a broader redefinition of state identity and behaviour through the elevation of a liberal global order, in which human rights has come to represent a new normative standard.[160]

Many political theorists began to stress the nexus between state legitimacy and internal, democratic order.[161] The new liberal state became defined by a series of traits, most notably representative government, separation of powers, and the constitutional guarantee of political rights. These new expectations of sovereignty in many ways evoke previous sovereign hierarchies as contingent upon the level of political advancement of the internal state. Most notably, John Rawls' influential work "The Law of Peoples" advanced five state archetypes based upon the operation of their domestic order: "reasonable liberal peoples," "decent peoples," the outlaw states, societies burdened by unfavourable conditions, and benevolent absolutims.[162] For some societies, Rawls

156 Australia 31–3 HRCOR (1987–8) I, SR.807, para. 19.

157 44 GAOR 3rd Cmttee 9th mtg., (A/C.3/44/SR.9) (1989).

158 Cassese (1996: 322), see also Christine Bell, "The New Law of Hybrid Self-Determination" *in On the Law of Peace* (Oxford: OUP *2008*).

159 Paul Sieghart, *The Lawful Rights of Mankind* (Oxford: OUP 1985).

160 See in particular: John Vincent, *Human Rights and International Relations* (Cambridge: CUP, 1986); Jack Donnelly, "Human Rights: A New Standard of Civilization?" *International Affairs* 74 (1) (1998): 1–23.

161 See Michael Reisman, "Sovereignty and Human Rights in Contemporary International Law." *The American Journal of International Law* 85, no. 4 (1990):866–876; John Rawls, "The Law of Peoples." *Critical Inquiry* 20, no. 1 (1993): 36–68. Anne-Marie Slaughter, "International law in a world of liberal States." *European Journal of International Law* 64 (1994): 503–38.

argued, support from other liberal states was crucial in order to preserve the possibility of "a people's self-determination."[163]

For the most part though as Brad Simpson has shown, Cold War and geopolitical considerations largely conditioned the West's deployment of the rhetoric of "democratic self-determination."[164] Anti-democratic regimes whose political alignment favoured Western interests were supported throughout the 1970s and 1980s, while interventionist politics reigned supreme. Despite the obvious geopolitical inconsistencies that accompanied this approach in practice, the link between self-determination and democratic governance as "the historic root from which the democratic entitlement grew"[165] was nevertheless to increasingly characterize applications of self-determination into the next period.

---

162 John Rawls, *The Law of Peoples.* (Cambridge, Mass: Harvard University Press, 1999).

163 *Ibid* 111–112.

164 Brad Simpson, 'Denying the 'First Right': The United States, Indonesia, and the Ranking of Human Rights by the Carter Administration, 1976–1980', 4 *International History Review* (2009) 798–826, 801; see also J.G. Taylor, "Encirclement and Annihilation': The Indonesian Occupation of East Timor', in R. Kiernan and B. Gellately (eds.), *The Specter of Genocide: Mass Murder in Historical Perspective* (Cambridge: CUP, 2003) 166–181.

165 Franck (1992: 52).

CHAPTER 5

# Sovereignty and Self-Determination at the End of History

The year 1991 marked the thirtieth anniversary of the United Nations Colonial Declaration, and the beginning of the Decade for the Eradication of Colonialism.[1] It was also the year in which the break-up of the Soviet Union began in earnest. The same year Franjo Tudjman proclaimed the independence of the Croatian state in the name of the "inalienable, indivisible, non-transferable and perpetual right of the Croatian nation to self-determination and state sovereignty."[2] The wave of independence claims that emanated from this period – and remain a staple of the international legal landscape to this day – underlined for many the failings of the "legalistic sleight-of-hand" that purported to keep "the self-determination genie" in check in the post-imperial period.[3] While anti-colonialists understood that colonial-era boundaries cut across ethnic and national groups, the bargain they had struck in their claim that all peoples had a right to self-determination was the acceptance of inherited colonial boundaries and territorial integrity. The oscillation between the conceptions of law and sovereignty which had preceded the independence of colonial peoples had closed with the assumption of *uti possedetis* and other legal mechanisms to refute any further 'gaps' in the sovereignty regime, excluding a new set of claimants from staking their own claims.

The new set of independence claims that emerged in the wake of the end of the Cold War, however, testified to the ongoing resonance of self-determination as a legal and political claim, particularly against the backdrop of the unfinished business of empire.[4] Formal decolonization may have

1 The title is taken from Francis Fukuyama's now infamous claim made in '*The End of History' and the Last Man* (New York: Free Press, 1992).

2 *Constitution of the Republic of Croatia,* Part I: Historical Foundations, adopted on December, 22nd, 1990.

3 Richard Falk, "Self-Determination Under International Law: The Coherence of Doctrine Versus the Incoherence of Experience" in Wolfgang Danspeckgruber (ed) *The Self-Determination of Peoples: Community, Nation and State in an Interdependent World* (Boulder: Lynne Rienner, 2002) 49.

4 As Marc Weller points out "while decolonisation has been applied in 72 cases of non-self-governing territories and 11 trust territories since 1945, this figure is nearly matched by the number of 78 major violent self-determination conflicts that have arisen out of the

 DOI:10.1163/9789004479197_007

been largely concluded, but the claims emanating from former colonial states underlined that many of the structures and legacies of imperial rule persisted. Self-determination assumed new significance, as groups seeking to legitimise their claims, appealed to its emancipatory logic to once again shift the goal posts of sovereignty. The accompanying conflicts that have followed have become some of the most pressing issues in the international arena.[5] In this climate, recognition practices, have become the determining factor in the resolution of self-determination claims.[6] According to Michael Addo, "the success of self-determination movements seems more often than not to depend on the fortunes of war and the strategic demands of the great powers than on the intrinsic legitimacy of their claims."[7]

As I will argue in this chapter, the contingency of new self-determination claims upon recognition took place against a backdrop of debate over the concept of sovereignty and increasing scrutiny over forms of governance, particularly human rights protection.[8] This new climate was summarised by former UN Secretary General Boutros Boutros-Ghali in his Agenda for Peace document, in which he pointed out that "[t]he time of absolute and exclusive

colonial context" Marc Weller, *Escaping the Self-Determination Trap*, (Leiden: Martinus Nijhoff 2009) 19.

5 The link between session and terrorism has been draw by many including Robert Pape who notes: "From Lebanon to Israel to Sri Lanka to Kashmir to Chechnya, every suicide terrorist campaign from 1980 to 2001 has been waged by terrorist groups whose main goal has been to establish or maintain self-determination for their community's homeland by compelling an enemy to withdraw," Robert A. Pape, 'The Strategic Logic of Suicide Terrorism', American Political Science Review, 97/3 (2002), 344.

6 As Brad Roth notes "International legal standing has traditionally been established by victory in a trial by ordeal: a region initially integral to an existing state successfully establishes itself as an independent sovereign unit only where its secession movement creates - usually by decisive victory in an armed struggle - facts on the ground that appear irreversible; an insurgent faction successfully establishes itself as a government where it overthrows an existing constitutional structure and secures - even if at bayonet-point - widespread popular acquiescence" (Roth: 2010, 34).

7 Quoted in Brad Simpson "Self-Determination in the Age of Putin" Foreign Policy (March 21st 2014) available http://www.foreignpolicy.com/articles/2014/03/21/self_determination_in_the_age_of_putin_crimea_referendum accessed June 28, 2022.

8 See e.g. Alexander Rosas, 'The Decline of Sovereignty: Legal Perspectives', in J.Iivonen (ed.), *The Future of the Nation State in Europe* (Aldershot: E. Elgar Pub. 1993), 149; Christoph Schreuer, 'The Waning of the Sovereign State: Towards a New Paradigm for International Law', EJIL 4 (1993), pp. 447–71; Rosalyn Higgins, Anne Marie. Slaughter, Thomas M. Franck, Stephen R. Ratner, Christine Chinkin, Panel on 'The End of Sovereignty', *ASIL Proceedings* 88 (1994), pp. 71–87; Greg Fox, and Brad Roth, 'Introduction: The Spread of Liberal Democracy and its Implications for International Law', in Greg Fox, and Brad Roth (eds.), *Democratic Governance and International Law*, (Cambridge: CUP 2000).

sovereignty…has passed; its theory was never matched by reality."[9] As a UN study on sovereignty released shortly after the publication of the Agenda clarified, "a shift in perceptions seems to be underway, suggesting that there may be limits to national sovereignty when human rights are grossly violated."[10] The resumption of standards of sovereignty was accompanied by new categories of statehood such as 'failed' and 'rogue' states, as well as a resurgence in concepts such as trusteeship, protectorates and international administrations to deal with entities falling short of these new standards.[11] It also saw the rise of military intervention. In Haiti,[12] Somalia,[13] and Bosnia, the UN Security Council found that the uniqueness of the situations justified the use of "all necessary means" to resolve the conflicts.

In this context a shift of emphasis to the association between self-determination and democratic governance, along with a commitment to human rights and minority rights, that had emerged in Western framings of the idea in the 1970s gained substantial ground.[14] As the European Community (EC) Commission on the dissolution of Yugoslavia asserted in its assessment of the relevance of self-determination to the conflict, "Article 1 of the two 1966 International Covenants on human rights established that the principle of the right to self-determination serves to safeguard human rights."[15] Particularly in the case of independence claims, these factors have become a new 'preparedness for sovereignty' standard upon which recognition by the international community its contingent. In the aftermath of the breakup up of the USSR and SFRY, recognition was often made contingent upon promotion of the rights of national and ethnic minorities. These developments were accompanied

9 Boutros Boutros-Ghali, Agenda for Peace, A/47/277, (New York: United Nations, 1992). para. 17.

10 United Nations (UN), 'The Limits of Sovereignty', DPI/1178 (February 1992).

11 Those scholars in defence of conditional or limited membership of international society include Jackson (1990); Anne-Marie Slaughter, "Security, Solidarity, and Sovereignty: The Grand Themes of UN Reform," *American Journal of International Law* 99 (July 2005): 619–31; Robert Keohane, "Political Authority after Intervention: Gradations in Sovereignty," in *Humanitarian Intervention: Ethical, Legal and Political Dilemmas*, ed. J. L. Holzgrefe and Robert O. Keohane (New York: CUP 2003). Those scholars who question these the new modes of unequal membership, include Gerry Simpson, *Great Powers and Outlaw States: Unequal Sovereigns in the International Legal Order* (Cambridge: CUP 2004); Koskenniemi, (2001: 480–509).

12 SC Res. 940 (1994).

13 SC Res. 794 (1992).

14 Hurst Hannum, 'Self-Determination, Yugoslavia, and Europe: Old Wine in New Bottles?' (1993) 3 *Transnat'l L. & Contemp. Probs* 69.

15 Quoted and discussed in Pellet, "The Opinions of the Badinter Arbitration Committee."

by the advancement of new standards of minority protection and autonomy for sub-state groups involving a wide variety of constitutional rights and protections, and power-sharing models.[16] Indigenous self-determination too is increasingly asserted against the territorial state, as a way of promoting and protecting indigenous peoples' rights and countering the colonial era exclusion of indigenous peoples from international law. The focus on internal self-determination, as well these new broadened categories of self-determination rights, were proposed as offering an alternative form of self-determination. Against this backdrop, a form of legal cohesion between the expectations of internal self-determination and territorial integrity was offered through a proposed 'remedial' right to self-determination. While this has sought to create doctrinal certainty, there are still questions over the logical end of this demand where a state fails to uphold its duty. These debates surround a broader reevaluation of the position of the state and the belief that, as Andrew Hurrell states "the problems of self-determination have at least as much to do with the triumph of a hard notion of sovereignty as it does with nationalism."[17]

## 1 New and Old Claims

By the end of the Cold War, despite a number of secessionist claims grounding their claims to independence in the rhetoric of self-determination, only Bangladesh had managed to gain recognition without the acquiescence of the state it was seceding from.[18] The breakup of the Soviet Union and later of Yugoslavia in 1991, however, returned the question of self-determination to the international agenda. As it became clear that self-determination was to be, once again, the principle at the base of a new wave of state formation, a new standard for its application had to be defined.

Just four months after the fall of the Berlin wall, the three Baltic union republics declared their independence from Moscow. The declarations were

16 See eg Document of the Copenhagen Meeting of the Conference on the Human Dimension of the CSCE in 29 ILM 1305 (1990); General Assembly Resolution and Declaration on the Right of Persons belong to National or Ethnic, Religious, Linguistic Minorities, GA Res 47/135 December 1992.

17 Hurrell (2007: 136).

18 Senegal is generally understood as having emerged from the dissolution Mali Federation in 1960 after agreement between the parties; Singapore achieved independence from Malaysia pursuant to a Separation Agreement in 1965 (see Government of Malaysia-Government of Singapore, Agreement Relating to the Separation of Singapore from Malaysia as an Independent and Sovereign State, 7 August 1965, 563 UNTS 89).

immediately rejected by Moscow and were unrecognized by the majority of states. Germany and France, backed by the US, supported a plan for a 'suspension' of the declaration of independence so as to enhance the chances for a negotiated settlement with Moscow. According to the UK the peoples of the Baltics did not have a right to independence, but rather "a right 'to resolve their future status through free negotiation with the Soviet authorities in a way which takes proper account of the legitimate rights and interests of the parties concerned'."[19] President George H.W. Bush announced that while his administration supported "the Baltic peoples' inalienable right to peaceful self-determination," the question of statehood would have to be left to the authorities of the states and Moscow.[20]

However, after the subsequent disintegration of the Soviet Union, states moved to establish diplomatic relations with the Baltic States. The did so, however, largely without invoking any reference to self-determination, instead appealing to the claim of a restoration of sovereignty, temporarily suspended by illegal Soviet annexation.[21] The EC in its statement welcomed "the restoration of the sovereignty and independence of the Baltic States which they lost in 1940,"[22] while Secretary of State James Baker pointed out that for the United States the Baltic republics had "never been Soviet republics but, instead, separate states for whom we helped keep alive the promise and diplomatic symbols of independence."[23] Western powers were quick to issue demands which would guide their recognition practice, the content of which reflected the shifting emphasis placed upon democratic governance as the new standard of political legitimacy. The previous year, member states of the Conference of Security and Cooperation in Europe (CSCE later the OCSE) had renewed their ideological commitment to democracy and human rights through the endorsement of the Paris Charter for a New Europe.[24] This was evident in the framework issued for recognition, which emphasised democratic processes,

---

19 James Crawford, *The Creation of States in International Law*, 2nd ed. (Cambridge: CUP, 2006) quoting Minister of State, Foreign and Commonwealth Office, *United Kingdom Materials on International Law* (Geoffrey Marston, ed.) (1991) at 395.

20 Quoted in Fabry (2010: 183).

21 Fabry (2010: 184).

22 See George Bush and Brent Scowcroft, *A World Transformed* (New York: Vintage Books, 1998), 538–539. R. Pullat, "The Restoration of Independence of Estonia 1991" 2 Finnish Yearbook of International Law (1991) 512–32 at. 516.

23 The UN General Assembly, for example, spoke in Resolution 47/21 of November 1992, of "particular satisfaction that independence was restored in Estonia, Latvia and Lithuania."

24 Charter of Paris for a New Europe, unanimously endorsed in Paris in 1990 by the members of the CSCE.

minority protection, along with the insistence that internal boundaries of the former constituent republics be recognized as the international boundaries of the new successor states.[25] These concerns – democratic governance and the maintenance of internal boundaries - along with an emphasis on minority rights, were reflected in the principles issued by the US, which were outlined by US Secretary of State James Baker in September 1991. "The West should stick to fundamentals and support those who put into practice our principles and values" he noted.[26] He appealed to leaders to conform to democratic values and practices of the Helsinki Final Act, support the rule of law and safeguard human rights, including equal treatment of minorities, and respect international law and obligations, especially the provisions of the Helsinki Final Act and the Charter of Paris.[27]

The emphasis on the retention of existing territorial boundaries may have solved the problem of the transition to independence of the former Soviet states in the short term, but it failed to address the larger issue of competing nationalist claims within the autonomous republics. As James Mayall notes "in sociological and empirical terms a strong case could be made that Chechnya had a better claim to independence than, say, Belarus, but as an autonomous region in the Russian Federation, it did not have the pre-existing legal credentials to fit easily into the conventional interpretation."[28] Independence claims emerged almost immediately. While many of these claims were based on allegations of ill treatment, forced jurisdictional or territorial transfers, or denial of constitutional status, many commentators saw these demands as a worrying return to the powder keg of nationalism of the pre-war period. "The tribes have returned" declared Michael Waltzer,[29] while Thomas Franck coined the phrase "postmodern tribalism" to describe the new era.[30] Cassese described the new iteration of demands for self-determination as a "Golem turned on its Creators."[31]

---

25 Musgrave (1997: 111).

26 Fabry (2010: 187) quoting 'America and the Collapse of the Soviet Empire: What Has to Be Done', December 12, 1991, *US Department of State Dispatch,* Vol. 2, No. 50 (1991).

27 'US Approach to Changes In the Soviet Union', September 4, 1991, *US Department of State Dispatch,* Vol. 2, No. 36(1991).

28 Mayall (2013: 56).

29 Michael Walzer, 'The New Tribalism', *Dissent* (1992) 164.

30 Thomas Franck, "Postmodern Tribalism and the Right to Secession" in Catherine Brölmann, René Lefeber and Marjoleine Zieck, eds., *Peoples and Minorities in International Law* (Dordrecht: Martinus Nijhoff, 1993) 3–27.

31 Cassese states that: "If, in the past, self-determination used the coin of 'progress', in its third apparition it has come to be seen increasingly as fuelling the currency of ethno-national

The events surrounding the breakup of Yugoslavia were to become emblematic for many commentators of the potential "pandora's box"[32] of ethnic strife and bloodshed that self-determination could carry with it. Yugoslavia had been a federal state comprising six Republics, representing the major 'nationalities', and two autonomous enclaves (Kosovo and Vojdvodina). A protracted power struggle between the republics following the death of Tito in 1980 was followed by declarations of independence being announced on the part of Slovenia and Croatia in 1991. Both leaders proclaimed independence in the name of the will of their respective people, explicitly framed as the right of their people to self-determination exercised through what they described "democratic elections."[33] However, both declarations contained explicit references to the rights of the "nation" defined in ethnic terms. The international community initially responded to the independence claims of Slovenia and Croatia in much the same fashion as they had to the crisis in the Soviet Union, by refusing to recognize the dissolution of the state, and attempting to preserve the territorial integrity of Yugoslavia. Secretary of State James Baker insisted that "self-determination cannot be unilateral and must be pursued by dialogue and peaceful means" and that, in this respect, "borders must not be changed except by consent."[34] However, these efforts to mediate conflict failed, leading to a shift in attitude towards the crisis.

As states began to indicate that they would support recognition, the question arose as to who would comprise the succeeding states, as well as what the broader implications of recognition would mean for the right to self-determination. The EC proceeded to convene a permanent conference on Yugoslavia in order to help mediate a settlement of the conflict and, more broadly, assist in negotiations on the future of the Yugoslav state.[35] An *ad hoc* arbitration panel was also created, headed by President of the French Constitutional Court Robert Badinter, which was to produce a series of non-binding

---

intolerance, rivalry, tribalism, xenophobia, and worse: a Golem turned on its Creators." Cassese (1998: 1).

32 Ibid.

33 Sabrina Ramet, *Nationalism and Federalism in Yugoslavia, 1962–1991*, (Bloomington: Indiana University Press, 1992) 178.

34 Quoted in Fabry (2010: 191). The United States declared already in May it "will not encourage or reward secession; it will respect any framework, federal, confederal, or other, on which the people of Yugoslavia peacefully and democratically decide. We firmly believe that Yugoslavia's external or internal borders should not be changed unless by peaceful consensual means."

35 Fabry (2010: 192).

advisory opinions on the issues involved.[36] Dubbed the "controversial modern classic" on the right to self-determination by Karen Knop,[37] the Opinions dealt with three questions which historically lay at the core of debates over self-determination's meaning: whose claims of self- determination should be recognised? What rights did self-determination entail? What would the implications be, once statehood would be recognised (and thus what should be the responsibilities correlative to such rights)?

Rejecting Serbia's claim that the declarations of independence were acts of illegal secession, the Commission declared that Yugoslavia was in a state of dissolution. This approach allowed the Commission to largely abdicate the question of secession from the question of self-determination, reducing it to one of fact regarding the existence or non-existence of the state. This ensured that any act of recognition could be made without seeking the consent of the federal government.[38] In answering the question "does the Serbian Population in Croatia and Bosnia and Herzegovina, as one of the constituent peoples of Yugoslavia, have a right to self-determination?" the Commission took a broad approach, upholding the rights of all groups to self-determination, but qualified by the principle of *uti possidetis juris*. This was the first time the principle had been applied outside of the colonial context. Declaring *uti possidetis* "a general principle, which is logically connected with the phenomenon of the obtaining of independence, wherever it occurs" the Commission concluded that any exercise of self-determination was prefaced upon the stability of borders, even ones that were constitutionally determined.[39] In this sense, the Commission formally acknowledged that independent statehood was possible only for the former constituent Yugoslav Republics. In the absence of any agreement regarding renegotiation of borders, the Commission contended that the Serbs in the two republics were only entitled "to all the rights accorded to minorities and ethnic groups under international law…" Drawing a link to Article 1 of the ICCPR, the Commission concluded that the ambit of self-determination

---

36 The Arbitration Commission of the European Community's Conference for Peace in Yugoslavia (hereinafter the 'Badinter Commission', named after Robert Badinter, the Commission's chairman) was established pursuant to the EC Declaration of 27 August 1991 and EC Ministerial Joint Statement of 3 September 1991 to promote peace between the various Yugoslav peoples. The Commission's decisions, which were not binding in nature, aimed "to resolve discrete issues through the application of legal principles."

37 Knop (2002: 167).

38 Matthew Craven, 'The European Community Arbitration Commission on Yugoslavia', 66 *British Yearbook of International Law* (1995) 333–413 at 367.

39 Conference on Yugoslavia, Arbitration Commission, Opinion No.3. 1 1 January 1992 in (1992) 3 1 L.L.M. 1499 at 1500.

also included the right of all individuals to choose their nationality, noting that self-determination "serves to safeguard human rights." In this sense, the newly independent states of the former Yugoslavia were expected to embody such an interpretation of self-determination in their new constitutional structure and state practices. This was also reflected in the EC's plan for recognition, which required the republics to commit themselves to the *Guidelines on the Recognition of New States in Eastern Europe and in the Soviet Union* and accept the provisions of the draft Convention on settling the conflict in Yugoslavia, especially those on human and minority rights.[40] In addition to being constituted on a democratic basis, the guidelines presented a list of other prerequisites, including the guarantee that they would comply with the provisions of the UN Charter, of the 1975 Helsinki Final Act, that they would respect the inviolability of international borders and, in particular, that they would comply with the 1990 Paris Charter and thereby accept "democracy as the only system of government of our nations."[41]

Despite warnings that pursuing this approach and proceeding with recognition would inflame tensions, the EC recognized Croatia and Slovenia, and eventually Bosnia in early 1992, leading to a protracted conflict that would lead to the deaths of thousands.[42] The Commission's opinions, particularly the events following their aftermath, provoked intense debate. According to David Owen, the Co-Chairman of the Steering Committee of the successor to the EC Conference on Yugoslavia, the approach worked against the attainment of a peaceful compromise.[43] While it was believed that applying *uti possidetis* to the Balkans might keep tensions at bay as they to some extent had done in the colonial context, the complicated federal structure of the SFRY presented a different set of problems.[44] The major difference was not only the fact that colonial borders been external rather than internal, and the newly decolonized entities liberated from the colonial powers rather than from one another, but, as Brad Roth says "*uti possidetis* in that context had represented maintenance of the *status quo inter se* rather than, as in the Yugoslav context, a drastic shift in power relations among the emergent states' constituent

40 Statement by an Extraordinary EPC Ministerial Meeting concerning Yugoslavia, December 16, 1991, *European Foreign Policy Bulletin,* Document 91/465.

41 Cornelia Navari, "Territoriality, Self-Determination and Crimea after Badinter," *International Affairs* 6(1) (2014) 1299–1318 at 1301.

42 Susan L. Woodward, *Balkan Tragedy: Chaos and Dissolution after the Cold War* (Washington, D.C: Brookings Institution, 1995), 184.

43 David Owen, *Balkan Odyssey,* (San Diego: Brace and Company, 1999) 34.

44 S. Ramer, "Drawing a Better Line: Uti Possidetis and the Borders of New States" (1996) 90 AJIL 590 at 6 1.

groups."[45] Hurst Hannum criticized the "ad hoc" and "unprincipled" approach to self-determination, leading to new minorities being trapped, "not by any comprehensible legal principle, but by the historical accident of administrative borders drawn by an undemocratic government…."[46] The endorsements of liberalism, democracy and human rights as the overarching framework for recognition also seemed to ring hollow given the heavy handed manner in which the conflict had been approached legally. This tension was best summed up by Tudjman's words when, in 1991, he claimed:

> (…) In their endorsement of human rights, democratic countries, including the entire United Nations are not sufficiently prepared for the present historical wave of creating national states. They have not found a satisfactory answer to the question of how to ensure the realisation of every nation's natural right to self-determination[47]

While the application of *uti possedetis* appeared in the eyers of many to have solved the issue of territorial distribution in the breakup of the SFRY, debates resumed again two years later with the attempted session of Kosovo, which led to the adoption of Security Council Resolution 1244 establishing the United Nations Interim Administration Mission (UNMIK). Between 1999 and 2008, when Kosovo unilaterally declared its independence, discussions raged about whether Kosovo was entitled to secede, underlining the continuing uncertainty surrounding self-determination's role in state creation. While Kosovo, an autonomous province within Serbia with a large Albanian majority, had largely escaped the violence of the early 1990s, the ascent of Milosevic saw the autonomy of Kosovo rescinded and the violent persecution of Kosovo Albanians. Though outside states resolutely refused to recognize Kosovo's claim to independence, following the breakdown of talks between the two sides and against fears of an "impending humanitarian catastrophe"[48] NATO, authorized the launching of military operations against the FRY. UN Security Council Resolution 1244 eventually placed Kosovo under a United Nations transitional administration, the United Nations Interim Administration Mission in Kosovo (UNMIK). In parallel to the handling of earlier independence claims, guidance

45 Brad Roth, *Sovereign Equality and Moral Disagreement: Premises of a Pluralist International Legal Order* (Oxford: OUP 2011) 192.

46 Hurst Hannum, Hurst, 'Self-Determination, Yugoslavia, and Europe: Old Wine in New Bottles?' 3 *Transnat'l L. & Contemp. Probs* (1993) 57–72.

47 Address Delivered by the President of the Republic of Croatia Franjo Tudjman to the Croatian Assembly, May 30, 1991, quoted in Fabry, *Recognizing States*, 191.

48 UN, S/Res/1199 (1998).

towards democratic self-governance was cited as the overarching principle of mission. Like the EC Guidelines on Recognition, the UNMIK 2000 Report referred explicitly to the endorsement of democracy as being conditional for "Kosovo's path to self-governance," which should be linked to "mature political and civic behaviour" in the area of "good governance, human rights, and equal opportunities."[49]

Ultimately, after a protracted assessment of the final outcome of Kosovo's status led by Martti Ahtisaari, Kosovo declared itself "an independent and sovereign state" on 17 February 2008 – a claim supported by its Western allies who had overseen Kosovo's transition to a democratic state. This was met with strong condemnation by the Serbian authorities as a distortion of international law. The US and its Western allies, wary of creating a precedent on self-determination, stressed that determining Kosovo's status had nothing to do with law or precedent, whilst deftly avoiding any reference to self-determination. In recognising Kosovo, Secretary of State Condoleezza Rice underlined "the unusual combination of factors found in the Kosovo situation—including the context of Yugoslavia's breakup, the history of ethnic cleansing and crimes against civilians in Kosovo, and the extended period of UN administration—are not found elsewhere and therefore make Kosovo a special case." Kosovo, she said, "cannot be seen as a precedent for any other situation in the world today."[50] Positions of the same kind were expressed by various other States.[51] Kosovo's own declaration of independence even observed, "Kosovo is a special case arising from Yugoslavia's non-consensual breakup and is not a precedent for any other situation."

The recourse to the claim of 'uniqueness' however, has left Kosovo's declaration of independence in a legal and moral grey area and kept the province in a near-permanent state of limbo since this time. It has also provoked an angry response from several states accusing the West of arbitrariness and double

49 Paragraph 108: http://www.un.org/en/ga/search/view_doc.asp?symbol=S/2000/1196.

50 Rice statements on Recognition of Kosovo as Independent State, American.gov (Feb 18, 2008), available online at <http://www.america.gov/st/texttrans-english/2008/February/20080218150254 bpuh5.512637e-02.html> (visited Apr 26, 2009). See also Rein Müllerson, *Precedents in the Mountains: On the Parallels and Uniqueness of the Cases of Kosovo, South Ossetia and Abkhazia*, 8 Chinese J Intl L 2, 2–5 (2009) (arguing the uniqueness of a case is in the eye of the beholder).

51 See Canada, Canada Joins International Recognition of Kosovo, Press Release no. 59, 18 March 2008, available at http://news.gc.ga; Latvia, Announcement by Minister of Foreign Affairs of Republic of Latvia on Recognition of Kosovo's independence, available at www.mfa.gov.lv/en/news/press-release/2008/february/20-february/; Peru, Peru decide reconocer indepencia de Kosovo, Communicaso Official 002-08, 22 February 2008, available at www.kosovothanksyou.com.

standards. "In international relations," Russian President Medvedev stated, "you cannot have one rule for some and another rule for others."[52] As the events in several former Soviet republics were to illustrate, the implications of Kosovo's independence were swiftly felt. In what was to emerge as a diplomatic game of tit for tat Russia was quick to invoke much of the same rhetoric used by the West in its recognition of Kosovo, in its decision to recognise Abkhazia and South Ossetia.[53] These joined a growing list of territories which have moved to declare their independence since the early 1990s, including Transnistria, Nagorno-Karabakh, the Republic of Crimea, the Donetsk Peoples' Republic' and the 'Luhansk People's Republic' – all of which were framed using some sort of claim to self-determination and involved some sort of referenda.[54] Unable to gain recognition from the majority of the international community, this has led to a series of frozen conflicts, the pitfalls of which are most keenly felt by the people of these territories.

## 2 Adjudicating Secession

In the aftermath of the Badinter Opinions and the events surrounding the Yugoslav conflict, the Pellet Report and the subsequent judgment rendered by the Canadian Supreme Court, offered a restatement of self-determination which sought to reconcile its increasing legal opacity against the backdrop of rising ethno-nationalism. A number of legal scholars had by this time begun to profess support for a new 'remedial' right, relying upon the so called 'safeguard' clause found in the 1970 *Declaration on Friendly Relations* as well as the Aaland Island Opinions.[55] This joined a growing chorus of normative political

---

52 Dmitry Medvedev, 'Why I had to recognise Georgia's breakaway regions'. Financial Times, 27 August 2008, 9.

53 Statement by Russian President Dmitry Medvedev, 26 August 2008, (Medvedev Recogniton Speech) www.un.int/russia/new/MainRoot/docs/off_news/260808/newen2.htm.

54 Matthew Craven & Rose Parfitt "Statehood, Self-Determination and Recognition" in Malcolm D. Evans, ed. *International Law.* (Oxford: OUP, 2018)

55 As Hurst Hannum puts it is: [the] norm of self-determination in the post-colonial era is both a shield that protects a state (in most cases) from secession and a spear that pierces the governmental veil of sovereignty behind which undemocratic and discriminatory regimes attempt to hide. Hurst Hannum, "Rethinking Self-Determination" 34 Va. J. Int'l L. (1993–1994) 1–69 *at* 40 (stressing that a right of secession will arise only in the most extreme circumstances). In the *Loizidou v Turkey* case, European Court of Human Rights, judgment of 18 December 1996, Judges Wilhaber and Ryssdal, in a concurring opinion, pronounced themselves strongly in favour of a right of secession.

theorists who had also proposed a conditional right of secession.[56] Against this backdrop, the Pellet report - prepared by five international lawyers in response by a request by the National Assembly of Québec, "to consider the territorial status of the province in the event of its separation from Canada"[57] - seemed to confirm self-determination's new conditional logic as directed towards the interior of the state, but within the safe limits of existing boundaries. The subsequent Supreme Court Judgement, however, indicated some limited support for an extended application of the principle in opposition to unfettered rights of sovereignty.

The Pellet report begins by correcting the "erroneous assumption" that self-determination implies the right to independence. Rather, they argue, outside of the colonial context, self-determination implies only the right of a people to participate in the definition of its political, economic, social and cultural future. While no right to secession derived from self-determination can be said to exist in international law, given "the legitimate desire of States to preserve their territorial integrity," they were also of the view that international law does not prevent secession either. The balance – between self-determination and territorial integrity, they explain, is particularly pertinent given the manner in which interpretations of self-determination have given way to broader understandings of 'peoples'. Viewed in this way, the experts note "self-determination has substance without being limited to a particular category of peoples." Instead, recourse to 'internal' self-determination, particularly democratic participation and minority rights, becomes the acceptable counterpoint to what is in essence the prohibition of secession, even if that position is not made explicit. This mirrors the Badinter Commission's reasoning, including its adept avoidance of the question of the nature of the 'self'.

The subsequent 1998 judgement by the Supreme Court of Canada reached a similar conclusion. They did, however, go on to affirm that 'a people' may include only a portion of the population of an existing state, arguing that "to

56 A vast amount of literature regarding both the moral and legal implications of secession and self-determination was disseminated following the end of the Cold War. Writings by Allen Buchanan, Lea Brilmayer and Diane F. Orentlicher, for instance, have sought to engage with the question of secession from a philosophical viewpoint. See Allen Buchanan, *Secession: The Morality of Political Divorce from Fort Sumter to Lithuania and Quebec* (Boulder, Colorado: Westview Press, 1991), 174; Lee Brilmayer, 'Secession and Self-Determination: A Territorial Interpretation', YJIL 16 (1991), 177–202; Diane F. Orentlicher, 'Separation Anxiety: International Responses to Ethno-Separatist Claims', YJIL 23 (1998), 1–78.

57 Thomas M. Franck, Rosalyn Higgins, Alain Pellet, Malcolm, N. Shaw and Christian Tomuschat, 'The territorial integrity of Quebec in the event of the attainment of sovereignty', in Quebec, Assemblée Nationale, Exposés et études, 1992, vol. 1, pp. 377–461.

restrict the definition of the term to the population of existing states would render the granting of a right to self- determination largely duplicative… and would frustrate its remedial purpose."[58] While emphasizing that self-determination is predominantly enjoyed through its 'internal' aspect which the Court articulated as "a people's pursuit of its political, economic, social and cultural development within the framework of an existing state" the Court held that in "exceptional" situations a right to external self-determination did exist. These, were 'at best' in "situations of former colonies; where a people is oppressed, as for example under foreign military occupation; or where a definable group is denied meaningful access to government to pursue their political, economic, social and cultural development."[59]

The link forged between the fact of alien rule, the denial of human rights and the lack of access to government, each of which is taken as expressive of the same denial of self-determination, seems to promote an idea of sovereignty as conditional upon the preservation and promotion of individual and collective rights and the maintenance of a system of government by consent. Indeed, as Matthew Craven notes "one might conclude from this that in cases where a determinate people have been oppressed, abused, or routinely denied their rights, a claim for secessionary self-determination might be sustained simply by reason of the fact that the parent state is no longer in the position of being able to justify its claim to sovereignty."[60] The Court did not expand upon the meaning of political, economic, social, or cultural development, but it concluded that since Quebec "did not meet the threshold of a colonial people or an oppressed people" and since the Quebecers had not been denied "meaningful access to government" they did not enjoy the right to secede from Canada unilaterally. Rather, they enjoyed a (Constitutional) right to negotiate the terms of their constitutional arrangement.[61] The Court also signaled that a "clear expression of a clear majority" would have to demonstrate the unambiguous willingness of the Québécois to secede from Canada.[62] Although the Court reaffirmed that "in itself and without more, [the holding of a referendum] has no direct legal effect, and could not in itself bring about unilateral secession."[63]

58 *Reference re Secession of Quebec* [1998] 2 SCR 217, para 124.

59 *Ibid* para 138.

60 Matthew Craven, "Statehood, Self-Determination and Recognition" in Malcolm Evans (ed.) *International Law* (Oxford: OUP 2014) 238.

61 *Reference re Secession of Quebec* [1998] 2 SCR 217, para 136.

62 *Ibid* para 92–100.

63 *Ibid* para 87.

While the Quebec decision seemed to indicate some limited support for the idea of remedial self-determination in international law, this position seemed to have receded ten years later, when the International Court of Justice was requested by the General Assembly to consider the lawfulness of the Kosovo Declaration of Independence.[64] Although the Court was presented with an opportunity to confront the question of remedial secession – particularly given the evidence of discrimination, violence and repression committed against the Kosovo Albanians - it adopted an exceedingly narrow interpretation of the request, focussing almost exclusively on the legality of the unilateral declaration of independence. In this respect it has been observed that the Opinion "might not enter into the judicial history of the Court for its answer to this question, but rather for what it did not say."[65] The decision was described by Richard Falk as "essentially an argument that combin[ed] legal positivism with political realism,"[66] arising from "a tortuous exercise of avoiding from commenting on complex and difficult legal issues, with its only objective of not stumbling into non liquet."[67]

During submissions a number of states expressed support for a remedial interpretation of self-determination.[68] Germany advocated for the secession of Kosovo on the basis of a denial of 'internal' self-determination.[69] Switzerland argued that secession in the case of Kosovo was lawful on the basis of the saving clause contained in principle 5, paragraph 7, of the Declaration on Friendly Relations.[70] The United Kingdom cautiously left open the possibility for the Court to find in favour of an exercise of self-determination in extremis, but it did not go so far as to endorse remedial secession.[71] Similar reasoning was exhibited by the US. China expressly rejected the doctrine, noting that it

64 *Accordance with International Law of the Unilateral Declaration of Independence in Respect of Kosovo*, Advisory Opinion, ICJ Reports 2010.

65 Bjorn Arp, 'The ICJ Advisory Opinion on the Accordance with International Law of the Unilateral Declaration of Independence in Respect of Kosovo and the International Protection of Minorities (2010), 11 German Law Journal 847.

66 Richard Falk, 'The Kosovo Advisory Opinion: Conflict Resolution and Precedent', (2011) 105 *American Journal of International Law*, at 54.

67 *Ibid.*

68 Albania, Verbatim Record, 2 December 2009, CR 2009/26, 22–3, para. 15 (Gill), Estonia, Written Statement by Estonia, p. 6, para. 2.1., Ireland, Written Statement of Ireland, p. 9, para. 30., the Netherlands, Verbatim Record, 10 December 2009, CR 2009/32, 15, paras. 27–8 (Lijnzaad)., Poland, Written Statement of Poland, p. 25, para. 6.5; Written Statement by Germany, 33–5.

69 Written Statement by Germany, 33–5.

70 Written Statement of Switzerland, p. 16, paras. 62–3.

71 10 December 2009, CR 2009/32, p. 54, para. 29 (Crawford).

'does not believe there is such a right under international law'.[72] Other States, many of which faced their own secessionist claims, also made clear their rejection of the doctrine of remedial secession.[73] States further argued that the question phrased by the General Assembly was political in nature rather than legal, and thus beyond the scope of the Court.

The Court seems to have accepted this position, concluding that it was not required to determine whether international law confers a positive right of secession. While rejecting the argument that declarations of independence were prohibited under international law, the Court ultimately refused to engage with the question of remedial session.[74] Two dissenting opinions, by Judges Yuusuf and Trindade, did however raise the possibility under "exceptional circumstances, the right of peoples to self-determination may support a claim to separate statehood."[75] Underlining that while no right to secession for ethnically or racially distinct groups within States exists, Judge Yuusuf notes that "this does not however meaning that international law turns a blind eye to the plight of such groups, particularly in those cases where the State not only denies the exercise of their internal right of self-determination." Emphasising the humane end of international law and the responsibility that States bears to their citizens, Judge Trindade, moreover argued that:

> The principle of self-determination has survived decolonization, in order to face nowadays new and violent manifestations of systematic oppression of peoples ... It is immaterial whether, in the framework of these new experiments, self-determination is given the qualification of 'remedial', or another qualification. The fact remains that people cannot be targeted for atrocities, cannot live under systematic oppression. The principle of self-determination applies in new situations of systematic oppression, subjugation and tyranny.[76]

While the judgement that the declaration of independence was not in violation of international law ultimately lent some legitimacy to Kosovo's claim, it failed to resolve the question of whether the subsequent recognition of its

72 7 December 2009, CR 2009/29, p. 35, para. 23 (Xue).

73 See submissions by Cyprus, 7 December 2009, CR 2009/29, pp. 47–8, paras. 58–61 (Droushiotis); Iran Written Statement of Iran, p. 6, para. 4.1; Serbia Written Comments of Serbia, 14 July 2009, pp. 142–5.; Slovakia Written Statement of Slovakia, para. 28. And Spain Verbatim Record, 8 December 2009, CR 2009/30, p. 17, paras. 37–44 (Escobar Hernández).

74 Ibid para. 82.

75 Ibid para. 11.

76 Kosovo Advisory Opinion, Separate Opinion of Judge Cançado Trindade, p. 53, para. 175.

independence might constitute a violation of Serbian sovereignty, leaving Kosovo's status no clearer, and with no clear resolution in sight. Despite the limitations of the court's approach however, many interpreted it as a necessary maintenance of self-determination's ambiguous status. As Craven argues the decision fulfilled an "essential function: that of keeping in play two apparently contradictory ideas namely that international law both sustains the possibility of an emancipatory national self-determination, but yet also serves to protect and secure a stable, ordered, society of States."[77]

## 3 Human Rights, Democracy and the New Standards of Sovereignty

If the decade following 1989 witnessed the avoidance of ethnic or national claims to independence based on self-determination, then support for self-determination as a democratic entitlement correspondingly grew in force. As became evident from the manner in which the international community responded to the dissolution of the USSR and SFRY, the solution to the problem of external self-determination in the non-colonial context lay, it was proposed, in extensive internal self-determination. This was reflected in the conditions associated with recognition given to the successor republics. It has also been evident in a number of approaches by intergovernmental organizations to secessionist conflicts, including Abkhazia, Chechnya and Kosovo.[78] As Dianne Orentlicher has noted an increased focus on global democratic entitlements has been perceived as the "best inoculation against" destabilizing forces.[79]

The nexus between human rights, democratic governance and self-determination that had become prominent in Western discourses in the late 1970s and 80s as seen in Chapter 4, were further developed and extended to encompass new forms of political arrangements and obligations on states. In this climate, self-determination assumed a more prevalent role in attempts by various actors to promote international standards of governmental legitimacy and sovereign responsibility. Political participation, democratic government, good governance, free and fair elections, and public accountability became increasingly referred to as falling within the rubric of 'internal'

---

77 Craven (2014: 232).

78 This was no less the premise of UN SC 688 (1991), which served as a basis for the establishment of a no-fly zone to protect the Iraqi Kurds. It called for the Iraqi government to support respect human and political rights of the Kurds, but, at the same time, declared the UN members' support for the territorial integrity of Iraq.

79 Diane F. Orentlicher, 'Separation Anxiety: International Responses to Ethno-Separatist Claims' (1998) 23 *Yale J. Int'l L.* 1 61.

self-determination, which was said to create international standards regarding the form and function of a state's internal political order.[80] As the International Commission on Intervention and State Sovereignty put it in 2001: "It is acknowledged that sovereignty implies a dual responsibility: externally, to respect the sovereignty of other states, and internally, to respect the dignity and basic rights of all the people within the state."[81]

The (1993) Vienna Declaration and Program of Action and (CERD) General Recommendation XXI (48) issued the same year, both focused on the right of 'internal' self-determination, a position also evident in the work of the Human Rights Committee.[82] Both documents underline that secession is generally excluded from the right of self-determination, asserting that the implementation of self-determination requires every State to promote universal respect for and observance of human rights and fundamental freedoms. In this context, the CERD Committee drew attention to the Declaration on the Rights of Persons Belonging to National or Ethnic, Religious and Linguistic Minorities, adopted by the General Assembly in its resolution 47/135 of 18 December 1992. A link was also made to the right of every citizen to take part in the conduct of public affairs of the state.

While the question of the universality of international human rights law has always been debated, the elaboration of models of 'democratic governance' and 'legitimate governance' through international human rights law was one of the most contentious developments to emerge from this period. International legal scholars were quick to interpret the fall of the Soviet Union as a sign that the post-Cold War international legal order had become more amenable to democracy. In 1992, Thomas Franck published 'The Emerging Right to Democratic Governance,' which posited the idea that democracy today

80 For example, UN Doc. E/CN.4/1995/60 (1995), Resolution 1995/60 on 'ways and means of overcoming obstacles to the establishment of a democratic society and requirements for the maintenance of democracy', UN Commission on Human Rights ESCOR Supp. (No. 4) p. 183, Preamble; section VI of the (1990) Document of the Copenhagen Meeting of the Conference on the Human Dimension of the CSCE, (1990) 11 Human Rights Law Journal 232; the (1990) CSCE Document of the Copenhagen Meeting of the Conference on the Human Dimension, paras 6–1.8; the (1991) Geneva CSCE Meeting of Experts on National Minorities, http://www.osce.org/; UN Doc.A/47/49 (1993), Declaration on the Rights of Persons Belonging to National or Ethnic, Religious or Linguistic Minorities, 1992, United Nations General Assembly Res. 47/135, Annex, 47 UNGAOR Supp.(No. 49) 210.

81 ICISS, The Responsibility to Protect: Report of the International Commission on Intervention and State Sovereignty (Ottawa: IRDC, 2001), 8.

82 For example, UN Doc. ICCPR/C/21/Add.3, General Comment 12(21), Human Rights Committee, GAOR, 39th Sess., Supp. 40, Annex VI; also, Doc. DPI/ 1394–39399, Vienna Declaration and Program of Action (1993).

plays a crucial role in the international legal order.[83] In the article, Franck pointed to two events which he argued inaugurated the transformation of self-determination from the right of overseas colonies to independence into a right of all to participate in democratic governance - the failed August 1991 coup in Moscow, and the international response to the overthrowal of President Aristide of Haiti in September 1991. In both these cases, Franck argued, "the leaders of states constituting the international community vigorously asserted that only democracy validates governance."[84] This "dramatic statement," he argues "attains even more potency if, as in the Haitian case, it is transposed from political philosophy, where it is "mere" moral prescription, to law, where a newly recognized "democratic entitlement" was used in both the OAS and the UN General Assembly to impose new and important legal obligations on states."[85] The UN mission to oversee the elections in Haiti in 1990 "may be understood," he wrote, "as the first instance in which the United Nations, acting at the request of a national government, intervened in the electoral process solely to validate the legitimacy of the outcome."[86] At the same time, he noted the way "monitoring by governmental and nongovernmental observers ... became an important ad hoc part of the post-1989 transition from Communist to democratic regimes in Eastern Europe."[87] "The symbiotic linkage among democracy, human rights and peace is now widely recognized," he asserted.[88] In concluding that secession is neither endorsed nor prohibited per se in international law—that secession is a factual situation to which international law responds but does not anticipate—Franck summarises the position of self-determination in international law as:

> [t]he probable redefinition of self-determination [in a post-Cold War/ post-decolonisation context] does recognize an international legal right, but it is not to secession but to democracy. In the transition from colonial to post-colonial contexts, the right is reinterpreted in the practice of states to take on new vigor as the instrument for regional and global enforcement of minimal standards of governmental legitimacy. This is

83 See Susan Marks, 'What has become of the emerging right to democratic governance?', 22 *Eur J Int Law* (2011) 2 pp. 507–524; see also David Kennedy, 'Tom Franck and the Manhattan School', 35 *NYU J Int'l Law & Politics* (2003) 432.

84 Thomas M. Franck, "The Emerging Right to Democratic Governance" 86 *American Journal of International Law* (1992) 47.

85 *Ibid.*

86 *Ibid* 72–73.

87 *Ibid* 74.

88 *Ibid* 89.

> rooted both in developing human rights law and in the evolution of the international community's thinking about the causes of war.[89]

While the debate about the emergence of a 'right to democratic governance' seems to have waned in recent years, the emphasis on 'meaningful participation' as an aspect of State obligations towards its people has become more pronounced in the post-Cold War era.[90] At the end of the Cold War, between 1988 and 1993, a set of General Assembly Resolutions, entitled 'Enhancing the Effectiveness of the Principle of Periodic and Genuine Elections' was adopted, which seek to affirm that governmental authority stems from the will of the people, expressed through periodic and genuine elections.[91] The resolutions calls for electoral processes which accommodate "distinct alternatives," whilst nothing that "there is no single political system or electoral method that is equally suited to all nations and their people." In this regard it is also recalled that "all States enjoy sovereign equality and that each State has the right freely to choose and develop its political, social, economic, and cultural system." The connection between the right of self-determination and the right of political participation has also been recorded by the Human Rights Committee.[92] Indeed, many states are eager to 'fill' the meaning of the right to self-determination with democracy and participation, as an attempt to set the external aspect of the right – and secession – aside. In its 1995 periodic report to the Human Rights Committee concerning self-determination, Cyprus stated that "in Cyprus democratic elections are held enabling its people to determine their political status and to pursue in a free manner their economic, social and cultural development."[93] Similarly in its report Mauritius referred to elections, referenda and the judicial control over the fairness of elections as falling within the ambit of self-determination. In 1999 Canada defined self-determination as "the right which can continue to be enjoyed in a functioning democracy in which citizens participate in the political system and have the opportunity to have input in the political processes that affect them."[94] The same year Norway favoured a similar understanding of the right as "the right of peoples to participate at all levels of decision-making in legislative and administrative

89 *Ibid* 21.

90 Edward Mansfield and Jack Snyder rightly warn that democratization does not necessarily lead to either peace or increased respect for human rights and often to the opposite of these. See Mansfield and Snyder, 'Democratization and War', 73 *Foreign Affairs*, 4 (1995).

91 GA Res 45/150 (18 December 1990). GA Res 45/151 (18 December 1990).

92 HRC General Comment on Article 25 (1999).

93 UN Doc. CCPR/C94/Add.1, 9.

94 Statement of Norway to the CHR intersessional working group, October 1999.

matters and the maintenance and development of their political and economic systems."[95]

The United Nations Declaration on the Rights of Indigenous Peoples includes several provisions on political participation including: Article 5, which follows the provision on self-determination, and Articles 18 and 19.[96] The distance between these provisions in the text derives from the different clusters to which provisions belong – the right to self-determination to the general and fundamental principles, the participation articles to the more detailed parts of the Declaration.[97] Effective participation is also required by the CSCE. The Flensburg Proposals also emphasise that decision makers must proactively consult members of minorities that are affected by their decisions and must also create opportunities for them to effectively participate in the decision-making process. Both the UN Declaration on Minorities,[98] the UN Commission on Human Rights[99] and the OSCE[100] have concluded that the issue of minorities can be resolved only within a democratic framework.

It should also be reiterated that recognition of the successor states of the USSR and the SFRY was made dependent upon the commitment to democratic values. After signaling the EC's "attachment to the principles of the Helsinki Final Act and the Charter of Paris, in particular the principle of self-determination"[101] the EC guidelines detailed "respect for [...] the rule of law, democracy and human rights" and "guarantees for the rights of ethnic and national groups and minorities in accordance with the commitments subscribed to in the framework of the CSCE," as commitments required of new states. As Cassese pointed out, "recognition was made dependent on

95 Statement of Norway to the CHR intersessional working group, October 1999.

96 United Nations Declaration on the Rights of Indigenous Persons, GA Resolution 61/295, 13 September 2007.

97 Caroline Foster, 'Articulating Self-Determination in the Draft Declaration on the Rights of Indigenous Peoples' (2001) 12 *European Journal of International Law* 141–57 at 151.

98 United Nations Declaration on the Rights of Persons belonging to National, Ethnic, Religious and Linguistic Minorities, GA Resolution 47/135, 18 December 1992, Preamble.

99 The UN Commission on Human Rights has concluded that the creation of the conditions for a democratic system of government are 'essential for the prevention of discrimination and the protection of minorities' E/CN.4/RES/1995/60, Preamble.

100 See the OSCE Guidelines to assist national minority participation in the electoral process, www.osce.org/odihr/documents/guidelines/gl_nmpa_eng.pdf. See also the CSCE Copenhagen document, which provides that 'questions relating to national minorities can only be satisfactorily resolved in a democratic political framework:' Copenhagen Meeting of the Human Dimension (1990) 29 ILM 1318, para. 30.

101 Declaration on 'Guidelines on the Recognition of New States in Eastern Europe and in the Soviet Union' (16 December 1991), *European Journal of International Law*, Vol. 4, 1993, p. 72.

democratic rule, that is, internal self-determination."[102] The European Community thus "affirmed the close link existing between external and internal self-determination" by making respect for the rule of law, democracy and human rights a '*sine qua non*' for the achievement of independence.[103]

In view of the interpretation of the "right to democratic governance" as the right to liberal democracy, many scholars have expressed concern about this development. Brad Roth argues that such an interpretation deprives international law "of its indispensable role as an overlapping consensus among societies that otherwise radically differ on fundamental matters."[104] While Susan Marks notes that "imperialism looms large" in this assessment.[105] David Kennedy problematizes these views as "post-enlightenment, rationalist, secular, Western, modern, capitalist"[106] and Gerry Simpson calls them "liberal anti-pluralism."[107] This situation highlights a broader concern about 'internal' self-determination and its promotion of western liberalism.[108] As has been pointed out by Jean Salmon:

> [t]he real difficulty of the matter is to define how a people exercises its internal right to self-determination. [...] In the Western countries, it is generally believed that the only right answer is a system of liberal regime coupled with market economy. Such reasoning is purely ideological; there are many regimes in the world which are not similar to Western parliamentarianism and which may, however be viewed as truly representative of the peoples concerned according to their own social and historic traditions.[109]

These discussions over self-determination's link to 'legitimate' forms of internal political functioning and democratic governance were also enmeshed in debates over the resurgence in concepts such as trusteeship, protectorate and

102 Cassese (1996: 268).

103 *Ibid.*

104 Roth (2000: 442).

105 Susan Marks, *The Riddle of All Constitutions: International Law, Democracy, and the Critique of Ideology* (Oxford: OUP 2003) 1.

106 David Kennedy, The International Human Rights Movement: Part of the Problem? (2002), http://www.law.harvard.edu/students/orgs/hrj/iss15/kennedy.shtml.

107 Gerry Simpson, Two Liberalisms, 21 *Euro. J. Int'l. L.* 537, 558 (2001).

108 In the words of Francis Fukuyama, Western liberal democracy is "the end point of mankind's ideological evolution and [...] the final form of human government, Francis Fukuyama, *The End of History and the Last Man* (Free Press, 1992).

109 Jean A Salmon, "Internal Aspects of the Right to Self-Determination," in Tomuschat (1993: 280).

international administration, which had retreated with decolonization, and the rise of post-conflict reconstruction missions.[110] Throughout the Cold War period there had been only a handful of peacekeeping missions authorised; by the end of the 1990s, however, the UN had established 42 peacekeeping operations. These included UN missions to Cambodia, Haiti and Somalia, and the institution of full international governance in cases such as Bosnia and Herzegovina, Kosovo and East Timor. Many of these situations involved widespread abuses of human rights and breaches of international humanitarian law. While these efforts are more or less willingly consented to by the state or authorized under specific peace plans by UN Security Council's powers to intervene when international peace and security is at stake, some commentators see these missions as evidence of a new normative conditioning in international law.[111] Given that they operate as precursors to independence, these missions seem to point to a new form of conditional sovereignty – or 'earned' sovereignty as it was also termed.[112] Others see them as a worrying return to the "civilising mission."[113] The link between the promotion of democracy even through the use of unilateral force was also seen in debates on the question of humanitarian intervention or the doctrine of Responsibility to Protect (R2P). Whilst the issue is an old one, the post–Cold War period saw a clear increase in the willingness of states to use force for humanitarian purpose.[114] This tendency can be seen in the interventions into Somalia in 1992 and Haiti in 1994 where due to the "unique character of the situation," as the Security Council reiterated, it authorized the use of "all necessary means" to put an end to existing humanitarian crises.[115] International lawyers, have in this context interpreted

---

110 See Ralph Wilde *International Territorial Administration: How Trusteeship and the Civilizing Mission Never Went Away* (Oxford: OUP 2008).

111 Ralph Wilde, 'From Danzig to East Timor and Beyond: the Role of International Territorial Administration', 95 *AJIL* 583 (2001).

112 See Paul Williams, Michael Scharf and James Hooper, 'Resolving Sovereignty-Based Conflicts: the Emerging Approach of Earned Sovereignty', 31 Denver JILP (2002–3) 349; Paul Williams, 'Earned Sovereignty: The Road to Resolving the Conflict over Kosovo's Final Status', 31 *Denver JILP* (2003) 387.

113 Wilde (2001: 261–2); Catriona Drew, 'The Meaning of Self-determination: "The Stealing of the Sahara" Redux?', in K Arts and P Pinto Leite, *International Law and the Question of Western Sahara* (Leiden: IPJET, 2007), 87.

114 See J. L. Holzgrefe and Robert Keohane (eds.), *Humanitarian Intervention: Ethical, Legal and Political Dilemmas* (Cambridge: Cambridge University Press, 2004); Jennifer Welsh (ed.), *Humanitarian Intervention and International Relations* (Oxford: Oxford University Press, 2004); Anne Orford, International Authority and the Responsibility to Protect (Cambridge: CUP, 2011).

115 Rein Mullerson "Precedents in the Mountains: On the Parallels and Uniqueness of the Cases of Kosovo, South Ossetia and Abkhazia," 8 *Chinese Journal of International Law* 1, 4

Article 2(4) of the UN Charter in a way that allowed intervention through the use of force if such intervention was meant for the "enhancement of the ongoing right of peoples to determine their own political destinies."[116] However, this position faced strong opposition, particularly from states within the Global South.[117] Events in the past decade indicate that pre-democratic intervention remains an ongoing question of debate.[118]

## 4 Re-working Sovereignty: Minority and Indigenous Rights

The shift towards internal self-determination as the logical counterpoint to self-determination's ongoing incarnation seemed to offer a general solution to the problem of its judicial status. However, for many this articulation of self-determination through the language of individual human rights, failed to account for the particular demands and protection of minority groups within states.[119] The dominant view that only the "*whole* of the people of a state or colonial territory – are beneficiaries of self-determination,"[120] writes James Anaya, had largely prevented its applicability to the vast number of sub-state groups whose concerns represent some of the most pressing in the post-imperial era.[121] Similarly, Antonio Cassese in his contemporary reassessment of the law self-determination in the post-Cold War era, proposed its broader applicability to the domestic situation of ethnic groups and minorities.[122]

116 Michael Reisman, for example, argued that: "The basic policy of contemporary international law has been to maintain the political independence of territorial communities so that they can continue to express their desire for political community in a form appropriate to them … Each application of Article 2(4) must enhance opportunities for ongoing self-determination." Michael Reisman, "Coercion and Self-Determination: Construing Charter Article 2(4)" 78 *American Journal of International Law* (1984) 642 at 643.

117 Ved P Nanda, "The Validity of United States Intervention in Panama under International Law" (1990) 84 *American Journal of International Law* 494.

118 As B.S. Chimni recently noted, the mission of imperialist powers is to "bring democracy, the rule of law and good governance to others … Towards this end suitable international law concepts are adopted or adapted" in B.S Chimini, "Legitimating the International Rule of Law" in James Crawford and Martti Koskenniemi, eds., The Cambridge Companion to International Law(Cambridge: CUP 2012).

119 Catherine Brolmann et al (eds.) *Peoples and Minorities in International Law*, (Dordrecht: Martinus Nijhoff, 1993), Preface.

120 James Anaya, "Self-Determination as a Collective Right under Contemporary International Law" in P. Aikio and M. Scheinin eds., *Operationalizing the Right of Indigenous Peoples to Self-Determination* (Turku: Åbo Akademi University, 2000) 100.

121 *Ibid.*

122 Cassese (1995: 348–359).

A position that would not, he argued, threaten the internal unity of states, but would instead enhance it through the empowerment of the claims and aspirations of groups.[123]

In place of a monolithic depiction of the people entitled to exercise self-determination, as attaching only to the population of a state as a whole, new variations emerged linking the right to ethnic, linguistic and cultural groups, at least in the internal dimension. This was accompanied by a shift in appreciation of self-determination in absolute terms, as solely authorizing complete sovereign independence for a people. Instead, as Patrick Macklem notes "the right is increasingly viewed dynamically as also housing a spectrum of constitutional and institutional possibilities that fall short of secession but which can nonetheless protect a community's identity, culture, territory and self-governing capacity."[124]

Throughout the post-war period, minority and indigenous rights regimes had been kept apart from legal articulations of self-determination, and minority concerns were largely subsumed within broader discussions of human rights. Against the backdrop of the breakup of the USSR and SFYR, discussions around self-determination began to return to the question of how to accommodate cultural and ethnic claims into statist theories to international law.[125] A shift occurred, not unlike the one during the interwar period, towards an expansion of minority rights. An early development was the concluding document of the Copenhagen meeting in 1990 on the "human dimensions" of the CSCE, which took a human rights-based approach to establish rights of national minorities.[126] This was followed in 1992 by the United Nations Declaration on the Rights of Persons Belonging to National, Ethnic, Religious and Linguistic Minorities,[127] which expanded the concept of protections for minority groups, beyond the text of Article 27 of the ICCPR. The Declaration obliged states to protect cultural diversity and identities; it stated that persons belonging to minorities had the right to enjoy their own culture, to profess and practice their own religion, and use their own language freely, and also stated

123 Cassese (1995: 349–350).

124 Patrick Macklem, 'Militant Democracy, Legal Pluralism, and the Paradox of Self-Determination', *International Journal of Constitutional Law*, 4 (3) (2006) 488–516.

125 See Will Kymlicka, Multicultural Citizenship: A Liberal Theory of Minority Rights (Oxford: Clarendon Press, 1996); Susan Okin, *Is Multiculturalism Bad for Women* (Princeton: Princeton University Press, 1999).

126 CSCE, Document on the Copenhagen Meeting of the Conference on the Human Dimensions of the CSCE 29 June 1990.

127 UN, Declaration on the Rights of Persons Belonging to National, Ethnic, Religious and Linguistic Minorities, A/Res./47/135 (1992).

that minorities had the right to exercise their individual and collective rights without discrimination. These were joined in 1995 by the Council of Europe's 1995 Framework Convention for the Protection of National Minorities, which places a positive duty on State parties to promote the continued existence and development of national minorities.

The human rights-based approach contained in these documents, however, was increasingly criticized as too limited in its protection of minorities as groups, rather than individuals. This was most notably stated in the 1983 report of Jose Martinez Cobo on the protection of indigenous populations.[128] The Martinez Cobo report concluded that existing human rights standards "are not fully applied" to Indigenous peoples and, moreover, are "not wholly adequate" to the task. These feelings were reinforced by the events surrounding Yugoslavia. Subsequently, the events of the post-Cold War period led to an increasing recognition that the term 'people' in international law applied to sub-state groups.[129] A broader definition of peoples was also endorsed by the African Commission on Human and Peoples' Rights in its decision regarding *Katangese Peoples' Congress v. Zaire*.[130]

128 In 1971 the Sub-Commission for Human Rights appointed Mexican Ambassador Jose R. Martinez Cobo to conduct a thorough study of "discrimination against indigenous populations." The Martinez Cobo report concludes that existing human rights standards "are not fully applied" to indigenous peoples and, moreover, are "not wholly adequate" to the task. Critically, the Special Rapporteur argued that "self-determination, in its many forms, must be recognized as the basic precondition for the enjoyment by indigenous peoples of their fundamental rights and the determination of their own future." "In essence," the report states, "self-determination constitutes the exercise of free choice by indigenous peoples, who must, to a large extent, create the specific content of this principle, in both its internal and external expressions, which do not necessarily include the right to secede from the State in which they may live and to set themselves up as sovereign entities. This right may in fact be expressed in various forms of autonomy within the State." Jose R Martinez Cobo, Study of the Problem of Discimination Against Indigenous Populations, Final Report, ("Final Report") UNESCOR, 43th Sess, UN Doc E/CV.4/Sub.2/1986/7 (1986) 580–581.

129 This is based partly on the provisions pertaining to self-determination within both the Friendly Relations Declaration and the Vienna Declaration and Programme of Action. The Friendly Relations Declaration stresses that the right to self-determination requires "a government representing the whole people of a territory without discrimination as to race, creed or colour;" The Vienna Declaration stipulates that States conduct themselves in compliance with the principle of equal rights and self-determination if they provide for "a government representing the whole people belonging to a territory without distinction of any kind."

130 African Commission on Human and Peoples' Rights, Communication 75/92, *Katangese Peoples' Congress v. Zaire,* Decision taken on its 16th session, Banjul, The Gambia 1994

Against this backdrop, Indigenous rights have become increasingly articulated within the framework of self-determination.[131] This is grounded in a claim that Indigenous peoples are "peoples" rather than minorities, who faced and continue to face the persecutory effects of colonial rule; a situation which has often been facilitated by international law.[132] As Chief Ted Moses articulated in 1997:

> … We are the victims of genocide in the most terrible and explicit meaning of that idea. Yet some of us have survived and are still here, along with the States that perpetrated these crimes against us. The world knows that the sovereignty, legitimacy, and territorial integrity of these States is tainted and fundamentally impaired because ofthe unjust, immoral, and murderous means employed in their establishment upon indigenous lands[133]

The question of self-determination's application to Indigenous peoples was raised repeatedly during the decolonisation debates, however the adoption of the so-called 'blue-water thesis' and *uti possedetis* explicitly excluded them from the ambit of the Colonial Declaration. The reluctance of the international community to extend or even refer to indigenous peoples as "peoples" was also made clear in subsequent UN documents, including the The Convention on the Rights of Child, which refers to the children of "persons of indigenous origin." An important shift occurred with the publication of the Martinez Cobo which referred to "indigenous populations,"[134] however in most

131 See James Crawford, ed., *The Rights of Peoples* (Oxford: Clarendon Press, 1988); R.L. Barsh, "Indigenous Peoples in the 1990s: From Object to Subject of International Law?" (1994) 7 *Harv. Hum. Rts J.* 33: 8. Benedict Kingsbury, "Claims by Non-State Groups in International Law" (1 992) 25 *Cornell Int'l L.J.* 48 1; Patrick Thornberry, *International Law and the Rights of Minorities* (Oxford: Clarendon Press, 1991) at pt.VI.

132 See Paul Keal, *European Conquest and the Rights of Indigenous Peoples: The Moral Backwardness of International Society* (Cambridge: CUP, 2003); James Anaya, *Indigenous Peoples in International Law* (2nd edition, New York: OUP, 2004); Alexandra Xanthaki, *Indigenous Rights and United Nations Standard: Self-Determination, Culture and Land* (Cambridge: CUP, 2007); Irene Watson (ed.), *Indigenous Peoples as Subjects of International Law* (London: Routledge, 2018), among others.

133 Ted Moses, Ambassador to the UN for the Grand Council ofthe Crees, Address at Indigenous Self-determination International Guest Panel, Plenary Session 2, Australian Reconciliation Convention at paras. 21 -23 (May 27, 1997), available at http://www.austlii.edu. au /au/other/IndigLRes/car/1997/3/speeches/plenary2/moses.htm.

134 José R. Martinez Cobo in his study of the problem of discrimination against indigenous populations: Indigenous communities, peoples and nations are those which, having a historical continuity [4] with pre-invasion and pre-colonial societies [2] that developed on

international forums there has been a clear attempt to restrict indigenous peoples to "people" rather than "peoples."[135] Even in declaring the "International Year of the World Indigenous People" in 1993 the UN assiduously avoided the word "peoples."[136]

The International Labour Organisation's Convention 169 of 1989 was crucial milestone in this regard, employing for the first time the term "peoples" in referring to indigenous groups, and laying out the entitlements of self-governance in relation to matters connected with their lands, beliefs, and economic and cultural development.[137] Indigenous self-determination was bolstered in 2006 with the adoption of the "United Nations Declaration on the Rights of Indigenous Peoples."[138] The Declaration was the result of a prolonged drafting process, involving hundreds of indigenous peoples and their representatives, during which time it was decided that the terms "peoples" and "self-determination" should be used without any reservation.[139] This broadened participation of indigenous peoples themselves in the articulation of their rights in international law including self-determination, in contrast to previous judicial and institutional discussions of indigenous peoples, leads Karen Knop too conclude that the Declaration integrates self-determination into both its credo and its methods.[140] Affirming their right to self-determination,[141] the Declaration also links the exercise of this right to self-government and autonomy "in matters relating to their internal and local affairs, as well as ways and means

---

their territories [3], consider themselves distinct [5] from other sectors of the societies now prevailing [5] in those territories, or parts of them. They form at present non-dominant sectors of society and are determined to preserve, develop and transmit to future generations their ancestral territories, and their ethnic identity, as the basis of their continued existence as peoples, in accordance with their own cultural patterns, social institutions and legal systems. Final Report, 379.

135 In the year 1992 the Earth Summit, frequently used the term "indigenous people and their communities" (AGENDA 21, Chapter 26, 1992). The UN World Conference on Human Rights (1993), the UN Conference on Population and Development (1994) all refer to indigenous "people."

136 Patrick Thornberry, *Indigenous Peoples and Human Rights* (Manchester: Manchester University Press, 2002) 41–42.

137 Art. 7 of ILO Convention 169 concerning Indigenous and Tribal Peoples in Independent Countries, adopted on 27 June 1989 by the General Conference of the International Labour Organisation at its 76th session. Prior to this ILO Convention 107 from 1957 used the term "populations."

138 GA resolution 61/295, adopted by 143 votes to 4, with 11 abstentions (A/61/PV.107, p. 19).

139 Report on Fifth Session, 14, quoted in Knop (2002: 259).

140 Knop (2002: 213–14).

141 UN General Assembly Resolution 61/295, A/RES/61/295, para 3. Full text available at http://www.undemocracy.com/A-RES-61-295.pdf.

for financing their autonomous functions."[142] In linking self-determination to its internal formulation, the Declaration also referred to aspects of the rights under which States are entrusted for its realisation through action and inaction. These includes right to life and liberty; right to preserve distinct identity based on culture, religion, language and spiritual belief; educational rights; self-governance and participatory rights; land resources and management.

Despite the emphasis on the internal aspect of the exercise of self-determination, however, its inclusion was nevertheless highly contentious, with several states voicing their strong opposition.[143] The majority of states acquiesced to its inclusion on the proviso that it was understood as not affecting the States' sovereignty, territorial integrity and political independence, national unity and organizational structure.[144] The Human Rights Committee has nevertheless repeatedly linked indigenous peoples to the right to self-determination;[145] and states have gradually started analysing indigenous issues within Article 1 of the International Covenants: for example, Finland discussed in its report to the Human Rights Committee in 2004 Sami issues within the realm of Article 1,[146] while Denmark stated in 2002 that the right of peoples to self-determination is applicable to indigenous peoples.[147] The Committee has referred to the right to self-determination of the indigenous peoples of both Norway[148] and Mexico.[149] It has also recommended, in relation to Article 1 of the ICCPR, that Australia "take the necessary steps in order to secure for the indigenous inhabitants, a stronger role in decision-making over their traditional lands and natural resources."[150]

142 *Ibid* Article 4.

143 A/61/PV.107, position of Australia, 11.

144 *Ibid.*, Argentina; Japan; UK; Jordan; Mexico; Sweden; Thailand; Suriname.

145 Concluding Observations of the Human Rights Committee, Canada, UN Doc. CCPR/C/79/Add.105(1999), paras 4, 7 and 8; also Norway, UN Doc.CCPR/C/79/Add.112 (1999), paras. 16 and 17; also Mexico, UN Doc.CCPR/C/ 79/Add.109, para. 19; and Australia, UN Doc. CCPR/CO/69/AUS (2000), para. 506.

146 Finland, Fifth Periodic Report, Consideration of Reports submitted by States Parties under Article 40 of the Covenant, Human Rights Committee, UN Doc. CCPR/C/FIN/2003/5 (2003), para. 93.

147 UN Committee on Economic, Social and Cultural Rights, Fourth Periodic Report submitted by States Parties under Articles 16 and 17 of the Covenant, Denmark, UN Doc. E/C.12/Add 12 (2003), para. 7.

148 Human Rights Committee, Concluding Observations, Norway, UN Doc CCPR/C/79/Add.112 (1999).

149 Human Rights Committee, Concluding Observations, Mexico, UN Doc CCPR/C/79/Add.109 (1999).

150 Human Rights Committee, Concluding Observations of the Human Rights Committee, Australia 24/07/2000. GA 55th sess, supp 40, UN Doc. A/55/40 vol. I (2000).

The emphasis within Indigenous self-determination on the idea of protection as one of "preservation" and "respect for" their status as peoples, has also allowed indigenous peoples to promote the crucial relationship between indigenous peoples and their ancestral lands.[151] In this sense the demand for Indigenous self-determination has been interpreted as an important restorative step towards redressing stolen sovereignty, as well challenging the legal fictions of colonial era international laws that reduced indigenous peoples to objects, facilitating the removal of their lands. As Robert Williams has put it, indigenous peoples have reversed "the controlling assumption that indigenous peoples are not proper legal subjects of international concern or sanction."[152]

Catherin Iorns draws a direct between the political and economic oppression indigenous peoples continue to face, as well as the loss of their lands and their cultural and ethnic traditions, to colonial ideas that "indigenous ways of life are backward and inferior and not appropriate for a 'civilized' society."[153] "The tragedy if the treatment of indigenous peoples is not merely historical" she says, "it continues today."[154] For Iorns, the indigenous claim to self-determination entails a fundamental challenge to international law, and more broadly, the "present world system of states."[155] The preamble to the 1992 Indigenous Peoples Earth Charter articulates the use of self-determination as a means to inform the broader historical context that informs the indigenous claim:

> We, the Indigenous Peoples, walk to the future in the footprints of our ancestors.
> From the smallest to the largest living being, from the four directions, from the air, the land and the mountains. The creator has placed us. The Indigenous peoples upon our Mother the earth.
> The footprints of our ancestors are permanently etched upon the lands of our peoples.

---

151 A representative of the World Council of Indigenous Peoples once remarked: "Next to shooting indigenous peoples, the surest way to kill us is to separate us from our part of the earth". Rights of the Indigenous Peoples to the Earth, paper submitted to the UN Working Group on Indigenous Populations; UN Doc E/CN.4/Sub. 2/AC.4.1985/WP.4 at 5.

152 Robert A. Williams Jr., "Encounters on the Frontiers of International Human Rights Law: Redefining the Terms of Indigenous Peoples' Survival in the World," DUKE L.J. 660, 663 n.4 (1990).

153 Catherine J. Iorns,"Indigenous Peoples and Self-Determination: Challenging State Sovereignty" 24 *Case W. Res. J. Int'l L.* 199 (1992) 201. See also Elena Cirkovic, "Self-Determination and Indigenous Peoples in International Law" *American Indian Law Review*, Vol. 31, No. 2, (2006/2007) 375–399.

154 *Ibid* 200.

155 Ibid 202.

> We, the Indigenous peoples, maintain our inherent rights to self-determination. We have always had the right to decide our own forms of government, to use our own laws, to raise and educate our children, to our own cultural identity without interference.
> We continue to maintain our rights as peoples despite centuries of deprivation, assimilation and genocide.
> We maintain our inalienable rights to our lands and territories, to all our resources -- above and below -- and to our waters. We assert our ongoing responsibility to pass these onto the future generations.
> We cannot be removed from our lands. We, the Indigenous peoples are connected by the circle of life to our lands and environments.
> We, the Indigenous peoples, walk to the future in the footprints of our ancestors.

Appeals to indigenous self-determination are thus taking place against the backdrop of broader debates the statist paradigm of international law, with autonomy rights and devolutionary arrangements directed towards the goal of 'unpacking' sovereignty.[156] Cleaving the internal dimension of self-determination from its external counterpart, has in this sense paved the way for a more a diffuse idea of where and with who sovereign authority rests.[157] This has given rise to new forms of rights to autonomy and to political decision making in order to allow indigenous groups to co-exist and develop as distinct peoples.[158] As Gunter Minnerup and Pia Solberg notes "self-determination has become a central tool for indigenous groups seeking to further a reconstruct the statist notion of sovereignty and nationhood to a vision more in keeping with their own needs as sub-state peoples."[159]

---

156 *ICISS Report*, International Commission on Intervention and State Sovereignty, *The Responsibility to Protect* (Ottawa: International Development Research Centre, 2001) [*ICISS Report*] at para. 4.38. See H–J. Heintze, 'On the Legal Understanding of Autonomy' in Suksi, *Autonomy: Applications and Implications*, 7–32; also Z. A. Skurbaty, 'Introduction' in Skurbaty, One-Dimensional State, XXXVIII.

157 Patrick Macklem, 'Distributing Sovereignty: Indian Nations and Equality of Peoples' (1992- 1993) 45 *Stan. L. Rev.* at 1346–7.

158 James Anaya, 'The Capacity of International Law to Advance Ethnic or Nationality Rights Claims' [1990] 75 *Iowa Law Review* 842.

159 Gunter Minnerup and Pia Solberg, *First World, First Nations: Internal Colonialism and Indigenous Self-Determination in Northern Europe and Australia* (Brighton, UK, 2011). See also See C. Temant, "Indigenous Peoples, International Institutions, and the International Legal Literature 60 1945–1993" (1994) 16 Hum. Rts Q. 1.

EPILOGUE

# Contesting Sovereignty

> Powerless people can sometimes trigger... a crisis by challenging an institution internally, that is by using its own logic against it. Such a crisis occurs when powerless people force open and politicize a contradiction between the dominant ideology and their reality.[1]
>
> KIMBERLEY CRENSHAW

∴

Diego Garcia looks like any of the Pentagon's other heavily militarized bases dotted around the world; its green vegetation dissected by a concrete landing strip, flecked with military jets. Now sparsely populated by US military personnel, the Islands were once home to 1500 islanders. In 1965, the Chagossians were forcibly removed by the governing UK authorities and relocated to neighbouring islands. In the intervening 50 years, the Islanders and their decedents have unsuccessfully petitioned the UK and the international community for their right to return to the islands, which have since become a lynchpin in the USA's Indo-Pacific Strategy. On February 25, 2019, the International Court of Justice (ICJ) issued an advisory opinion finding that the UK had wrongfully kept control of the Chagos Islands after Mauritius asserted its independence, in breach of the islanders' right to self-determination.[2] Given that this book began by invoking the image of Indonesia's declaration of independence from colonial rule, it is only fitting that it should close with a case that evokes not only the remnants of empire in our present,[3] but highlights how people continue to appeal to self-determination to demand change in the international legal system.

---

1 Kimberley Crenshaw, "Race, Reform and Retrenchment: Transformation and Legitimation in Antidiscrimination Law" 101 *Harvard Law Review* (1988) 1367.

2 ICJ, *Legal Consequences of the Separation of the Chagos Archipelago from Mauritius in 1965*, Advisory Opinion (25 February 2019).

3 For a discussion of how the Chagos Island case illustrates the ongoing norms of colonialism in our present see Kinnari Bhatt, "A post-colonial legal approach to the Chagos case and the (dis)application of land rights norms" *International Journal of Law in Context* 15(1) (2019) 1–19.

 | DOI:10.1163/9789004479197_008

The history of the Chagos Islands spans a story of displacement and dispossession that mirrors that experienced by many colonized peoples. Indeed, its history in many ways bares not only the injustices of European imperialism, but its imperfect completion in the 20th century – a legacy that continues to the present. Passed from colonial power to colonial power – Holland then France – the islands fell under British control in the early 19th century. Britain continued its administration of the islands as part of the greater colony of Mauritius until the 1960s, by which time the decolonisation process had begun to gain momentum. With the adoption of the Colonial Declaration, outlawing colonialism "in all its forms and manifestations," Mauritius' independence became a foregone conclusion. "Existing colonies may linger on," noted Kwame Nkrumah, "but no new colonies will be created."[4] This was to prove a somewhat short-sighted assessment. Despite the Declaration's prohibition of "partial or total disruption of the national unity and the territorial integrity of any country" during the transition to independence, Britain began to draw up plans to separate the Chagos Islands from Mauritius. In 1964 the UK began to discuss the future of the Chagos Islands with the United States, who had expressed an interest in establishing military facilities on the island of Diego Garcia, which was "thrilled at the idea of a base with no civilian population within almost 500 miles."[5] A few months later, using a combination of diplomatic pressure and bullying, Britain convinced the government of Mauritius to hand the Islands over to British control as part of a newly constructed 'British Indian Ocean Territory'. Prime Minister Ramgoolam was later to tell the Mauritian Parliament: "we had no choice." Between 1967 and 1973, the entire population of the Chagos Archipelago - referred to in official UK documents as "some few Tarzans and Man Fridays" – was forcibly removed by the United Kingdom. A Foreign Office legal adviser advised the government to 'continue to argue that the local people are only a floating population', advising that:

> the longer that such a population remains, and perhaps increases, the greater the risk of our being accused of setting up a mini-colony about which we would have to report to the UN and fulfil our obligations to inhabitants living in non-self-governing territories under Article 73 of the UN Charter. Therefore, immigration legislation giving such labourers and

4 Kwame Nkrumah, *Neo-Colonialism: The Last Stage of Imperialism* (Thomas Nelson & Sons, 1965) ix. quoted in John Reynolds "Decolonising the Chagos Islands?" *Nigerian Yearbook of International Law* 2 (2019) 456.

5 David Vine, *Island of Shame: The Secret History of the U.S. Military Base on Diego Garcia* (Princeton: Princeton University Press, 2009) 90.

> their families very restricted rights of residence would bolster our arguments that the territory has no Indigenous population.[6]

Fearful of international condemnation, particularly by the UN Committee of Twenty-Four, officials were encouraged to "maintain the fiction that the inhabitants of Chagos are not a permanent or semi-permanent population' but rather itinerant workers with no connection to the islands."[7] In a confidential memo, Paul Gore-Booth, Permanent Under-Secretary of State in the Foreign Office wrote: "We must surely be very tough about this. The object of the exercise was to get some rocks which will remain ours; there will be no indigenous population except seagulls who have not yet got a Committee (the Status of Women does not cover the rights of Birds)."[8]

Decades of lobbying and legal challenges by the Chagossians challenging their exile followed, including a bid before the UK High Court in 2000. This led to an emphatic win, and a short-lived decision to permit the Chagossians to return. Following the September 11 terrorist attacks, however, the Chagos Islands assumed a new strategic importance for US strategic activities in the Middle East. The UK issued a new order barring the return of the Chagossians to the Archipelago. A case brought before the European Court of Human Rights in 2012, was rejected on the ground of jurisdiction, with the ECHR holding that the UK had not extended its European human rights law obligations over the territory.[9] Following the announcement by the UK in 2016 that the Chagos Islands lease had been extended by twenty years, and with the support of the African Union, in 2017 Mauritius successfully petitioned the UN to seek an ICJ advisory opinion on the legality of the separation.[10] The hearings before the ICJ became a rallying point for states eager to confront the ongoing legacies of colonialism and the injustices it had wrought. Twenty-two interested parties, among them the African Union and many former colonies, took part. Many underlined the duty of all member states of the UN "to assist the general

---

6 Bancoult, R. (on the application of) v. Secretary of State for Foreign and Commonwealth Office [2000] EWHC 413 (Admin) (3 November 2000), para. 18.

7 Anthony Aust, 'Immigration Legislation for BIOT', Memorandum, 16 January 1970, quoted in John Reynolds "Decolonising the Chagos Islands?" *Nigerian Yearbook of International Law* 2 (2019) 457.

8 Foreign Office confidential memo ZD4/56, 'British Indian Ocean Territory', 24 August 1966, cited in R (on the application of Bancoult) v. Secretary of State for Foreign & Commonwealth Affairs Rev 1 [2006] EWHC 1038 (Admin), Judgment, 11 May 2006, para. 27.

9 Chagos Islanders v. UK, *European Court of Human Rights*, Application No. 35622/04, Fourth Section Decision, 11 December 2012.

10 General Assembly Resolution 71/292, UN Doc. A/RES/71/292, 22 June 2017.

assembly to remove the last vestiges of colonialism." Namira Negm, legal counsel of the African Union, said: "It is unthinkable that today, in the 21st century, there is a part of Africa that still remains subject to European colonial rule." Refuting the assertion that self-determination had become an established part of international law in 1964, the UK insisted that the matter should never have been brought before the ICJ, arguing that the matter had been resolved in a 1982 agreement on compensation. Against the backdrop of the rhetoric surrounding the Brexit debate, the irony of the UK's position could not be more evident. "No country wishes to be a colony," noted Philippe Sands, representing Mauritius. "The UK does not wish to be a colony, yet it stands before this court to defend a status as coloniser of others."

The Opinion affirmed what was already a political and material reality for the Islanders: that the UK had wrongly detached and maintained control of the islands after Mauritius asserted its independence given that self-determination was a customary right by this time.[11] While not casting the UK's actions explicitly in terms of coercion or duress, the Court concluded that "the detachment was not based on the free and genuine expression of the will of the people concerned."[12] As such: "it follows that any detachment by the administering Power of part of a nonself-governing territory, unless based on the freely expressed and genuine will of the people of the territory concerned, is contrary to the right to self-determination."[13] The UK's ongoing administration of the territory therefore constitutes an internationally wrongful act which should be ended as quickly as possible.[14]

The ICJ Opinion can be criticised in many respects, not least its failure to sufficiently account for the human and material experience of the Chagossians,[15] by focussing overwhelmingly on Mauritius's territorial sovereignty rather than the Chagossians' right to return. Indeed, as John Reynolds notes "the substantive findings section of the Court's advisory opinion devotes just a single sentence to the uprooted Chagossians" and it largely deflects the issue of the islanders' right of return.[16] While highlighting the Chagossians' long struggle for justice, the Court casts their situation as a human rights issue, and beyond the scope of the ICJ itself. This stance has been criticised as a missedopportunity

---

11 ICJ, *Legal Consequences of the Separation of the Chagos Archipelago from Mauritius in 1965*, Advisory Opinion (25 February 2019) para. 182.

12 *Legal Consequences of the Separation of the Chagos Archipelago*, para. 182.

13 *Legal Consequences of the Separation of the Chagos Archipelago*, 160.

14 *Legal Consequences of the Separation of the Chagos Archipelago*, paras. 139–182.

15 John Reynolds "Decolonising the Chagos Islands?" *Nigerian Yearbook of International Law* 2 (2019).

16 Ibid.

to draw a closer nexus between issues of sovereignty and questions of human rights.[17] Indeed as Irini Papanicolopulu and Thomas Burri note, by largely glossing over these human rights implications (which include not only the right to self-determination, but the freedom of movement and the right of abode, the fundamental prohibition of forced displacement and the violation of the economic rights of the islanders) and providing little guidance about the consequences of the breach for states and other actors, including the specific individuals who have been deported from Chagos and denied the right to return, the Court missed the chance to extend its usual narrow, statist approach to redressing self-determination conflicts.[18] Nevertheless, the Opinion was received by the islanders themselves as a victory, not least as a broad international legitimisation of the international wrong that was committed against them in 1965.[19] In the words of Mauritius's prime minister, Pravind Kumar Jugnauth: "This is a historic moment for Mauritius and all its people, including the Chagossians who were unconscionably removed from their homeland and prevented from returning for the last half century. Our territorial integrity will now be made complete, and when that occurs, the Chagossians and their descendants will finally be able to return home."

The *Chagos Opinion* is an excellent reminder of international law's complicity in the erasure of peoples and cultures – but also of its ability to redress these injustices. In this setting, self-determination came to provide both the legal and moral frame to assert the Chagossian claim to their ancestral land. Legally, through the unextinguished right to self-determination owed to them under international law, and morally through the assertion of their deep cultural and spiritual connection to their land and traditional ownership. The written statement of Mauritius, while stressing the legal and constitutional basis of sovereignty over the Chagos Islands, also relayed the deep social, cultural and material link to the land held by the Chagossian people. In many ways, therefore, the Chagossian claim represents a new post-colonial framing of self-determination; one that chips away at the Eurocentric conditioning of

17 Irini Papanicolopulu and Thomas Burri, 'Human Rights and the Chagos Islands Opinion' in Thomas Burri, Jamie Trinidad (eds) *The International Court of Justice and Decolonisation: New Directions from the Chagos Advisory Opinion* (Cambridge: CUP, 2021), 260.

18 *Ibid.*

19 Owen Bowcott, "UN court rejects UK's claim of sovereignty over Chagos Islands," The Guardian, 25 February 2019. Marlis SIMONS, "U.N. Court Tells Britain to End Control of Chagos Islands, Home to U.S. Air Base," The New York Times, 25 February 2019. "UK should leave Chagos Islands colony in Indian Ocean as soon as possible, top UN court says," South China Morning Post, 25 February 2019. Kamlesh BHUCKORY, "World Court Says U.K. Should Return Control of Indian Ocean Islands," Bloomberg, 25 February 2019.

Indigenous identity that has largely excluded Indigenous peoples from the ambit of self-determination.

While it remains to be seen whether the UK's bitter rejection of the Opinion will preclude the Chagossians possibility of return,[20] the Opinion marks a broader shift against the tacit acceptance and naturalisation of colonialism's legacy, including its ongoing effects. The project of considering how international law might understand its relationship to colonialism, and how the law has been used to contain the irregularities and injustices of the postcolonial period remains a fundamental one for present day international law. This includes the imperative to redress the material and conceptual legacy of colonialism, not least by involving the perspectives of those who have largely been marginalized from its institutions and processes. No longer relegated to a distant past, the material effects of colonialism have been aired before the world court, signalling a symbolic rejection of a world order that would defer peoples' rights to the "brutal realities of global politics."[21] The UK's appeal to the strategic importance of the islands for western defence efforts has held little sway either for the Court or the wider international community. The UK "unlawful occupation" of the islands has been roundly condemned by the majority of states. The General Assembly voted to welcome the ICJ advisory opinion and demand that Britain "withdraw its colonial administration unconditionally within a period of no more than six months."[22] 116 member states voted in favour of the resolution, with just 6 voting against. For all its weaknesses, the Opinion nevertheless reaffirms the rights of communities to lands from which they have been dispossessed; even those caught in the crossfire (literally) of the strategic interests of major powers. In doing so, the Opinion also raises the prospect that other cases of decolonisation could be reopened, and that territorial disputes that arose as a result of the failure to complete the process of decolonization after 1965 could bring their disputes before the ICJ.[23] In this sense, the struggle for the Chagossian claim to self-determination forms part of a broader struggle to counter not

---

20 Foreign and Commonwealth Office, 'British Indian Ocean Territory: Written statement – HCWS 1528', 30 April 2019.

21 *R* (*On the application of Bancoult*) v *Secretary of State for Foreign and Commonwealth Affairs* (*No 1*) [2001] QB 1067, para 6 (per Lord Hoffmann). Which held that a 1971 Immigration Ordinance prohibiting access to the islands by anyone without a permit was invalid.

22 UN General Assembly Resolution 73/295, UN Doc. A/RES/73/295, 22 May 2019, para. 3.

23 Victor Kattan raises this as a possibility. Victor Kattan "The Chagos Advisory Opinion and the Law of Self Determination" *Asian Journal of International Law* 10(1) 2020 12–20.

only the legacy of colonial rule but the ongoing structures of imperial sovereignty into the present.

∴

Asked by Brigitte Stern in 1997 whether he had any regrets arising from his time as an international lawyer, Oscar Schachter mentioned chairs. Or, more precisely, the number of them:

> In 1948, nearly fifty years ago, at the United Nations, the architects planning the future headquarters asked me how many seats they should make in the General Assembly. Now is that a lawyer's question? Probably only a lawyer was thought able to answer. The United Nations then had only fifty-one members. An international lawyer would be expected to know how many sovereign states existed and were potential members. I confidently answered the architects (after checking some text books) that they could safely add twenty seats to the fifty-one. It did not take long for my estimate to be mistaken and for costly renovations to be needed. A simple point, perhaps, but can lawyers confidently take the world as it is at a given moment when we know that it is in constant change? Could anyone have foreseen the breakup of colonial empires and the Soviet Union? The real problem, of course, does not involve guessing numbers but how to develop ideas and proceedings to cope with the unexpected changes that are inevitable. International lawyers and international organization specialists could give that challenge more attention.[24]

Schachter's anecdote underlines the inevitability of change in an international system, which is in now largely prefaced on upholding the status quo. Yet as the preceding account has underlined sovereignty is a contested and complex notion that continues to evolve against an ever-changing backdrop of international relations.[25] As Alexander Wendt, puts it, "the reproduction of sovereign states is an ongoing accomplishment of knowledgeable practice, not a natural, exogenously given fact of international life."[26] Sovereignty is not a static

24 A Conversation with Oscar Schachter, *ASIL Proceedings* (1997) p. 344.

25 Marcel Kohen records that whereas the growth in the membership of the United Nations from 51 member states in 1945 to 149 in 1984 was due to decolonization, the increase in membership from 151 in 1990 to 191 at present, is essentially due to secession. The history of self-determination" wrote Alfred Cobban "is a history of the making of nations and the breaking of states." Cobban, *The Nation State and National Self-Determination*, (London: Collins 1969) 42–43.

26 Alexander Wendt, "Sovereignty and the Social Construction of Power Politics" 24 (1990) cited in Iorns (1992: 342).

notion, but merely a convenient description of a host of varying identities, political, social and cultural aspirations and articulations which may be present in addition to the basic political structure of a community.[27]

Similarly, as I have has argued, self-determination is not a settled idea either legally, morally or politically, but operates as a discursive means of challenging existing legal orders – including the concept of sovereignty. Due to both its inherent ambiguity as a legal and political term, and its broader resonance as a conceptual idea, self-determination maintains the possibility of this dynamism; thereby ensuring the possibility of an international legal order that can be responsive to the ever-evolving demands of groups and individuals in response to changing geo-political conditions. As this analysis has underlined, self-determination has been reinvented in various juridical and normative iterations to create the conditions for global transformation, not least the entry of groups of states into international society. What may have started as a weighty political claim in the philosophy of Kant and Fichte, morphed into a powerful political rallying cry in the hands of Lenin and Wilson to shape the geopolitical aftermath of WWI. It was its eventual judicial crystallisation into a foundational principle of international law in the United Nations Charter, however, that truly provided the normative and legal possibility to further challenge the boundaries of international law. Far from being symbolic, self-determination assumed a crucial role in the process of unpicking the fabric of the colonial international order by Third World Activists (which was then rapidly stitched back together again) to enable colonial peoples to attain independence. The conflict and struggle for authoritative meaning of the self-determination has continued in the half century since the height of the decolonization period – where the discursive and judicial power of the principle continues to be mobilized in aid of various political and social causes.

The story of self-determination is not, however, one driven by statesman and political elites, but by people who have staked a claim to self-determination in order to shape their own future. From nationalist movements under the yoke of European empire, to minorities and communities caught in the crossfire of the redivision of national borders in the wake of the Paris Peace Conference, to colonial independence leaders and activists, self-determination has provided a powerful platform for change. It can be seen in the appeals

---

27 In the words of Brad Roth, '[c]ontrary to what is sometimes imagined, the international legal order is not a legal order of legal orders; it is a legal order of sovereign political communities, each of which bears an "inalienable" capacity.... to overthrow any existing order by any means.' Brad Roth (2021) "Legitimacy in the International Order: They Continuing Relevance of Sovereign States," *Notre Dame Journal of International & Comparative Law* 11(1) 73.

to self-determination by groups like the Chagossians or Indigenous Peoples to highlight the blind spots of international law and challenge the seeming permanency of discriminating and exclusionary practices. Peoples around the world continue to appeal to self-determination in the hope of changing their lives. As Upendra Baxi surmises, self-determination in the contemporary landscape of human rights: "insists that every human person has a right to a *voice* ... the right to bear witness to violation, a right to immunity against *disarticulation* by concentrations of economic, social, and political formations... thus opening up sites of resistance."[28]

28 Upendra Baxi, *The Future of Human Rights* (Oxford: OUP, 2002) 36.

# References


Abi-Saab, Georges, "The Newly Independent States and the Scope of Domestic Jurisdiction," in *Proceedings of the American Society of International Law* at Its Annual Meeting (1921–1969), Vol. 54 (APRIL 28–30, 1960).

Abi-Saab, Georges, "The Newly Independent States and the Rules of International Law: An Outline," 8 *Howard Law Journal* (1962) pp. 95–113.

Abi-Saab, Georges, "Wars of National Liberation and the Laws of War" 3 *Annale d'Etudes Internationales* (1972) pp. 93–117.

Abi-Saab, Georges, "The Third World and the Future of the International Legal Order" 29 *Revue Egyptienne de Droit International* (1973) pp. 27–66.

Abi-Saab, Georges, "Wars of National Liberation and the Development of Humanitarian Law" in Akkermann, van Krieken and Panneborg (eds), *Declaration on Principles: A Quest for Universal Peace* (Sijthoff, Leiden, 1977).

Acheson, D., The Foreign Policy of the United States," 18 *Arkansas Law Review and Bar Association Journal*, 3, (1964) pp. 232–254.

Acton, John Emerich Edward Dalberg, "Nationality" in *The History of Freedom and Other Essays* (Figgis, John Neville, and Vere, Laurence Reginald, eds.), (MacMillan & Co., London, 1922) pp. 270–300.

Adler-Nissen Rebecca., *Bourdieu in International Relations: Rethinking Key Concepts in IR*. (Routledge, Taylor & Francis Group, London, 2012).

Adu Boahen, A., *African Perspectives on Colonialism* (Johns Hopkins University Press, Baltimore, 1987).

Akehurst, Michael, *A Modern Introduction to International Law* (George Allen and Unwin, London, 1982).

Alexandowitz, C.H, *An Introduction to the History of the Law of Nations in the East Indies* (Clarendon Press, Oxford, 1967.

Alfredsson, Gudmundur, "The Right of Self-Determination and Indigenous Peoples" in Tomuschat, Christian, ed., *Modern Law of Self-Determination* (Martinus Nijhoff, Dordrecht, 1993) pp. 41–54.

Alfredsson, Gudmundur, "The Right of Self-Determination and Indigenous Peoples" in C. Tomuschat ed., *Modern Law of Self-Determination* (Martinus Nijhoff, Dordrecht, 1993).

Allott, Philip, "Self-Determination – Absolute Right or Social Poetry?" in Tomuschat, Christian, ed., *Modern Law of Self-Determination* (Martinus Nijhoff, Dordrecht, 1993) pp. 177–210.

Allott, Philip, "Peoples' Rights: Their Rise and Fall" in Alston, Philip, ed., *Peoples' Rights* (Oxford University Press, Oxford, 2001) pp. 259–293.

Amankwah, H.A., "Self-determination in the Spanish Sahara: a credibility gap in the United Nations' practice and procedure in the decolonisation process" 14 *C.I.L.S.A.* 34 (1981).

Ambrose, S.E, *Eisenhower, vol. 2: The President* (Simon and Schuster, New York, 1984)

Anand, R. P. "Role of the "New" Asian--African Countries in The Present International Legal Order", 56 *American Journal of International Law* (1962) pp. 383–401.

Anand, R. P. Attitude of the Asian-African States toward Certain Problems of International Law", *The International and Comparative Law Quarterly*, Vol. 15, No. 1 (Jan., 1966), 55–75, 59.

Anabtawi, Samir, "The Afro-Asian States and the Hungarian Question," 17 *International Organisation* 4 (1963) pp. 872–900.

Anaya, James, "The Capacity of International Law to Advance Ethnic or Nationality Rights Claims" 13 *Human Rights Quarterly* (1991), pp. 403–411.

Anaya, James, "Self-Determination as a Collective Human Right under Contemporary International Law" in Aikio, Pekka, and Scheinin, Martin, eds., *Operationalizing the Right of Indigenous Peoples to Self-Determination* (Åbo Akademi University, Turku, 2000) pp. 3–18.

Anderson, M.S (ed.), *Documents of Modern History: The Great Powers and the Near East 1774–1923* (London: Edward Arnold, 1970).

Anghie, Antony, "Franciso de Vitoria and the Colonial Origins of International Law" 5 *Social and Legal Studies* 3 pp. 321–336.

Anghie, Antony, "Colonialism and the Birth of Institutions: Sovereignty, Economy and the Mandate System of the League of Nations," 34 *N.Y.U.J. International & Pol.* (2001–2002) 513 at 518.

Anghie, Antony, *Imperialism, Sovereignty and the Making of International Law* (Cambridge, Cambridge University Press, 2005).

Arangio-Ruiz, Gaetano, "Human Rights and Non-Intervention in the Helsinki Final Act" 157 *Recueil des Cours* (1977) IV pp. 195–328.

Archibugi, Daniele, 'A critical analysis of the self-determination of peoples: a cosmopolitan perspective', *Constellations*, 10.4 (2003).

Arendt, Hannah, *The Origins of Totalitarianism* (George Allen & Unwin, London, 1958).

Arendt, Hannah, *Imperialism: Part Two Of The Origins Of Totalitarianism* (Houghton Mifflin Harcourt, Mar 20, 1968).

Arendt, Hannah, *The Life of the Mind* (Harcourt, San Diego, 1978).

Armitage, David, *The Declaration of Independence: A Global History* (Harvard University Press, Cambridge, MA, 2007).

Armstrong, John A., "Contemporary Ethnicity: The Moral Dimension in Comparative Perspective" 52 *Review of Politics* (1990) pp. 163–188.

de Araújo, Caio Simões, "A Crisis of Confidence: The postcolonial moment and the diplomacy of decolonization at the United Nations, ca. 1961" in Nicole Eggers,

Jessica Lynne Pearson, Aurora Almada e Santos (eds.) *The United Nations and Decolonization* (London: Routledge, 2020).

Backer, John H, *The Decision to Divide Germany: American Foreign Policy in Transition* (Durham, NC, 1978).

Bak McKenna, Miriam, 'The Means to the End and the End of the Means: Self-Determination, Decolonization and International Law', 2:1 *Jus Gentium* (2017) 93–132.

Baker, James III with Frank, Thomas D, *The Politics of Diplomacy: Revolution, War and Peace 1989–1992* (G.P. Putnam's Sons, New York, 1995).

Bain, William, *Between Anarchy and Society: Trusteeship and the Obligations of Power* (Oxford University Press, Oxford, 2003).

Barraclough, Geoffrey, *An Introduction to Contemporary History* (Penguin, Harmondsworth, 1967)

Barros, James, *The Aaland Islands Question: Its Settlement by the League of Nations* (Yale University Press, New Haven, 1968).

Barsh, R.L. "Indigenous Peoples in the 1990s: From Object to Subject of International Law?" (1994) 7 Harv. Hum. Rts J. 33.

Bartelson, Jens, *A Genealogy of Sovereignty* (Cambridge University Press, Cambridge, 1995).

Bassiouni, "Self-Determination and the Palestinians", 65 *Proceedings of the American Society of International Law* 31, 33 (1971).

Bayefsky, Anne F., *Self-Determination in International Law: Quebec and Lessons Learned* (Kluwer, The Hague, 2000).

Baxi, Upendra, *The Future of Human Rights* (Oxford: OUP, 2002).

Beaulac, Stephane, 'The Westphalian Legal Orthodoxy - Myth or Reality?', *Journal of the History of International Law, 2* (2000), 148–177.

Becker Lorca, Arnul, *Mestizo International Law: A Global Intellectual History 1842–1933* (Cambridge University Press 2016)

Bedjaoui, Mohammed, ed., *International Law: Achievements and Prospects* (UNESCO, Paris, 1991) 1177–1203.

Bedjaoui, Mohammed, ed., *Towards a New International Economic Order* (Holmes and Meier, New York, 1979) p. 184.

Beer, George Loui, *African Questions at the Paris Peace Conference* (Macmillan, New York, 1923).

Bell, Christine, "The New Law of Hybrid Self-Determination" *in On the Law of Peace (Oxford University Press, Oxford, 2008).*

Bell Duncan, "John Stuart Mill on Colonies." *Political Theory* 38, no. 1 (2009): 36–64.

Beloff, Max, ed., *The Debate on the American Revolution 1761–1783* (Nicholas Kaye, London, 1949).

Benes, E., *Memoirs of Dr Eduard Benes* (George Allen Unwin, London, 1954).

Bengoa, Jose, "Existence and Recognition of Minorities", 6th sess, Sub-Commission on Promotion and Protections of Human Rights, Working Group on Minorities, 81, *UN Doc E/CN.4/Sub.2/AC.5/2000/WP.2* (2000).

Bentham, Jeremy, "Principles of International Law" in Bowring, John, ed., *The Works of Jeremy Bentham* (William Tait, Edinburgh, 1838) volume II, pp. 535–571.

Benton, Lauren, 'From International Law to Imperial Constitutions: The Problems of Quasi-Sovereignty', Law and History Review 26(3) (2008) 595–619.

Benton, Lauren, *Law and Colonial Cultures: Legal Regimes in World History, 1400–1900* (Cambridge: CUP, 2002).

Berlin, Isaiah, "Two Concepts of Liberty", in *Four Essays on Liberty* (Oxford University Press, Oxford, 1969).

Berman, Nathaniel, "Sovereignty in Abeyance: Self-Determination and International Law" 7 *Wisconsin International Law Journal* (1988) 51, at 61 –62.

Berman, Nathaniel, "Modernism, Nationalism, and the Rhetoric of Reconstruction", *Yale Journal of Law & the Humanities: Vol. 4: Iss. 2,* (1992) pp. 351–379.

Berman, Nathaniel, "'But the Alternative is Despair': European Nationalism and the Modernist Renewal of International Law" 106 *Harvard Law Review* (1993) pp. 1792–1903.

Berman, Nathaniel, "Beyond Colonialism and Nationalism? Ethiopia, Czechoslovakia, and 'Peaceful Change'" 65 *Nordic Journal of International Law* (1996) pp. 421–479.

Berman, Nathaniel, *Passion and Ambivalence, Colonialism, Nationalism, and International Law* (Martinus Nijhoff, Leiden, 2012).

Berman, Nathaniel, "The International Law of Nationalism: Group Identity and Legal History" in Wippman, David, ed., *International Law and Ethnic Conflict* (Cornell University Press, Ithaca, 1998) pp. 25–57.

Bernhardt, R., "Federalism and Autonomy", in Y. Dinstein (ed.), *Models of Autonomy*, (New Brunswick, 1981).

Betts, Alexander and Loeshcer, Gill (eds.) *Refugees in International Relations* (Oxford University Press, Oxford, 2010).

Bhalla, R. S., "The Right of Self-Determination in International Law" in Twining, William, ed., *Issues of Self-Determination* (Aberdeen University Press, Aberdeen, 1991) pp. 91–101.

Bhatt, Kinnari, "A post-colonial legal approach to the Chagos case and the (dis)application of land rights norms" *International Journal of Law in Context* 15(1) (2019) 1–19.

Bigo, D and Walker, RBJ, "International, Political, Sociology", *International Political Sociology* (2007) 1: 1–5.

Binder, Guyora, "The Case for Self-Determination", 29 *Stanford Journal of International Law* (1993) pp. 223–270.

Black, Cyril, "Challenges to an Evolving Order" in Richard Falk & Cyril Black, eds., *The Future of International Legal Order, vol. 1* (Princeton, NJ: Princeton University Press, 1969).

Blay, Sam, "Self-Determination: A Reassessment in the Post-Communist Era" 22 *Denver Journal of International Law and Policy* (1993–94) pp. 275–315.

Blaydes, Lonnie E., Jr., "International Court of Justice Does Not Find 'Legal Ties' of Such a Nature to Affect Self-Determination in the Decolnization Process of Western Sahara" 11 *Texas International Law Journal* (1976) pp. 354–368.

Blum, Yehuda Z., "Reflections on the Changing Concept of Self-Determination", 10 *Israel Law Review* (1975) pp. 509–514.

Bluntschli, J. K., *The Theory of the State* (Clarendon Press, Oxford, 1885).

Bodin, Jean, *The Six Books of a Commonwealth* (McRae, Kenneth Douglas, ed.), (Harvard University Press, Cambridge, 1962).

Borstelmann, Thomas, *The Cold War and the Color Line; American Race Relations in the Global Arena* (Harvard Uni. Press, Cambridge Massachusetts, 2001).

Bourdieu, Pierre, The Force of Law: Toward a Sociology of the Juridical Field, *The Hastings Law Journal* 38 (1987), pp. 805–853.

Bourdieu, Pierre, *La Noblesse de L'Etat*, (Miniut, Paris, 1989).

Boutros Ghali, Boutros, "An Agenda for Peace: Preventative Diplomacy, Peacemaking and Peace-Keeping", *UN Doc. A/47/277 - S/24111* (1992).

Bowett, DW, "Self-Determination and Political Rights in the Developing Countries", 60 *ASIL Proceedings*, (1966) pp. 129–135.

Bowring, Bill, "Burial and Resurrection: Karl Renner's controversial influence on the 'National Question' in Russia", in E. Nimni (ed.), *National-Cultural Autonomy and its Contemporary Critics*(London: Routledge, 2005).

Bowring, Bill, "Positivism versus Self-Determination" in Susan Marks (ed) *International Law on the Left: Re-Examining Marxist Legacies* (Cambridge University Press, Cambridge, 2008).

Brietzke, Paul H., "Self-Determination, or Jurisprudential Confusion: Exaccerbating Political Conflict" in McCorquodale, Robert, ed., *Self-Determination in International Law* (Dartmouth, Aldershot, 2000) pp. 77–140.

Brilmayer, Lea, "Secession and Self-Determination: A Territorial Interpretation", 16 *Yale Journal of International Law* (1991) pp. 177–202.

Brölmann, C. M., and Zieck, M. Y. A., "Indigenous Peoples" in Brölmann, Catherine, Lefeber, René, and Zieck, Marjoleine, eds., *Peoples and Minorities in International Law* (Martinus Nijhoff, Dordrecht, 1993) pp. 187–220.

Brown, Philip Marshall, "The Aaland Islands Question", 15 *American Journal of International Law* (1921) pp. 268–72.

Brownlie, Ian, "An Essay in the History of the Principle of Self-Determination" in Alexandrowicz, C. H., ed., *Grotian Society Papers* (Martinus Nijhoff, The Hague, 1968) pp. 90–99.

Brownlie, Ian, *Basic Documents on African Affairs* (Clarendon Press, Oxford, 1971).

Brownlie, Ian, *African Boundaries: A Legal and Diplomatic Encyclopedia*, (Hurst & Co, London, 1979).

Brownlie, Ian, "The Rights of Peoples in International Law", 9 *Bull. Austl. Soc. Leg. Phil.* (1985) pp. 104–119.

Brownlie, Ian, "The Rights of Peoples in Modern International Law" in Crawford, James, ed., *The Rights of Peoples* (Clarendon Press, Oxford, 1988) pp. 1–16.

Brownlie, Ian, *Principles of Public International Law* (Fourth Edition), (Clarendon Press, Oxford, 1990).

Buccheit, Lee C., *Secession: The Legitimacy of Self-Determination* (Yale University Press, New Haven, 1978).

Buchanan, Allen, "Toward a Theory of Secession", 101 *Ethics* (1991) pp. 322–342.

Buchanan, Allen, *Secession: The Morality of Political Divorce from Fort Sumter to Lithuania and Quebec* (Boulder, Colorado: Westview Press, 1991).

Buchanan, Allen, "Democracy and Secession" in Moore, Margaret, ed., *National Self-Determination and Secession* (Oxford University Press, Oxford, 1991) pp. 14–33.

Buchanan, Allen, "The International Institutional Dimension of Secession", in P. B. Lehning (ed.), *Theories of Secession* (London/New York 1998).

Buchanan, Allen, "The Quebec Secession Issue: Democracy, Minority Rights, and the Rule of Law" in Macedo, Stephen, and Buchanan, Allen, ed., *Secession and Self-Determination* (New York University Press, New York, 2003) pp. 238–71.

Bull, Hedley, "Society and Anarchy in International Relations", in H. Butterfield and M. Wight (eds), *Diplomatic Investigations: Essays on the Theory of International Politics* (London, 1966).

Bull, Hedley, "The revolt against the West", in Bull and Watson (eds.), *The Expansion of International Society*, (Oxford University Press, Oxford, 1984).

Bull, Hedley, "The Importance of Grotius in the Study of International Relations" in Bull, Hedley, Kingsbury, Benedict, and Roberts, Adam, eds., *Hugo Grotius and International Relations* (Clarendon Press, Oxford, 1990) pp. 65–93.

Bull, Hedley and Adam Watson (eds.), *The Expansion of International Society* (Oxford University Press, New York, 1984).

Burbank, Jane and Frederick Cooper. *Empires in World History: Power and the Politics of Difference* (Princeton: Princeton University Press, 2010).

Burke, Edmund, "Reflections on the Revolution in France, and on the Proceedings in Certain Societies in London Relative to that Event" in Burke, Edmund, *The Works of Edmund Burke* (George Bell and Sons, London, 1876) volume II, pp. 277–518.

Burke, Roland, "From Individual Rights to National Development: The First UN International Conference on Human Rights", Tehran, 1968', 19 *Journal of World History*, 3 (2008), 288.

Burke, Roland, *Decolonization and the Evolution of International Human Rights* (University of Pennsylvania Press, Philadelphia, 2010).

Burke, Roland, "Competing for the Last Utopia?: The NIEO, Human Rights, and the World Conference for the International Women's Year, Mexico City, June 1975" (2015)

6(1) *Humanity: An Interdisciplinary Journal of Human Rights, Humanitarianism, and Development*.

Bush, George and Scowcroft, Brent, *A World Transformed* (Vintage Books, New York, 1998).

Butler, Judith, "Indefinite Detention" in *Precarious Life: The Powers of Mourning and Violence* (2004), 50–100.

Cabral, Amilcar, "Anonymous Soldiers for the United Nations", in *Revolution in Guinea: An African People's Struggle* (London: Love and Malcomson, 1969).

Carlton J. H. Hayes, *A Generation of Materialism* (New York, 1941).

Carrington, C.E., *The Liquidation of the British Empire* (Harrap, Toronto and Vancouver, 1962).

Cass, Deborah Z., "Re-Thinking Self-Determination: A Critical Analysis of Current International Law Theories" 18 *Syracuse Journal of International Law and* Commerce (1992) pp. 21–40.

Cass, Deborah Z., 'Navigating the New Stream: Recent Critical Legal Scholarship in International Law' 65 *Nordic Journal of International Law* (1995) 341–383.

Cassese, Antonio, "The Helsinki Declaration and Self-Determination" in Buergenthal, Thomas, ed., *Human Rights, International Law and the Helsinki Accord* (Allanheld, Osmun & Co., Montclair, 1977) pp. 83–110.

Cassese, Antonio, "Political Self-Determination: Old Concepts and New Developments" in Antonio Cassese, ed., *UN Law/Fundamental Rights: Two Topics in International Law* (Sijthoff & Noordhoff, Alphen aan den Rijn, 1979).

Cassese, Antonio, "The Self-Determination of Peoples" in Henkin, Louis, ed., *The International Bill of Rights: The Covenant on Civil and Political Rights* (Columbia University Press, New York, 1981) pp. 92–113.

Cassese, Antonio, *Self-Determination of Peoples: A Legal Reappraisal* (Cambridge University Press, Cambridge, 1995).

Cassese, Antonio, "The ICJ and Self-Determination", in V. Lowe & M. Fitzmaurice, eds., *Fifty Years of the International Court of Justice: Essays in Honour of Sir Robert Jennings* (Cambridge: Grotius Publications, 1996).

Cassese, Antonio, *International Law* (Oxford University Press, Oxford, 2005).

Chadwick, Elizabeth, *Self-Determination, Terrorism and the International Humanitarian Law of Armed Conflict* (Martinus Nijhoff, The Hague, 1996).

Charlesworth, Hilary, and Chinkin, Christine, *The Boundaries of International Law: A Feminist Analysis* (Manchester University Press, Manchester, 2000).

Chen, Lung-Chu, "Self-Determination as a Human Right", in *Towards World Order and Human Dignity*, W Michael Reisman and Burns H Weston eds. (The Free Press, New York, 1976).

Chimni, B.S, *International Law and World Order* (New Delhi: Sage Publications, 1993).

Chimni, B.S, "An Outline of a Marxist Course on Public International Law", 17 *Leiden Journal of International Law* (2004), pp. 1–30.

Chimni, B.S, "Legitimating the International Rule of Law" in James Crawford and Martti Koskenniemi, eds., The Cambridge Companion to International Law(Cambridge: Cambridge University Press, 2012).

Chinkin, Christine, "The East Timor Case (Portugal v. Australia)" 45 *International and Comparative Law Quarterly* (1996) pp. 712–725.

Chinkin, Christine, "The Potential and Pitfalls of the Right to Self-Determination for Women" in Bowen, Stephen, ed., *Human Rights, Self-determination and Political Change in the Occupied Palestinian Territories* (Martinus Nijhoff, The Hague, 1997) pp. 93–117.

Chinkin, Christine & Wright, Susan, "The Hunger Trap: Women, Food and Self-Determination" (1993) 14 *Mich. J. Int'l L.* 262 at 294.

Chinkin, C., R. Higgins, A. M. Slaughter, T. M. Franck, S. R. Ratner, Panel on "The End of Sovereignty", *ASIL Proceedings 88* (1994), pp. 71–87.

Chowdhury, Subrata Roy, "The Status and Norms of Self-Determination in Contemporary International Law" 24 *Netherlands International Law Review* (1977) pp. 72–84.

Churchill, Winston S., *The World Crisis: The Aftermath* (Thornton Butterworth Limited, London, 1929).

Clapham, Christopher, "The Foreign Policies of Ethiopia and Eritrea" in Wright, Stephen, ed., *African Foreign Policies* (Westview, Boulder, 1999) pp. 84–99.

Clark, D & Williamson, R. eds., *Self-Determination: International Perspectives* (New York: St. Martin's Press, 1996).

Claude, Inis, *National Minorities* (Harvard University Press, Cambridge, 1955).

Cmiel, Kenneth, 'The Recent History of Human Rights', 109 American Historical Review (2004), 117–136.

Cobban, Alfred, *The Nation-State and National Self-Determination* (Collins, London, 1969).

Connell, Dan, *Against All Odds: A Chronicle of the Eritrean Revolution* (Red Sea Press, Trenton, 1993).

Connor, Walker, "Self-Determination: The New Phase" 20 *World Politics* (1967–8) pp. 30–53.

Corbett, P. E., 'What is the League of Nations?' 5 *British Yearbook of International Law* pp. 119–136.

Coursier, Henri, *Le Statut international du territoire de la Sarre* 5 (1925).

Cover, Robert, "Nomos and Narrative" in M. Minow, M. Ryan & A. Sarat, eds., *Narrative, Violence, and the Law: The Essays of Robert Cover* (Am Arbor: University of Michigan Press, 1992).

Cranston, Ruth, *The Story of Woodrow Wilson: Twenty-Eighth President of the United States, Pioneer of World Democracy* (Simon & Schuster, New York, 1945).

Craven, Matthew C. R., "The European Community Arbitration Commission on Yugoslavia", 66 *British Yearbook of International Law* (1995) pp. 333–413.

Craven, Matthew C. R., "Statehood, Self-Determination and Recognition" in Malcolm Evans (ed) *International Law* (Oxford University Press, Oxford, 2010).

Craven, Matthew C. R., 'On Foucault and Wolff or from Law to Political Economy', *Leiden Journal of International Law* 25 (2012) 627–645.

Craven, Matthew & Rose Parfitt "Statehood, Self-Determination and Recognition" in Malcolm D. Evans, ed. International Law. (Oxford: OUP, 2018).

Crawford, James, *The Creation of States in International Law* (Clarendon Press, Oxford, 1979).

Crawford, James, "Rights of Peoples: Peoples or Governments", 9 Bull. Austl. Soc. Leg. Phil (1985) pp. 136–49.

Crawford, James, "The Rights of Peoples: Some Conclusions" in Crawford, James, ed., *The Rights of Peoples* (Clarendon Press, Oxford, 1988) pp. 159–175.

Crawford, James, "Book Review of Antonio Cassese, Self-Determination of Peoples: A Legal Reappraisal" 90 *American Journal of International Law* (1996) pp. 331–3.

Crawford, James, "The General Assembly, the International Court and self-determination" in V. Lowe & M. Fitzmaurice, eds., *Fifty Years of the International Court of Justice: Essays in Honour of Sir Robert Jennings* (Cambridge: Grotius Publications, 1996).

Crawford, James, "The Dissolution of Yugoslavia and the Emergence of its Constituent Republics," *Attachment 1 I to State Practice and International Law in Relation to Unilateral Secession* (Expert Report, Reference re Secession of Quebec, S.C.C. No. 25506) ~http://canada.justice.gc.ca/News/Communiques/1997~frtctum/craw-en.html>

Crawford, James, "The Right of Self-Determination in International Law: Its Development and Future" in Alston, Philip, ed., *Peoples' Rights* (Oxford University Press, Oxford, 2001) pp. 7–67.

Crawford, James, *The Creation of States in International Law* (OUP, Oxford, 2006).

Crawford, Neta C., *Argument and Change in World Politics: Ethics, Decolonization, and Humanitarian Intervention* (Cambridge University Press, Cambridge, 2002).

Crawford Young, "Comparative Claims to Political Sovereignty: Biafra, Katanga, Eritrea," in Donald Rothchild and Victor A. Olorunsola, eds., *State Versus Ethnic Claims: African Policy Dilemmas* (Westview Press, Boulder, 1983).

Crenshaw, Kimberley, "Race, Reform and Retrenchment: Transformation and Legitimation in Antidiscrimination Law" 101 Harvard Law Review (1988) 1367.

Cristescu, A., *The Right to Self-Determination*, UN Doc. E/CN.4/Sub.2/404/Rev.1.

Cronjie, S., *The World and Nigeria: The Diplomatic History of the Biafran War 1967–1970* (Sidwick and Jackson, London, 1972).

Crossman, R., *Government and the Governed: A History of Political Ideas and Political Practice* (London, 1969).

Croxton, Derek "The Peace of Westphalia of 1648 and the Origins of Sovereignty", *The International History Review,* 21 (1999), 569–591.

Damrosch, Lori Fisler, " Politics Across Borders: Nonintervention and Nonforcible Influence over Domestic Affairs" 83 *Am. J. Int'l L. 1* (1989)

Danspeckgruber, W. and Watts, Sir A. eds., *Self-determination and Self-administration: A Sourcebook*, (Lynne Rienner, Boulder, 2000).

Darwin, John, *The End of the British Empire: The Historical Debate* (Basil Blackwell, Oxford, 1991).

Dehm, Julia, 'Highlighting Inequalities in the Histories of Human Rights: Contestations over Justice, Needs and Rights in the 1970s', *Leiden Journal of International Law* 31:4 (2018) 871–895

Derrida, Jacques "Force of Law: The "Mystical Foundation of Authority" (1990) *Cardozo Law Review* 11 at 991

Deutscher, Isaac, *Stalin: A Political Biography, revised edition* (Harmondsworth, 1966).

Dinstein, Yoram, *Collective Human Rights of peoples and Minorities,* 25 INT'L & CoMP. L.Q. 102 (1976)

Djadjadiningrat, Idrus Nasir, *The Beginnings of the Indonesian-Dutch Negotiations and the Hoge Veluwe Talks* (Ithaca: Southeast Asia Program Cornell University, 1958)

Doehring, Karl, "Self-Determination" in Simma, Bruno, ed., *The Charter of the United Nations: A Commentary* (Oxford University Press, Oxford, 1994) pp. 56–72.

Dolzer, Rudolf, "New Foundations of the Law of Expropriation of Alien Property", 75 *American Journal of International Law* (1981) pp. 553–589.

Doyle, Michael, "Kant, Liberal Legacies, and Foreign Affairs" 12 *Phil. & Pub. Affairs* 205, 207–8 (1983).

Drachmann, SS., "The War in Cambodia and the Case for Judicial Enforcement of Human Rights Conditions on Foreign Aid", 30 *Columbia of Transnational Law* (1992) pp. 661–695.

Drew, Catriona J., "Self-Determination, Population Transfer and the Middle East Peace Accords" in Bowen, Stephen, ed., *Human Rights, Self-determination and Political Change in the Occupied Palestinian Territories* (Martinus Nijhoff, the Hague, 1997) pp. 119–168.

Drew, Catriona J., *Population Transfer: The Untold Story of the International Law of Self-Determination,* unpublished thesis on file with the author

Drew, Catriona J., "The East Timor Story: International Law on Trial" 12 *EJIL* (2001) 651 at 658.

Du Bois, W.E.B, "To the Nations of the World" in W.E.B. Du Bois: A Reader., ed. David Levering Lewis (New York: Henry Holt, 1995)

Dugard, John, "The South West Africa Cases, Second Phase, 1966" 83 *S. African L.J.* (1966)

Dugard, John, "Namibia (South West Africa: The Court's Opinion, South Africa's Response, and Prospects for the Future" 11 *Columbia Journal of Transnational Law* (1972) pp. 14–49.

Dugard, John, *The South West Africa/Namibia Dispute: Documents and Scholarly Writing on the Controversy Between South Africa and the United Nations* (University of California Press, Berkeley, 1973).

Dugard, John, "1966 and All That: The South West Africa Judgment Revisited in the East Timor Case" 8 *African Journal of International and Comparative Law* (1996) pp. 549–563.

Duursma, J.C. *Fragmentation and the International Relations of Micro-States: Self-Determination and Statehood* (Cambridge: Cambridge University Press, 1996)

Eagleton, Clyde, "Excesses of Self-Determination" 31 *Foreign Affairs* (1953) pp. 592–604.

Eckel, Jan, "Human Rights and Decolonization: New Perspectives and Open Questions', 1:1 *Humanity* (2010)

Eckel, Jan, 'Human rights and decolonization: new perspectives and open questions', *Humanity: An International Journal of Human Rights, Humanitarianism, and Development*, 1.1 (2010)

Eckert, Andreas. 'African nationalists and human rights, 1940s and 1970s', in Stefan-Ludwig Hoffmann (ed.), *Human Rights in the Twentieth Century* (Cambridge University Press, 2011).

Edwards, Jr., R. W., "Contributions of the Genocide Convention to the Development of International Law," *Ohio NUL Review*, 8 (1981), 300–314.

Eide, Asbjørn, "In Search of Constructive Alternatives to Secession" in Tomuschat, Christian, ed., *Modern Law of Self-Determination* (Martinus Nijhoff, Dordrecht, 1993) pp. 139–176.

Eisner, Michael, "A Procedural Model for the Resolution of Secessionist Disputes" 33 *Harvard International Law Journal* (1992) pp. 407–425.

Eisenhower, D.D., *The White House Years: Waging Peace* (Doubleday, Garden City, 1965).

Elias, T.O., "The Charter of the Organization of African Unity", *American Journal of International Law*, 59, 2 (1965), p. 248.

Elster, Jon, "Majoritarian Rule and Individual Rights", in Stephen Shute and Susan Hurley (eds.), *On Human Rights: The Oxford Amnesty Lectures* (Basic Books, New York, 1993).

Emerson, Rupert, *From Empire to Nation: The Rise of Self-assertion of Asian and African Peoples* (Harvard University Press, Cambridge Mass., 1960).

Emerson, Rupert, "Nation-Building in Africa" in Deutsch, Karl W., and Foltz, William J., eds., *Nation-Building* (Atherton Press, New York, 1963) pp. 95–116.

Emerson, Rupert, *Self-Determination Revisited in the Era of Decolonization* (Harvard University Center for International Affairs, Occasional Papers in International Affairs, No. 9, 1964).

Emerson, Rupert, "Colonialism, Political Development, and the UN", 19 *International Organization* (1965) pp. 484–503.

Emerson, Rupert, "The New Higher Law of Anti-Colonialism", in Karl W. Deutsch and Stanley Hoffmann (eds.), *The Relevance of International Law: Essays in Honor of Leo Gross* (Cambridge, MA: Schenkman Publishing, 1968), p. 157.

Emerson, Rupert, "Self-Determination", 65 *American Journal of International Law* (1971) pp. 459–475.

Emerson, Rupert, "The Fate of Human Rights in the Third World", 27 *World Politics* (1974–5) pp. 201–226.

Ermacora, Felix, "The Protection of Minorities before the United Nations", 182 *Recueil des Cours* (1983) IV, pp. 255–370.

Eslava, Luis, Michael Fakhri and Vasuki Nesiah (eds), *Bandung, Global History, and International Law: Critical Pasts and Pending Futures* (Cambridge: Cambridge University Press, 2017).

Fabry, Miklas, *Recognizing States: International Society and the Establishment of New States since 1776* (Oxford University Press, Oxford, 2010).

Fain, Haskell, *Normative Politics and the Community of Nations* (Temple University Press, Philadelphia, PA, 1987).

Falk, Richard A, "The South West Africa Cases: An Appraisal", 21 *Int'l Org.* 1 (1967).

Falk, Richard A, "The Interplay of Westphalia and Charter Conceptions of International Legal Order" in Richard Falk & Cyril Black, eds., *The Future of International Legal Order*, (Princeton University Press, Princeton, 1969).

Falk, Richard A, *The Status of Law in International Society* (Princeton University Press, Princeton, 1970).

Falk, Richard A, "The Rights of Peoples (In Particular Indigenous Peoples)" in Crawford, James, ed., *The Rights of Peoples* (Clarendon Press, Oxford, 1988) pp. 17–37.

Falk, Richard A, "Self-Determination Under International Law: The Coherence of Doctrine Versus the Incoherence of Experience" in Wolfgang Danspeckgruber (ed) *The Self-Determination of Peoples: Community, Nation and State in an Interdependent World* (Lynne Rienner, Boulder, 2002)

Fanon, Frantz, *The Wretched of the Earth*. Trans. Richard Philcox. (Grove Press, New York, 2004).

Fassebender, Bardo and Peters, Anne (eds) *Oxford Handbook of the History of International Law* (Oxford University Press, Oxford, 2012)

Fastenrath, Ulrich, "Declaration Regarding Non-Self-Governing Territories" in Simma, Bruno, ed., *The Charter of the United Nations: A Commentary* (Oxford University Press, Oxford, 1994) pp. 923–931.

Fichte, Johann Gottlieb, "Addresses to the German Nation" in Reiss, H. S. ed., *The Political Thought of the German Romantics 1793–1815* (Basil Blackwell, Oxford, 1955) pp. 102–118.

Finkelstein, N., Vegh, G., & Joly, C., "Does Quebec Have the Right to Secede at International Law?" 74 *Can. Bar Rev.* (1995) pp. 245–247

Fink, Caroline, *Defending the Rights of Others, The Great Powers, the Jews, and International Minority Protection, 1878–1938*. Cambridge; New York: Cambridge University Press, 2004)

Fitzgerald, Brian F., "Portugal v. Australia: Deploying the Missiles of Sovereign Autonomy and Sovereign Community" 37 *Harvard International Law Journal* (1996) pp. 260–271.

Fitzmaurice, "The Future of Public International Law and the International Legal System in the Circumstances of Today", *Institut de Droit International, Evolution et Perspectives du Droit International* (1973) 196, at 233.

Foster, C., "Articulating Self-Determination in the Draft Declaration on the Rights of Indigenous Peoples" 12 *European Journal of International Law* (2001) pp. 141–57.

Fox, Gregory H., "The Right to Political Participation in International Law" in Fox, Gregory H., and Roth, Brad R., eds., *Democratic Governance and International Law* (Cambridge University Press, Cambridge, 2000) pp. 48–90.

Fox, Gregory H., "Introduction: The Spread of Liberal Democracy and its Implications for International Law", in G. Fox, and B. Roth (eds.), *Democratic Governance and International Law*, (Cambridge: Cambridge University Press, 2000)

Fradera, Josep Maria, *The Imperial Nation: Citizens and Subjects in the British, French, Spanish, and American Empires* (Princeton: Princeton University Press 2018)

Franck, Thomas M., "Legitimacy in the International System" 82 *American Journal of International Law* (1988) pp. 705–759.

Franck, Thomas M., *The Power of Legitimacy among Nations* (Oxford University Press, Oxford, 1990).

Franck, Thomas M., "The Emerging Right to Democratic Governance" 86 *American Journal of International Law* (1992) pp. 46–91.

Franck, Thomas M., "Postmodern Tribalism and the Right to Secession" in Brölmann, Catherine, Lefeber, René, and Zieck, Marjoleine, eds., *Peoples and Minorities in International Law* (Martinus Nijhoff, Dordrecht, 1993) pp. 3–27.

Franck, Thomas M., *Fairness in International Law and Institutions* (Clarendon Press, Oxford, 1995).

Franck, Thomas M., "Clan and Superclan: Loyalty, Identity and Community in Law and Practice" 90 *American Journal of International Law* (1996) pp. 359–383.

Franck, Thomas M., *The Empowered Self Law and Society in the Age of Individualism* (Oxford University Press, New York, 1999).

Franck, Thomas M., "Legitimacy and the Democratic Entitlement" in Fox, Gregory H., and Roth, Brad R., eds., *Democratic Governance and International Law* (Cambridge University Press, Cambridge, 2000).

Frankland, N. (ed.), *Documents on International Affairs 1955* (Oxford University Press, Oxford, 1958).

Freedman, Lawrence and Karsh, Efraim, *The Guld Conflict 1990–1991* (Faber and Faber, London, 1993).

Friedlander, *Self-Determination: A Legal-Political Inquiry, 1* DET. C.L. REV. 71 (1975)

Friedlander, "The Jurisprudential Implications of the South West Ahca Case" 6 *Col. J. Transnat'l L. 1* (1967).

Frowein, Jochen A., "Self-Determination as a Limit to Obligations under International Law" in Tomuschat, Christian, ed., *Modern Law of Self-Determination* (Martinus Nijhoff, Dordrecht, 1993) pp. 211–223.

Furtado, Jr. Charles F. and Andrea Chandler (eds.), *Perestroika in the Soviet Republics: Documents on the National Question* (Westview Press, Boulder, 1992).

Fukuyama, Francis, "The End of History?" *The National Interest* 16(1989) 3–18.

Gallagher, John, *The Decline, Revival and Fall of the British Empire* (Cambridge University Press, Cambridge, 1982).

Gayim, Eyassu, *The Principle of Self-Determination: A Study of its Historical and Contemporary Legal Evolution* (Norwegian Institute of Human Rights, Publication No. 5, Oslo, 1990).

Gayim, Eyassu, *The Eritrean Question: The Conflict between the Right of Self-Determination and the Interests of States* (Iustus Förlag, Uppsala, 1993).

Friedlander, *The UN Draft Declaration on Indigenous Peoples: Assessment of the Draft Prepared by the Working Group on Indigenous Populations* (University of Lapland, Rovaniemi, 1994).

Gayimm Eyassu, & Myntti, K eds. *Indigenous and Tribal Peoples ' Rights - 1993 and After* (Juridica Lapponica No. I 1) (Northern Institute for Environmental and Minority Law, Rovaniemi, Finland, 1995)

Gellner, Ernest, *Nations and Nationalism* (Basil Blackwell, Oxford, 1983).

Gellner, Ernest, *Culture, Identity, and Politics* (Cambridge University Press, Cambridge, 1987).

George, Lloyd, *The Truth About Peace Treaties* (1938) Vol 1. 31.

George, Richard T. de, "The Myth of the Right of Collective Self-Determination" in Twining, William, ed., *Issues of Self-Determination* (Aberdeen University Press, Aberdeen, 1991) pp. 1–7.

Gerard, Emmanuel and Bruce Kuklic, *Death in the Congo: Murdering Patrice Lumumba* (Cambridge, MA: Harvard University Press, 2015).

Gess, Karol N., "Permanent Sovereignty over Natural Resources: An Analytical Review of the United Nations Declaration and its Genesis" 13 *International Comparative Law Quarterly* (1964) pp. 398–449.

Getachew, Adom, *Worldmaking After Empire: The Rise and Fall of Self-Determination* (Princeton: Princeton University Press, 2019).

Ghai, Yash, (ed.), *Autonomy and Ethnicity*, (Cambridge University Press, Cambridge, 2000).

Gibson, Richard, *African Liberation Movements: Contemporary Struggles against White Minority Rule* (Oxford University Press, London, 1972).

Gilchrist, Huntington "Colonial Questions at the San Francisco Conference", 39 *The American Political Science Review*, 5 (1945)

Gilman, Nils, 'The New International Economic Order: A Reintroduction', 6:1 *Humanity* (2015) 1–16.

Gleijeses, Piero, *Shattered Hope: The Guatemalan Revolution and the United States, 1944–1954* (Princeton, University Press, Princeton, 1992).

Glendon, Mary Ann, *A World Made New: Eleanor Roosevelt and the Universal Declaration of Human Rights*. (New York: Random House, 2001)

Godechot, Jacques, Hyslop, Beatrice F., Dowd, David L., *The Napoleonic Era in Europe* (Holt, Rinehart and Winston, New York, 1971).

Gong, G., *The Standard of 'Civilisation in International Society* (Clarendon Press, Oxford, 1984).

Goodin, Robert, "Enfranchising All Affected Interests, and Its Alternative" *Philosophy & Public Affairs* 35, no. 1 (2007), 43

Gordon, Ruth E. "Some Legal Problems with Trusteeship" 23 *Cornell International Law Journal* (1995)

Gould, Carol *Globalizing Democracy and Human Rights*, (Cambridge University Press, Cambridge, 2004).

Green, T. H., *Lectures on the Principles of Political Organisation* (Longmans, Green and Co., London, 1917).

Green, T. H., *Self-Determination and Settlement of the Arab-Israeli Conflict*, PROc.AM. Soc. INT'L L. 40 (1971)

Grewe, William, *The Epochs of International Law*, (Walter de Gruyter, Berlin, 2000)

Grimal, Henri, *Decolonisation: The British, Dutch and Belgian Empires, 1919–1963*, (Routledge, London, 1978)

Gros Espiell, Héctor, *The Right to Self-Determination: Implementation of United Nations Resolutions* (United Nations, New York, 1980), E/CN.4/Sub.2/404/Rev.1

Gross, Leo, "The Peace of Westphalia, 1648–1948" 42 *American Journal of International Law* (1948) pp. 20–41.

Gross, Leo, "The Right of Self-Determination in International Law," in *New States in the Modem World*, Martin Kilson ed., (Harvard University Press, Cambridge MA, 1975)

Grovogui, S.N. *Sovereigns, Quasi-Sovereigns, and Africans: Race and Self-Determination in International Law* (University of Minnesota Press, Minneapolis, 1996)

Grotius, Hugo, De Jure Belli ac *Pacis Libri Tres* (Kelsey, Francis W. trans.) (Carnegie Endowment for International Peace, Washington, 1925).

Guzman, Raul P. de, and Reforma, Mila A. eds., *Government and Politics of the Philippines* (Oxford University Press, Singapore, 1988).

Habermas, Jurgen, *The Philosophical Discourse of Modernity.* (Polity Press, Cambridge, 1987)

Habermas, Jurgen, "A Genealogical Analysis of the Cognitive Content of Morality", *The Inclusion of the Other: Studies in Political Theory.* (MIT Press, Cambridge, 1998)

Hale, James C., "The Reform and Extension of the Mandates System: A Legal Solution to the Colonial Problem," in *Transactions of the Grotius Society*, vol. XXVI (Grotius Society, London, 1941), pp. 153–210: 161.

Haljan, David P., "Negotiating Quebec Secession", *RBDI 31* (1998), pp. 191–216.

Hall, Duncan, *The Trusteeship System*, 24 BYIL 33, 37 (1947)

Hall, Duncan, *Mandates, Dependencies and Trusteeship* (Carnegie Endowment Fund for International Peace, Washington, 1948)

Hall Stewart, John (ed.), *A Documentary Survey of the French Revolution* (The Macmillan Company, New York, 1951)

Halperin, Morton, Scheffer, David, and Small, Patricia, *Self-Determination and the New World Order* (Carnegie Endowment for International Peace, Washington, 1992).

Hannum, Autonomy, *Sovereignty, and Self-Determination: The Accomodation of Conflicting Rights* (University of Pennsylvania Press, Philadelphia, 1996).

Hannum, Autonomy, *Documents on Autonomy and Minority Rights* (Martinus Nijhoff, Dordrecht, 1993).

Hannum, Autonomy, 'Self-Determination, Yugoslavia, and Europe: Old Wine in New Bottles?' 3 *Transnat'l L. & Contemp. Probs* (1993) pp. 57–72.

Hannum, Autonomy, "Rethinking Self-Determination", 34 *Virginia Journal of International Law* (1994) pp. 1–69.

Hannum, Autonomy, "Self-Determination in the Post-Colonial Era" in Clark, Donald, and Williamson, Robert, eds., *Self-Determination: International Perspectives* (St. Martin's Press, New York, 1996) pp. 12–44.

Harhoff, Frederick, "Institutions of Autonomy", 55 *Nordic J. Int'l L.* (1986), pp. 31–40.

Harris, D J, *Cases and Materials on International Law* (London: Sweet and Maxwell, Sixth edition, 2004)

Harris, Nigel, *National Liberation* (I.B. Taurus, London, 1990).

Hart, H. L. A., *The Concept of Law* (2nd ed)(Clarendon, Oxford, 1994)

Hassan, *Collected Documents from the Asian-African Conference*, (Agency for Research and Development, Department of Foreign Affairs, 1983)

Havn, Steven 'Slave Rebellions and Mutinies Shaped the Age of Revolution', *Boston Review*, 2021.

Heater, Derek, *National Self-Determination: Woodrow Wilson and His Legacy* (St. Martin's Press, New York, 1994).

Henkin, Louis, "The United Nations and Human Rights", *International Organization* 19(3) (1965)

Henrard, Kristin, *Devising an Adequate System of Minority Protection: Individual Human Rights, Minority Rights and the Right to Self-Determination* (Martinus Nijhoff, The Hague, 2000).

Henson, Eric et al., eds.,*The State of the Native Nations: Conditions under U.S. Policies of Self-Determination* (Oxford University Press, New York, 2007).

Heraclides, Alexis, *The Self-Determination of Minorities in International Politics* (Frank Cass, London, 1991).

Herbst, Jeffrey "The Creation and Maintenance of Borders in Africa", 43 *International Organisation* 4 (1989) pp. 673–692.

Hicks, Frederick C, *The New World Order: International Organization, International Law, International Cooperation* (Doubleday, London, 1920).

Higgins, Rosalyn, *The Development of International Law Through the Political Organs of the United Nations* (Oxford University Press, London, 1963).

Higgins, Rosalyn, "The United Nations and Law Making: The Political Organs", 64 AJIL 43 (1970)

Higgins, Rosalyn, *United Nations Peacekeeping 1964–67: Documents and Commentary. The United Nations Operation in the Congo (ONUC) 1960–1964* (London, 1980)

Higgins, Rosalyn, "Judge Dillard and the Right to Self-Determination", 23 *Virginia Journal of International Law* (1983) pp. 387–394.

Higgins, Rosalyn, "International Law and the Avoidance, Containment and Resolution of Disputes», 230 *Rec. des Cours* 9 (1991) pp. 159–160.

Higgins, Rosalyn, "Postmodern Tribalism and the Right to Secession: Comments" in Brölmann, Catherine, Lefeber, René, and Zieck, Marjoleine, eds., *Peoples and Minorities in International Law* (Martinus Nijhoff, Dordrecht, 1993) pp. 29–35.

Higgins, Rosalyn, *Problems and Process: International Law and How We Use It* (Clarendon Press, Oxford, 1994).

Higgins, Rosalyn, "Self-Determination and Secession" in *Secession and International Law* (J. Dahlitz ed) (TMC Asser Press 2003)

Hillebrink, Stephen, *The Right of Self-Determination and Post-Colonial Governance: The Case of the Netherlnds Antilles and Aruba* (TMC Asser Press, London, 2008) p. 13

Hobsbawn, Eric, *The Age of Revolution 1789 -1848* (Mentor, New York, 1962)

Hobsbawn, Eric, "Marx, Engels and Politics", in E. J. Hobsbawm (ed.) *The History of Marxism: Volume One: Marxism in Marx's Day* (Indiana University Press, Bloomington, 1982)

Hobsbawn, Eric, *Nations and Nationalism Since 1780: Programme, Myth, Reality* (Cambridge University Press, Cambridge, 1990).

Hoff, Joan, "From Sarajevo to Sarajevo" in Michael Hogan (ed), *The Ambiguous Legacy: US Foreign Relations in the America Century* (Cambridge University Press, Cambridge, 1999)

Hoffmann, Stefan-Ludwig (ed) *Human Rights in the Twentieth Century* (Cambridge University Press, Cambridge, 2011)

Holbraad, Carsten, *The Concert of Europe: A Study in German and British International Theory 1815–1914* (Barnes and Noble, New York, 1971).

Holland, R. F. *European Decolonization, 1918–1981* (Macmillan, London, 1985).

Holsti, K. J., *The State, War and the State of War* (Cambridge University Press, Cambridge, 1996).

Holzgrefe, J. L. and Keohane, Robert (eds.), *Humanitarian Intervention: Ethical, Legal and Political Dilemmas* (Cambridge University Press, Cambridge, 2004).

Horowitz, Donald, *Ethnic Groups in Conflict* (University of California Press, Berkley, 1985)

Horowitz, Donald, "Self-Determination: Politics, Philosophy, and Law" in Moore, Margaret, ed., *National Self-Determination and Secession* (Oxford University Press, Oxford, 1998) pp. 181–214.

Hoskyns, Catherine. *The Congo since Independence: January 1960 to December 1961.* (Oxford University Press, London, 1965.)

Howse, Robert, and Malkin, Alissa, "Canadians are a Sovereign People: How the Supreme Court Should Approach the Reference on Quebec Secession", 76 *Canadian Bar Review* (1997) pp. 186–227.

Huberman, Leo, *Man's Worldly Goods* (Monthly Review Press, New York, 1936).

Hull, Cordell, *The Memoirs of Cordell Hull*, vol 2 (Macmillan, New York, 1948)

Humphrey, John, *The Great Adventure: Human Rights & the United Nations*, (Transnational Publishers, Michigan, 1984)

Humphrey, John, *On the Edge of Greatness*, vol. 2, (McGill University Libraries, Toronto, 1994).

Huntington Gilchrist, "Colonial Questions at the San Francisco Conference", 39 *The American Political Science Review, 5*, (October 1945) p. 987

Hurrell, Andrew, "The Making and Unmaking of Boundaries in International Law", in A. Buchanan, M. Moore (eds.) States, Nations and Borders: The Ethics of Making Boundaries (Cambridge University Press, Cambridge, 2003)

Hurrell, Andrew, *On Global Order: Power, Values and the Constitution of International Society* (Oxford University Press, Oxford, 2007)

Ibhawoh, Bonny, "Imperialism and Human Rights: Colonial Discourses of Rights and Liberties in African History", *Left History* (2007)

Ijalaye, David A., "Was 'Biafra' at Any Time a State in International Law?" 65 *American Journal of International Law* (1971) pp. 551–559.

Iorns, Catherine J., "Indigenous Peoples and Self Determination: Challenging State Sovereignty", 24 *CASE W. RES. J. INT'L L.* 199, 239–44 (1992).

Irwin, Ryan, "A Wind of Change? White Redoubt and the Postcolonial Moment, 1960–1963," Diplomatic History 33(5) (2009)

Islam, M. Rafiqul "Secession Crisis in Papua New Guinea: The Proclaimed Republic of Bougainville in International Law", *U. Haw. L. R 13* (1991).

Jackson, Robert, *Quasi States: Sovereignty, International Relations and the Third World*, (Cambridge University Press, Cambridge, 1990)

Jackson, Robert, "Negative Sovereignty in Sub-Saharan Africa", 12 *Review of International Studies* 4 (1986) pp. 250–251.

Jackson, Robert, "Sovereignty in World Politics: A Glance at the Historical and Conceptual Landscape", *Political Studies* 47 (1999), 435–439.

Jacobson, Harold Karan, "The United Nations and Colonialism: A Tenative Appraisal", *16 International Organization* (1967) pp. 786–811.

Janis, Mark W., "The International Court of Justice: Advisory Opinion on the Western Sahara" 17 *Harvard International Law Journal* (1976) pp. 609–621.

Jennings, Sir Ivor, *The Approach to Self-Government* (Cambridge University Press, Cambridge, 1956).

Jennings, Sir Robert, and Watts, Sir Arthur, *Oppenheim's International Law* (Ninth Edition), (Longman, London, 1992) volume I.

Jensen, Steven, *The Making of international Human Rights: The 1960s, Decolonization, and the Reconstruction of Global Values* (New York: CUP, 2016)

Johnson, Harold S., *Self-Determination within the Community of Nations* (A. W. Sijthoff, Leyden, 1967).

Johns, Andrew and Satler, Kathryn, eds, *The Eisenhower Administration, the Thirld World and the Globalization of the Cold War* (New York, Rowman and Littlefield, 2006)

Kamanu, Onyeonoro, "Secession and the Right of Self-Determination: An OAU Dilemma" 12 *The Journal of Modern African Studies* 3 (1974) pp. 355–376.

Kamenka, Eugene, "Human Rights, Peoples' Rights" in Crawford, James, ed., *The Rights of Peoples* (Clarendon Press, Oxford, 1988) pp. 127–139.

Kattan, Victor, "The Chagos Advisory Opinion and the Law of Self Determination" Asian Journal of International Law 10(1) 2020 12–20.

Kayaoglu, Turan, *Legal Imperialism: Sovereignty and Extraterritoriality in Japan, the Ottoman Empire and China*, (Cambridge: Cambridge University Press, 2010).

Kayaoglu, Turan, 'Westphalian Eurocentrism in International Relations Theory', *International Studies Review* 12(2) (2010) 193–217.

Keal, P. European Conquest and the Rights of Indigenous Peoples: The Moral Backwardness of International Society (Cambridge: CUP, 2003).

Kedourie, Elie, ed., *Nationalism in Asia and Africa* (Frank Cass, London, 1970).

Keesing's *Contemporary Archives* (Longman, Harlow) 16–23 Feb 1952.

Keene, Edward, *Beyond the Anarchical State: Grotius, Colonialism and Order in World Politics* (Cambridge University Press, Cambridge 2002)

Keitner, Chimene, *The Paradoxes of Nationalism: The French Revolution and its Meaning for Contemporary Nation Building* (State University of New York Press, New York, 2007)

Kelsen, Hans, *The Law of the United Nations: A Critical Analysis of its Fundamental Problems* (Stevens and Sons, London, 1950).

Kennedy, David, "Law's Literature" in Marjorie Garber, Rebecca L. Walkowitz and Paul B. Franklin (eds.), *Field Work* (New York, 1996), pp. 207–13 at p. 212.

Kennedy, David, *The International Human Rights Movement: Part of the Problem?* (2002), http://www.law.harvard.edu/students/orgs/hrj/iss15/kennedy.shtml.

Kennedy, David, 'Tom Franck and the Manhattan School', 35 *NYU J Int'l Law & Politics* (2003) pp. 397–432.

Kingsbury, Benedict, "Claims by Non-State Groups in International Law" 25 *Cornell International Law Journal* (1992) pp. 481–513.

Kingsbury, Benedict, "Self-Determination and 'Indigenous Peoples'" 86 *Proceedings of the American Society of International Law* (1992) pp. 383–394.

Kingsbury, Benedict, "Sovereignty and Inequality", 9 *European Journal of International Law* (1998) 599 at 608

Kingsbury, Benedict, "Reconstructing Self-Determination: A Relational Approach" in Aikio, Pekka, and Scheinin, Martin, eds., *Operationalizing the Right of Indigenous Peoples to Self-Determination* (Åbo Akademi University, Turku, 2000) pp. 19–37.

Kionka, Riina, and Vetik, Raivo, "Estonia and the Estonians" in Smith, Graham, ed., *The Nationalities Question in the Post-Soviet States* (Longman, London, 1996) pp. 129–146.

Kirgis, Frederic L. Jr., "The Degrees of Self-determination in the United Nations Era" 88 *American Journal of International Law* (1994) pp. 304–310.

Kirkpatrick, Jeane J. & Gerson, Allan, "The Reagan Doctrine, Human Rights and International Law", in Louis Henkin, éd., *Right v. Might: International Law and the Use of Force* (New York: Council on Foreign Relations, 2d ed. 1991).

Kiss, Alexandre, "The Peoples' Right to Self-Determination" 7 *Human Rights Law Journal* (1986) pp. 165–175.

Kiwanuka, Richard N., "The Meaning of 'People' in the African Charter on Human and Peoples' Rights" 82 *American Journal of International Law* (1988) pp. 80–101.

Klabbers, Jan, and Lefeber, René, "Africa: Lost between Self-determination and Uti Possidetis" in Brölmann, Catherine, Lefeber, René, and Zieck, Marjoleine, eds., *Peoples and Minorities in International Law* (Martinus Nijhoff, Dordrecht, 1993) pp. 37–76.

Klabbers, Jan, and Lefeber, René, "The Scope of International Law: Erga Omnes Obligations and the Turn to Morality" in Tupamäki, Matti, ed., *Liber Amicorum Bengt Broms: Celebrating his 70th Birthday 16 October 1999* (Finnish Branch of the International Law Association, Helsinki, 1999) pp. 149–179.

Knop, Karen, *Diversity and Self-Determination in International Law* (Cambibge University Press, Cambridge, 2002).

Knop, Karen, 'Statehood: Territory, People, Government' in J. Crawford and M. Koskenniemi (eds), *The Cambridge Companion to International Law* (Cambridge University Press, Cambridge, 2012)

Knorr, Klaus, 'Is International Coercion Waning or Rising?', 1 *International Security*, 4 (1975), pp. 92–110.

Kohn, Hans, *American Nationalism: An Interpretative Essay* (MacMillan, New York, 1957).

Kohn, Hans, *Nationalism: Its Meaning and History* (D. van Nostrand, Princeton, 1965).

Kohen, Marcelo G, *Secession: International Law Perspectives* (Cambridge, Cambridge University Press, 2006)

Kohen, Marcelo, "The Principle of Non-Intervention 25 years after the Nicaragua Judgement", 25 *Leiden Journal of International Law*, (2012) pp. 157–164

Korman, Sharon, *The Right of Conquest: The Acquisition of Territory by Force in International Law and Practice* (Clarendon Press, Oxford, 1996).

Koskenniemi, Martti, *From Apology to Utopia: The Structure of International Legal Argument* (Finnish Lawyers' Publishing Company, Helsinki, 1989).

Koskenniemi, Martti, "National Self-Determination Today: Problems of Legal Theory and Practice" 43 *International and Comparative Law Quarterly* (1994) pp. 241–269.

Koskenniemi, Martti, *The Gentle Civilizer of Nations: The Rise and Fall of International Law 1870–1960* (Cambridge University Press, Cambridge, 2001).

Koskenniemi, Martti, "The Lady Doth Protest Too Much: Kosovo, and the Turn to Ethics in International Law". *Modern Law Review*, 65, (2002) pp. 159–175.

Krasner, Stephen, "Westphalia and All That", in Judith Goldstein and Robert Keohane (eds.), *Ideas and Foreign Policy: Beliefs, Institutions and Political Change* (Ithaca, New York: Cornell University Press, 1993)

Krasner, Stephen, "Compromising Westphalia", 20(3) *Int'l Security* 115 (Winter 1995 -1996)

Kymlicka, Will, *Multicultural Citizenship: A Liberal Theory of Minority Rights* (Clarendon Press, Oxford, 1995).

Kymlicka, Will, *Multicultural Odysseys* (Oxford University Press, Oxford, 2007)

Lachs, Manfred, "The Law in and of the United Nations (Some Reflections on the Principle of Self-Determination)" 1 *Indian Journal of International Law* (1960–1) pp. 429–442.

Lake, Marilyn and Henry Reynolds. *Drawing the Global Colour Line: White Men's Countries and the International Challenge of Racial Equality*. (Cambridge; New York: Cambridge University Press, 2008)

Lalonde, Suzanne, *Determining Boundaries in a Conflicted World: The role of uti possedetis juris*, (McGill-Queen's University Press, Montreal, 2002.)

Landheer, B, *On the Sociology of International Law and International Society* (The Hague, The Netherlands: Nijhoff, 1966)

Lansing, Robert, *The Peace Negotiations: A Personal Narrative* (Houghton Mifflin, Boston, 1921)

Lapidoth, R, *Autonomy: Flexible Solutions to Ethnic Conflicts*, (United States Institute of Peace Press, Washington, 1997)

Lauterpacht, Sir Hersch, *Recognition in International Law* (Cambridge University Press, Cambridge, 1947)

Lawey, A., "Contemporary Efforts to Guarantee Indigenous Rights Under International Law" 23 in Vand. J. *Transnat'l L.* (1990)

Lawrence, T. J., *The Principles of International Law* (Macmillan, London, 1910)

Legum, Colin, "The Organisation of African Unity—success or failure?", 51 *International Affairs*, 2 (1975).

Lenin, V.I., *Imperialism: The Highest State of Capitalism*, (International Publishers, New York, 1939)

Lenin, V.I., "The Right of Nations to Self-Determination" in Lenin, V. I., *Selected Works* (Foreign Languages Publishing, Moscow, 1946) volume I, pp. 564–611.

Lenin, V.I., "The Revolutionary Proletariat and the Right of Nations to Self-Determination", *Collected Works*, vol. 21, pp. 407–14.

Lieber, Francis, *Fragments of Political Science on Nationalism and Inter-Nationalism* (Charles Scribner and Co., New York, 1868).

Lieven, Anatol, *The Baltic Revolution: Estonia, Latvia, Lithuania and the Path to Independence* (Yale University Press, New Haven, 1993).

Liu, Lydia H, 'Shadows of Universalism: The Untold Story of Human Rights around 1948' *Critical Inquiry* 40 (Summer 2014) 400

Lloyd George, David, *The Truth About The Peace Treaties* (Victor Gollancz, London 1938).

Locke, John, *Two Treatises of Government: A Critical Edition with an Introduction and Apparatus Criticus* (Laslett, Peter, ed.), (Second Edition), (Cambridge University Press, Cambridge, 1967).

Louis, WR, *Imperialism at Bay, 1941–1945: The United States and the Decolonization of the British Empire* (Oxford University Press, New York, 1978).

Low, D. A., *Eclipse of Empire* (Cambridge University Press, Cambridge, 1993).

Lukacs, Georg, *Lenin: A Study in the Unity of His Thought* (New Left Books, London, 1970)

Lumumba, Patrice, "Speech at Leopoldville", December 28, 1958, in Lumumba Speaks: The Speeches and Writings of Patrice Lumumba, 1958–1961 (Boston: Little, Brown, 1972)

Macartney, C. A., *National States and National Minorities* (Oxford University Press, London, 1934).

Macklem, Patrick, 'Militant Democracy, Legal Pluralism, and the Paradox of Self-Determination', *International Journal of Constitutional Law*, 4 (3) (2006) 488–516

Macklem, Patrick, "Distributing Sovereignty: Indian Nations and Equality of Peoples", 45 *Stan. L. Rev.* (1992–1993) pp. 1311–1347.

Madsen, Mikael Rask, "Reflexivity and the Construction of the International Object: The Case of Human Rights", *International Political Sociology* 5 (2011) pp. 259–275.

Makinson, David, "The Rights of Peoples: Point of View of a Logician" in Crawford, James, ed., *The Rights of Peoples* (Clarendon Press, Oxford, 1988) pp. 69–92.

Makonnen, Yilma, *International Law and the New States of Africa*, (UNESCO, 1983)

Manela, Erez, *The Wilsonian Moment: Self-Determination and the International Origins of Anticolonial Nationalism* (Oxford: University Press, Oxford, 2007).

Marcum, John, "Government-in-Exile Versus Government-in-Insurgency: The Case of Angola", in Yossi Shain, ed., *Governments-in-Exile in Contemporary World Politics* (Routledge, Chapman & Hall, Inc., New York, 1991)

Marks, Susan, "International Law, Democracy, and the End of History" in Gregory H. Fox & Brad R. Roth eds., *Democratic Governance and International Law* (Cambridge University Press, Cambridge, 2000)

Marks, Susan, *The Riddle of All Constitutions: International Law, Democracy, and the Critique of Ideology* (Oxford Univeristy Press, Oxford, 2003).

Marks, Susan, "Empire"s Law" 10 *Ind. J. Global Legal Stud.* (2003) 449 at 451.

Marks, Susan, "What has Become of the Emerging Right to Democratic Governance?," 22 *Eur. J. Int'l. L.* 507, 522 (2011).

Marshall, M.G. and Gurr T.R., *Peace and Conflict 2005, Centre for International Development and Conflict Management*, (University of Maryland, Maryland 2005)

Marston, G. "United Kingdom Materials on International Law 1985", 56 *BYIL* (1985) 460.

Mason, A, "Themes and Prospects" in P D Finn (ed), *Essays in Equity*, (Sydney: Law Book Co, 1985)

Maaui, A.A. "The African State as a Political Refugee: Institutional Collapse and Human Displacement", 21 *Int'l J. Refugee L.* (1995)

Mayall, James (ed.), *The Community of States* (Allen & Unwin, London, 1982).

Mayall, James (ed.), *Nationalism and International Society* (Cambridge University Press, Cambridge, 1990).

Mayall, James (ed.), "Non-intervention, self-determination and the `new world order.'" 67 *International Affairs*, 3, (1991)

Mayall, James (ed.), *World Politics: Progress and its Limits* (James Wiley & Sons, London, 2013)

Mazower, Mark, *Governing the World: The History of an Idea*, (Penguin, New York, 2012)

Mazzini, Giuseppe, "On the Superiority of Representative Government", in S Recchia and N Urbinati (eds) *A Cosmopolitanism of Nations: Giuseppe Mazzini's Writing on*

*Democracy, Nation Building and International Relations* (Princeton University Press, Princeton, 2009) 43–44.

McCorquodale, Robert, "Self-Determination: A Human Rights Approach" 43 *International and Comparative Law Quarterly* (1994) pp. 857–885.

McDougal, Myres S., and Reismanm, W. Michael, "Rhodesia and the United Nations: The Lawfulness of International Concern", 62 *The American Journal of International Law*, 1 (1968), pp. 1–19.

McDougal, Lasswell, & Chen, "The Protection of Respect and Human Rights: Freedom of Choice and World Public Order", 24 *American University Law Review* (1975)

McGoldrick, D. "Canadian Indians, Cultural Rights and the Human Rights Committee" 40 *Int'l & Cornp. L.Q.* (1991).

McGoldrick, Dominic, "Yugoslavia – The Responses of the International Community and of International Law", 49 *Current Legal Problems* (1996) pp. 375–394.

McGowan, Patrick J., "African military coups d'e'tats, 1956–2001", 41 *Journal of Modern African Studies*, 3 (2003), pp. 339–70

McWhinney, Edward, "Friendly Relations and Co-operation among States: Debate at the Twentieth General Assembly, United Nations" 60 *American Journal of International Law* (1966) pp. 356–61.

Meyer, John W, Boli, John and Thomas, George M., "Ontology and rationalization", in George M. Thomas, John W. Meyer, Francesco Ramirez, and John Boli (eds.), *Institutional Structure: Constraining State, Society, and the Individual* (London: Sage, 1987), p. 12.

Meyers, David, "Intraregional Conflict Management by the Organisation of African Unity" 28 *International Organisation* 3 (1974) pp. 345–373.

Mieville, China, *Between Equal Rights: A Marxist Theory of International Law* (Brill, Leiden, 2005)

Mill, John Stuart, "Considerations on Representative Government" in *Utilitarianism, Liberty, Representative Government* (J. M. Dent & Sons, London 1954) pp. 171–393.

Miller, Russell A., "Self-Determination in International Law and the Demise of Democracy?" 41 *Columbia Journal of Transnational Law* (2003) pp. 601–48.

Milton, John, "The Tenure of Kings and Magistrates" in *Complete Prose Works of John Milton* (Yale University Press, New Haven, 1962) volume III, pp. 189–258.

Modeen, Tore, *The International Protection of National Minorities in Europe* (Åbo Akademi, Åbo/Turku, 1969).

Molony, Tom and King, Tom eds., *Nyerere: Student, Teacher, Humanist, Statesman* (Edinburgh University Press, Edinburgh 2000).

Moynihan, Daniel P, "Was Woodrow Wilson Right? Morality and American Foreign Policy" 57 *Commentary* (1974) pp. 23–31.

Montesquieu, Charles de, *The Spirit of The Laws* (Cohler, Anne M., Miller, Basia Carolyn, and Stone, Harold Samuel, trans. and ed.), (Cambridge University Press, Cambridge, 1989).

Moore, John, "Toward an Applied Theory for the Regulation of Intervention", in *Law and Civil War in the Modern World*, John Moore ed, (The Lawbook Exchange, 1974)

Moore, Margaret, "Introduction: The Self-Determination Principle and the Ethics of Secession" in Moore, Margaret, ed., *National Self-Determination and Secession* (Oxford University Press, Oxford, 1998) pp. 1–13.

Moore, Margaret, "The Territorial Dimension of Self-Determination" in Moore, Margaret, ed., *National Self-Determination and Secession* (Oxford University Press, Oxford, 1998) pp. 134–157.

Morgan, D.J., *The Official History of Colonial Development, Vol. 5: Guidance Towards Self-Government in British Colonies, 1941–1971*(London: Macmillan, 1980), pp. 1–5.

Morgan, Edward M., "The Imagery and Meaning of Self-Determination" 20 *New York University Journal of International Law and Politics* (1987–8) pp. 355–403.

Morgenthau, Hans J., "The Paradoxes of Nationalism" 46 *Yale Review* (1957) pp. 481–496.

Morgenthau, Hans J., *Politics Among Nations: The Struggle for Power and Peace*, 5th ed (Alfred A Knopf, New York, 1978)

Morsink, Johannes. *The Universal Declaration of Human Rights: Origins, Drafting and Intent.* (University of Pennsylvania Press, Philadelphia, PA, 1999)

Mosley, Leonard, *On Borrowed Time: How World War II Began* (Random House, London, 1969)

Mountz, William "The Congo Crisis: A Reexamintion," *The Journal of the Middle East and Africa* 5(2) (2014): 151–165.

Moyn, Samuel, *The Last Utopia* (Harvard University Press, Cambridge, MA, 2010)

Mullerson, Rein, "The Continuity and Succession of States, by Reference to the Former USSR and Yugoslavia" 42 *International and Comparative Law Quarterly* (1993) pp. 473–493.

Millerson, Rein, *International Law, Rights and Politics: Developments in Eastern Europe* (Routledge, London, 1994)

Mullerson, Rein, *Ordering Anarchy in International Society* (Martinus Nijhoff, The Hague, 2000).

Mullerson, Rein, "Precedents in the Mountains: On the Parallels and Uniqueness of the Cases of Kosovo, South Ossetia and Abkhazia", 8 *Chinese J Intl L* (2009)

Murphy, "Self-Determination: United States Perspectives" in Y. Alexander & R. Friedlander eds., *Self-Determination: National, Regional and Global Dimensions,* (Westview Press, Boulder, 1978)

Murray, Gilbert, "Self-Determination of Nationalities" 1 *Journal of the British Institute of International Affairs* (1922) pp. 6–13.

Murray, Rachel, and Evans, Malcolm, ed., *Documents of the African Commission on Human and Peoples' Rights* (Hart Publishing, Oxford, 2001).

Murswiek, Dietrich, "The Issue of a Right of, Christian, ed., *Modern Law of Self-Determination* (Martinus Nijhoff Secession – Reconsidered" in Tomuschat, Dordrecht, 1993) pp. 21–39.

Musgrave, Thomas D., *Self-Determination and National Minorities* (Clarendon Press, Oxford, 1997).

Mustafa, "The Principle of Self-Determination in International Law", 5 *International Law*, 479 (1971)

Mutua, Makau, "Putting Humpty Dumpty Back Together Again: The Dilemmas of the Post-Colonial African State" 21 *Brooklyn Journal International* Law (1995).

Mutua, Makau, "Why Redraw the Map of Africa: A Moral and Legal Inquiry" 16 *Mich. J. International Law*, (1995)

Mutua, Makau, *Conflicting Conceptions of Human Rights: Rethinking the Post-Colonial State*, 89 ASIL Proc. 487 (1995)

Mutua, Makau, "What is TWAIL?" ASIL, Proceedings of the 94th Annual Meeting, April 2000, online: University of Buffalo http://www.law.buffalo.edu/Faculty_And_Staff/submenu/MutuaM/reports/asil040500.pdfS

Mwakikagil, Godfrey, *Ethnic Politics in Kenya and Nigeria* (Nova, Huntington, 2001)

Nagengast, Emil, "German and U.S. Intervention Against Yugoslav Sovereignty", in Andrew Vails (ed.), *Ethics in International Affairs* (Rowman and Littlefield, Lanham, 2000).

Naimark, Norman, *Fires of Hatred: Ethnic Cleansing in Twentieth-Century Europe*, (Harvard University Press, Cambridge, 2002)

Nanda, Ved P., "Self-Determination in International Law: The Tragic Tale of Two Cities Islamabad (West Pakistan) and Dacca (East Pakistan)" 66 *American Journal of International Law* (1972) pp. 321–336.

Nanda, Ved P., "Self-Determination Outside the Colonial Context: The Birth of Bangladesh",1 *Hous J Int'l L* 71 (1978–1979) pp. 71–93.

Nanda, Ved P., "Self-Determination under International Law: Validity of Claims to Secede" 13 *Case Western Reserve Journal of International Law* (1981) pp. 257–280.

N'Zatioula Grovogui, Siba, *Sovereigns, Quasi-Sovereigns and Africans*, (Minneapolis: University of Minnesota Press, 1996)

Naqvi, A., "West Pakistan's Struggle for Power", 4 *South Asian Rev.* 213 (April 1971), at 224

Navari, Cornelia. "Territoriality, Self-Determination and Crimea after Badinter." *International Affairs* 90, no. 6 (2014) 1299–1318.

Nawaz, M. K., "The Meaning and Range of the Principle of Self-Determination", 82 *Duke Law Journal* (1965) pp. 82–101.

Nayar, M. G. Kaladharan, "Self-Determination Beyond the Colonial Context: Biafra in Retrospect", 10 *Texas International Law Journal* (1975) pp. 321–345.

Nayar, M. G. Kaladharan, «Self-Determination: The Bangladesh Experience», *Revue des Droits de L'homme*, Vol. 7 (1974), pp. 231, 233

Nietzsche, Frederich, *A Genealogy of Morals,* (London: Random House, 2009).

Nixon, Charles R., "Self-Determination: The Nigeria/Biafra Case" 24 *World Politics* (1972) pp. 473–497.

Normand, Roger and Sarah Zaidi, Human Rights at the UN: The Political History of Universal Justice (Bloomington: Indiana University Press, 2008), 212–20; Burke (2010: 35–59).

Nowak, Manfred, "The Right of Self-Determination and Protection of Minorities in Central and Eastern Europe in Light of the Case-Law of the Human Rights Committee" 1 *International Journal on Minority and Group Rights* (1993) pp. 7–16.

Nkrumah, Kwame, *Neo-Colonialism: The Last Stage of Imperialism* (Thomas Nelson & Sons, 1965) ix.

Nwaubani, Ebere, "The United States and the Liquidation of European Colonial Rule in Tropical Africa, 1941–1963 », *Cahiers d'études africaines*, 171 | 2003, mis en ligne le 15 février 2007, consulté le 10 octobre 2012.

Nyerere, Julius K. "A United States of Africa", 1 *Journal of Modern African Studies*, 1 (1963).

Nyerere, Julius K. "Individual Human Rights", in Nyerere, Freedom and Unity/Uhuruna Umoja: *A Selection from Writings and Speeches 1952–65* (Dar es Salaam, 1966).

O'Malley, Alanna, "Ghana, India and the Transnational Dynamics of the Congo Crisis at the United Nations, 1960–1," *The International History Review* 37(5) (2015): 984.

O'Malley, Alanna, What an Awful Body the UN Have Become!!'Anglo-American–UN Relations during the Congo crisis, February–December 1961,"*Journal of Transatlantic Studies* 14,1 (2016): 26–46

Ofuatey-Kodjoe, W., "Self-Determination" in Schachter, Oscar, and Joyner, Christopher C., eds., *United Nations Legal Order* (Cambridge University Press, Cambridge, 1995) volume I, pp. 349–389.

Orentlicher, Diane F., "Separation Anxiety: International Responses to Ethno-Separatist Claims", 23 *Yale J. Int'l L.* 1 (1998).

Orentlicher, Diane F., "International Responses to Separatist Claims: Are Democratic Principles Relevant?" in Macedo, Stephen, and Buchanan, Allen, eds., *Secession and Self Determination* (New York University Press, New York, 2003) pp. 19–49.

Osiander, Andreas, "Sovereignty, International Relations, and the Westphalian Myth", *International Organization,* 55 (2001), 251–287.

Osterhammel, Jürgen, Europe, the 'West' and the Civilizing Mission (German Historical Inst 2006)

Otto, D, "Subalternity and International Law: The Problems of Global Community and the Incommensurability of Difference", 5 *Social & L. Studies* 3 (1996) pp. 339–348.

Otto, D, "A question of law or politics-Indigenous claims to sovereignty in Australia." *Syracuse Journal of International and Commerce*, 21 (1995) 65–104

Őzsu, Umut, 'Neoliberalism and the New International Economic Order: A History of Contemporary Legal Thought', in C. Tomlins and J. Desautels-Stein (eds.), *In Search of Contemporary Legal Thought* (Cambridge: CUP, 2016)

Őzsu, Umut, *Formalizing Displacement: International Law and Population Transfer* (Oxford: Oxford University Press, 2014)

Padelford, Norman J., and Andersson, K. Gösta A., "The Aaland Islands Question", 33 *American Journal of International Law* (1939) pp. 465–487.

Padmore, George, *Pan-Africanism or Communism* (Garden City, NY: Anchor Books, 1971),

Pagden, Anthony, *Lords of All the World: Ideologies of Empire in Spain, Britain and France c. 1500-c. 1800* (Yale University Press 1995)

Pahuja, Sundhya, *Decolonising International Law: Development, Economic Growth, and the Politics of Universality* (Cambridge: CUP 2011).

Panther-Brick, "The Right to Self-Determination: Its application to Nigeria", *Int.Affairs*, Vol. 44 (1958), 262.

Pape, Robert A., "The Strategic Logic of Suicide Terrorism", *American Political Science Review*, 97/3 (2002).

Rose Parfitt, "Empire des. Negres Blancs: The Hybridity of International Legal Personality in the Abyssinia Crisis of 1935–1936", *Leiden Journal of International Law* 24 (2911) 849–72.

Rose Parfitt, *The Process of International Legal Reproduction* (Cambridge: CUP, 2019).

Partsch, Karl Josef, "Fundamental Principles and Human Rights: Self-Determination, Equality and Non-Discrimination" in Vasak, Karel, and Alston, Philip, eds., *The International Dimensions of Human Rights* (Greenwood Press, Westport, 1982) volume I, pp. 61–86.

Paust, "Self-Determination: A Definitional Focus", in *Self-Determination: National, Regional and Global Dimensions*, Y. Alexander & R. Friedlander eds., (Westview Press, Boulder, 1978)

Pavkovic, Aleksandar and Radan, Peter, *The Ashgate Research Companion to Secession*, (Ashgate, London, 2011)

Pearson, Raymond, *The Turning Point in Africa: British Colonial Policy 1938–48* (Frank Cass, London, 1982).

Pearson, Raymond, *National Minorities in Eastern Europe, 1848–1945* (Macmillan, London, 1983).

Pellet, Alain, "The Opinions of the Badinter Arbitration Committee: A Second Breath for the Self-Determination of Peoples" 3 *European Journal of International Law* (1992) pp. 178–185

Pellet, Alain, «Note sur la Commission d'arbitrage de la Confirence europeenne pour la paix en Yougoslavie» 37 *Ann. fr. dr. int.* (1991)

Pellet, Alain, «L'Activite de la Commission d'arbitrage de la Conference europeenne pour la paix en Yougoslavie» 38 *Ann. fr. dr. int.* 220 (1992)

Pellet, Alain, «L'Activite de la Commission d'arbitrage de la Conference internationale pour l'ancienne Yougoslavie» 39 *Ann. fr. dr. int.* (1993)

Pitts, Jennifer, *A Turn to Empire: The Rise of Imperial Liberalism in Britain and France* (Princeton NJ: Princeton University Press 2006)

Philpott, Daniel, "*Revolutions in Sovereignty: How Ideas Shaped Modern International Relations* (Princeton: Princeton University Press, 2001)

Philpott, Daniel, "Self-Determination in Practice" in Moore, Margaret, ed., *Self-Determination and Secession* (Oxford University Press, Oxford, 1998)

Plamenatz, John, *On Alien Rule and Self-Government,* (Longmans, Michigan, 1960)

Polanco, Hector, *Indigenous Peoples in Latin America: The Quest for Self-determination* (Westview Press, Boulder, CO, 1997)

Pomerance, Michla, "The United States and Self-Determination: Perspectives on the Wilsonian Conception" 70 *American Journal of International Law* (1976) pp. 1–27.

Pomerance, Michla, *Self-Determination in Law and Practice: The New Doctrine of the United Nations* (Martinus Nijhoff, The Hague, 1982).

Pomerance, Michla, "Self-Determination Today: The Metamorphosis of an Ideal", 19 *Israel Law Review* (1984) pp. 310–339.

Porter, A.L & Stockwell, A.J., *British Imperial Policy and Decolonization, 1938–64,* vol. 1: *1938–1951* (St Martin's Press, New York, 1987).

Post, "Is there a Case for Biafra?" *Int. L Affairs*, Vol. 44 (1968), 32.

Poulio, V and Merand, F, "Bourdieu Concepts" in Rebecca Adler-Nissen, *Bourdieu in International Relations: Rethinking Key Concepts in IR*. (Routledge, Taylor & Francis Group, London, 2012)

Proceedings of the Summit Conference of Independent African States, Addis Ababa, vol. 1, section 2, *Summit CIAS/GEN/INF/36*, May 1963.

Pullat, Risto, "The Restoration of the Independence of Estonia 1991", 2 *Finnish Yearbook of International Law* (1991) pp. 512–532.

Quane, Helen, "The United Nations and the Evolving Right to Self-Determination", 47 *International and Comparative Law Quarterly* (1998) pp. 537–572.

Quane, Helen, "A Right to Self-Determination for the Kosovo Albanians?" 13 *Leiden Journal of International Law* (2000) pp. 219–27.

Quaye, Christopher O, *Liberation Struggles in International Law*, (Temple University Press, Philledelphia, 1991)

Quereshi, Asif H. ed., *Perspectives in International Economic Law* (Kluwer Law International, London, 2002).

Ramcharan, BG, "The Principle of Legality in International Human Rights Institutions", 64 *NJIL* (1995) pp. 1–24.

Ragazzi, Maurizio, "Conference on Yugoslavia Arbitration Commission: Opinions on Questions Arising from the Dissolution of Yugoslavia: introductory Note", 3 1 *ILM* (1992).

Raic, David, *Statehood and the Law of Self-Determination* (Kluwer, The Hague, 2002).

Ramer, S., "Drawing a Better Line: Uti Possidetis and the Borders of New States", 90 *AJIL* (1996)

Rapoport, David C., "The Four Waves of Modern Terrorism", in Audrey Kurth Cronin and James M. Ludes (eds.), *Attacking Terrorism: Elements of Grand Strategy* (Georgetown University Press, Washington, DC, 2004).

Ratner, Steven R., "The Cambodia Settlement Agreements", 87 *AM. J. INT'L. L.* 1, 3 (1993)

Ratner, Steven R., "Drawing a Better Line: Uti possidetis and the Borders of New States", 90 *American Journal of International Law* (1996) pp. 590–624.

Ratner, Steven R., "Ethnic Conflict and Territorial Claims: Where Do We Draw the Line" in Wippman, David, ed., *International Law and Ethnic Conflict* (Cornell University Press, Ithaca, 1998) pp. 112–127.

Rauschning, Dietrich, "International Trusteeship System" in Simma, Bruno, ed., *The Charter of the United Nations: A Commentary* (Oxford University Press, Oxford, 1994) pp. 933–948.

Ravenhill, John, "Redrawing the Map of Africa," in Donald Rothchild and Naomi Chazan, eds., *The Precarious Balance: State and Society in Africa* (Westview Press, Boulder, 1988), pp. 282–83.

Rawls, John, *The Law of Peoples* (Harvard University Press, Cambridge: Mass., 1999).

Raz, Joseph, and Margalit, Avishai, "National Self-Determination" in Raz, Joseph, ed., *Ethics in the Public Domain* (Clarendon Press, Oxford, 1994) pp. 110–130.

Redslob, Robert, "The Problem of Nationalities", 17 *Transactions of the Grotius Society* (1932) pp. 21–34.

Reid, John Phillip, *The Concept of Representation in the Age of the American Revolution* (University of Chicago Press, Chicago, 1989).

Reid, R., "Caught in the Headlights of History: Eritrea, the EPLF and the Post-war Nation-state", 43 *Journal of Modern African Studies 3*, (2005) pp. 467–88.

Reus-Smit, Christian, *The Moral Purpose of the State: Culture, Social Identity, and Institutional Rationality in International Relations* (Princeton University Press, Princeton, NJ, 1999)

Reus-Smit, Christian, *Individual Rights and the Making of the International System* (Cambridge University Press, Cambridge, 2013)

Reynolds, A. (ed.), *The Architecture of Democracy*, (Oxford University Press, Oxford, 2001)

Rézette, Robert, *The Western Sahara and the Frontiers of Morocco* (Nouvelles Éditions Latines, Paris, 1975).

Rich, Roland, "Recognition of States: The Collapse of Yugoslavia and the Soviet Union" 4 *European Journal of International Law* (1993) pp. 36–65.

Richardson, Henry J. III, "Constitutive Questions in the Negotiations for Namibian Independence" 78 *American Journal of International Law* (1984) pp. 76–120.

Richardson, Henry J. III, "Self-Determination, International Law and the South African Bantustan Policy", 17 *Columbia Journal Transnational Law* (1978)

Riedel, E.H., "Confrontation in Western Sahara in the Light of the Advisory Opinion of the International Coun of Justice of 16 October 1975. A Critical Appraisal", 19 *German Y.B. Int'l L.* (1976) pp. 407–418.

Rigo-Sureda, A., *Evolution of the Right to Self-Determination* (A. W. Sijthoff, Leiden, 1973).

Robinson, Jacob, *Were the Minorities Treaties a Failure?*, (Institute of Jewish Affairs, 1943)

Roepstorff, Kristina, *The Politics of Self-Determination Beyond the Decolonisation Process*, (Routledge, London, 2012)

Rohozinski, Rafal, "The August Coup: A Thirty Day Chronology, 18 August - 17 September 1991", in J.L. Black (ed.), *USSR Document Annual 1991*, Vol. 2 (Academic International Press, Gulf Breeze, 1993).

Roling, B. V. A., *International Law in an Expanded World* (Djambatan, Amsterdam, 1960)

Ronen, Dov, *The Quest for Self-Determination* (Yale University Press, New Haven, 1979).

Rosas, Allan, "Internal Self-Determination" in Tomuschat, Christian, ed., *Modern Law of Self- determination* (Martinus Nijhoff, Dordrecht, 1993) pp. 225–252.

Rosas, Allan, "The Decline of Sovereignty: Legal Perspectives', in J.Iivonen (ed.), The Future of the Nation State in Europe(Aldershot: E. Elgar Pub. 1993), p. 131, at p. 149

Rosas, Allan, "The Right of Self-Determination" in Eide, Asbjørn, Krause Catarina, and Rosas, Allan eds., *Economic, Social and Cultural Rights: A Textbook* (Martinus Nijhoff, Dordrecht, 1995) pp. 79–86.

Rosas, Allan, "Article 21" in Alfredsson, Gudmunder, and Eide, Asbjørn, eds., *The Universal Declaration of Human Rights: A Common Standard of Achievement* (Martinus Nijhoff, The Hague, 1999) pp. 431–451.

Rosenstock, Robert, "The Declaration of Principles of International Law Concerning Friendly Relations: A Survey" 65 *American Journal of International Law* (1971) pp. 713–735.

Roth, Brad, *Governmental Illegitimacy in International Law* (Oxford University Press, Oxford, 1999)

Roth, Brad, *Sovereign Equality and Moral Disagreement: Premises of a Pluralist International Legal Order* (Oxford University Press, Oxford, 2011).

Rousseau, Jean-Jacques, *The Social Contract* (Cranston, Maurice, trans.), (Penguin Books, Harmondsworth, 1980).

Rousseau, J. J., *Considérations sur le Governement de Pologne, et sur sa Réformation Projettée* (London, 1782).

Ruskin, John, *Sesame and Lilies,* (Yale University Press, New Haven, 2002), p. 36

Russell, Ruth B., and Muther, Jeanette E., *A History of the United Nations Charter: The Role of the United States 1940–1945* (The Brookings Institution, Washington, 1958).

Salmon, Jean, "Internal Aspects of the Right to Self-Determination: Towards a Democratic Legitimacy Principle?" in Tomuschat, Christian, ed., *Modern Law of Self-Determination* (Martinus Nijhoff, Dordrecht, 1993) pp. 253–82.

Sanders, Douglas, "Self-Determination and Indigenous Peoples" in Tomuschat, Christian, ed., *Modern Law of Self-Determination* (Martinus Nijhoff, Dordrecht, 1993) pp. 55–81.

Sauvant, Karl P. *The Group of 77: Evolution, Structure, Organization,* (Oceana Publications, Inc., New York, London, Rome, 1981)

Sayre, Francis B., "Legal Problems Arising from the United Nations Trusteeship System", 42 *American Journal of International Law* (1948) pp. 263–298.

Schachter, Oscar, "The Relation of Law, Politics and Action in the United Nations", 109 *Recueil des Cours* (1963) II, pp. 163–256.

Schachter, Oscar, "Sovereignty – Then and Now" in St. John MacDonald, Ronald, ed., *Essays in Honour of Wang Tieya* (Martinus Nijhoff, Dordrecht, 1994) pp. 671–688.

Scheinin, Martin, "The Right to Self-Determination under the Covenant on Civil and Political Rights" in Aikio, Pekka, and Scheinin, Martin, eds., *Operationalizing the Right of Indigenous Peoples to Self-Determination* (Åbo Akademi University, Turku, 2000) pp. 179–199.

Scheinin, Martin, "The Right to Enjoy a Distinct Culture: Indigenous and Competing Uses of Land", in Theodore S. Orlin, Alan Rosas, and Martin Scheinin, eds., *The Jurisprudence of Human Rights Law: A Comparative Interpretive Approach* (Turku: Institute for Human Rights Abo Akademi University, 2000), 159–222, at 182–183.

Schmitt, Carl, *The Concept of the Political* (University of Chicago Press, Chicago, 1995).

Schmitt, Carl, "The Land Appropriation of a New World", 109 *Telos*, pp. 29–80.

Schmidt, E., *Foreign Intervention in Africa: From the Cold War to the War on Terror,* (Cambridge University Press, Cambridge, 2013)

Schreuer, C. "The Waning of the Sovereign State: Towards a New Paradigm for International Law", EJIL 4 (1993), pp. 447–71.

Schrijver, Nico, *Sovereignty over Natural Resources: Balancing Rights and Duties* (Cambridge University Press, Cambridge, 1997).

Schwarzenberger Georg, *Power Politics: An Introduction to the Study of International Relations and Post-War Planning* (The Camelot Press Ltd, 1941).

Schwegmann, C., *The Contact Group And Its Impact On The European Institutional Structure* (2000), available at http://www.iss.europa.eu/uploads/media/occ016.pdf

Scott, C., "Indigenous Self- Determination and Decolonization of the International Imagination: A Plea", 18 *Mum. Rts. Q.* 8 14 (1996)

Sargent, Daniel, '*Oasis in the Desert? America's Human Rights Rediscovery*', *in* Jan Eckel and Samuel Moyn (eds.) *The Breakthrough: Human Rights in the 1970s* (Philadelphia: University of Pennsylvania Press, 2014)

Seton-Watson, Hugh, *Neither War nor Peace: The Struggle for Power in the Postwar World* (London, 1960).

Shaw, Malcolm, "The Western Sahara Case", *British Yearbook of International Law* (1978) pp. 119–154.

Shaw, Malcolm, "The International Status of National Liberation Movements", 5 *Liverpool Law Review* 19 (1983)

Shaw, Malcolm, *Title to Territory in Africa: The International Legal Issues* (Clarendon Press, Oxford, 1986)

Shaw, Malcolm, "The Heritage of States: The Principle of Uti Possidetis Today" 67 *BYIL* (1996).

Shaw, Malcolm, "Peoples, Territorialism and Boundaries", 8 *European Journal of International Law* (1997) pp. 478–507.

Shaw, Malcolm, Report by Malcolm Shaw: "Re: Order in Council P.C 1996–1497 of 30 September 1996" in AF Bayefsky (ed.) *Self-Determination in International Law. Quebec and Lessons Learned* (Kluwer Law International, The Hague 2000) p. 138.

Shaw, Malcolm, "The Role of Recognition with Respect to Secession: Notes on Some Relevant Issues" in J Dahlitz (ed.) *Secession and International Law* (TMC Asser Press, The Hague 2003) p. 248.

Shaw, Malcolm, *International Law* (CUP, Cambridge 2003)

Shlaim, Avi, "The partition of Germany and the origins of the Cold War", *Review of International Studies*, 11, (1985) pp. 123–137.

Sieghart, Paul, *The International Law of Human Rights* (Clarendon Press, Oxford, 1983).

Sieghart, Paul, *The Lawful Rights of Mankind* (Oxford: Oxford University Press, 1985)

Simma, Bruno, and Alston, Philip, "The Sources of Human Rights Law: Custom, Jus Cogens, and General Principles", 12 *Australian Yearbook of International Law* (1991) pp. 82–108.

Simons, William B., ed., *The Constitutions of the Communist World* (Sijthoff and Noordhoff, Alphen Aan Den Rijn, 1980) pp. 582–624.

Simpson, Brad, "The United States And The Curious History Of Self-Determination" The United States And The Curious History Of Self-Determination." *Diplomatic History* 36.4 (2012): 675–694, 684.

Simpson, Brad, 'Denying the 'First Right': The United States, Indonesia, and the Ranking of Human Rights by the Carter Administration, 1976–1980', 4 International History Review (2009) 798–826.

Simpson, Brad, 'Self-Determination, Human Rights, and the End of Empire in the 1970s', 4:2 *Humanity* (2013) 239–260.

Simpson, Brad, The Biafran Secession and the Limits of Self-Determination," Journal of Genocide Research 16 (August 2014): 337–54, 343.

Simpson, Gerry J., "The Diffusion of Sovereignty: Self-Determination in the Post-Colonial Age" in McCorquodale, Robert, ed., *Self-Determination in International Law* (Dartmouth, Aldershot, 2000) pp. 585–616.

Simpson, Gerry, "Two Liberalisms", 21 *Euro. J. Int'l.* L. 537, 558 (2001).

Sinclair, Ian, "The Significance of the Friendly Relations Declarations", in *The United Nations and the Principles of International Law: Essays in Memory of Michel Akehurst*, Vaughan Lowe & Colin Warbrick eds., (Routledge, London, 1994)

Sindha, S. Prakash, "Perspective of the Newly Independent States on the Binding Quality of International Law", 14 *International and Comparative Law Quarterly* (1965) 127.

Sindha, S. Prakash, "Is Self-Determination Passé?" 12 *Columbia Journal of Transnational Law* (1973) pp. 260–273.

Skordas, Achilles, "Self-determination of peoples and transnational regimes: a foundational principle of global governance" in *Transnational Constitutionalism : International and European Perspectives*, Nicholas Tsagourias (ed) (Cambridge University Press, Cambridge, 2007)

Skurbaty, Zelim, *As If Peoples Mattered...: Critical Appraisal of 'Peoples' and 'Minorities' from the International Human Rights Perspective and Beyond* (Martinus Nijhoff, The Hague, 2000).

Slaughter, Anne-Marie, "International law in a world of liberal States." *European journal of international law.* 64 (1994): 503–38.

Smith, M.A., "Sovereignty Over Unoccupied Territories - The Western Sahara Decision", 9 *Case W. Res. J. Int'l. Law* (1997) 135

Smuts, J. C., "The League of Nations: A Practical Suggestion" in Miller, David Hunter, ed., *The Drafting of the Covenant* (G. P. Putnam's Sons, New York, 1928) volume. 2, pp. 23–60.

Snyder, F.E. & Sathirathai, S. eds., *Third World Attitudes Towards International Law: An Introduction* (Martinus Nijhoff, Dordrecht, 1987).

Spanu, Maja, "The hierarchical society: the politics of self-determination and the constitution of new states after 1919" *European Journal of International Relations, 26* (2), 372–396.

Spanu, Maja, *The Idea of Self-Determination: Hierarchy and Order after Empire* (PhD thesis 2014, European University Institute)

Spooner, K.A., *Canada, the Congo Crisis, and UN Peacekeeping, 1960–64*. (UBC Press, Vancouver, 2009)

Spruyt, Hendrick, *The Sovereign State and Its Competitors: An Analysis of Systems Change* (Princeton University Press, Princeton, 1994).

Stacy, H., "Relational Sovereignty" *SLR* 55 (2003) pp. 2029–45.

Stern, G, *The Structure of International Society*, 2d ed. (Pinter, London, 2000).

Strauss, Leo, *The City and Man*, (University of Chicago, Chicago, 1978)

Streseman, Gustav, *Gustav Streseman: His Diaries, Letters and Papers* (1935)

Stromseth, Jane E., "Self-Determination, Secession and Humanitarian Intervention by the United Nations", 86 *Proceedings of the American Society of International Law* (1992) pp. 370–374.

Suksi, M., *Autonomy: Applications and Implications*, (Kluwer Law International, The Hague, 1998)

Summers, James, *Peoples and International Law: How Nationalism and Self-Determination Shape A Contemporary Law of Nations* (Martinus Nijhoff, Dordrecht, 2007)

Suzuki, Eisuke, "Self-Determination and World Public Order: Community Response to Territorial Separation", 16 *Virginia Journal of International Law* (1975–6) pp. 779–862.

Swan, George Steven, "Self-Determination and the United Nations Charter", 22 *Indian Journal of International Law* (1982) pp. 264–277.

Tamir, Yael, "The Right to National Self-Determination", 58 *Social Research* (1991) pp. 565–590.

Tams, Christian and Malgosia Fitzmaurice, *Legacies of the Permanent Court of International Justice*, (Leiden; Brill, 2013)

Tarling, Nicholas, *The Fall of Imperial Britain in South-East Asia* (Oxford University Press, Oxford, 1993).

Temperley, H. W. V., ed., *A History of the Peace Conference of Paris (Six Volumes)*, (Henry Frowde & Hodder & Stoughton, London, 1924).

Tennant, C., "Indigenous Peoples, International Institutions, and the International Legal Literature 1945–1993", 16 *Hum. Rts Q. 1.* (1994)

Teschke, Benno, *The Myth of 1648: Class, Geopolitics and the Making of Modern International Relations*, (London: Verso, 2003)

Thiam, Doudou, *The Foreign Policy of African States* (Phoenix House, London, 1965).

Thornberry, Patrick, "Is There a Phoenix in the Ashes? – International Law and Minority Rights", 15 *Texas International Law Journal* (1980) pp. 421–458.

Thornberry, Patrick, "Self-Determination, Minorities, Human Rights: A Review of International Instruments", 38 *International and Comparative Law Quarterly* (1989) pp. 867–889.

Thornberry, Patrick, *International Law and the Rights of Minorities* (Clarendon Press, Oxford, 1991).

Thornberry, Patrick, "The Democratic or Internal Aspect of Self-Determination with Some Remarks on Federalism" in Tomuschat, Christian, ed., *Modern Law of Self-Determination* (Martinus Nijhoff, Dordrecht, 1993) pp. 101–38.

Thornberry, Patrick, "The Principle of Self-Determination", in *The United Nations and the Principles of International Law: Essays in Memory of Michel Akehurst*, Vaughan Lowe & Colin Warbrick eds. (Routledge, London, 1994)

Thorne, Christopher, *The Issue of War: States, Societies, and the Far East Conflict of 1941–45* (Oxford University Press, London, 1985)

Tierney, Stephen, "In a State of Flux: Self-Determination and the Collapse of Yugoslavia", 6 *International Journal on Minority and Group Rights* (1999) pp. 197–233.

Tiirk, D., "Recognition of States: A Comment", 4 *Eur. J. Int'l L. 66* (1993).

Tilly, Charles, "Reflections on the History of European State-Making" in Tilly, Charles, ed., *The Formation of National States in Western Europe* (Princeton University Press, Princeton, 1975) pp. 3–83.

Tillman, S. *Anglo-American Relations at the Paris Conference of 1919* (Princeton University Press, Princeton, 1961)

Tolley, Jr, Howard, *The U.N. Commission on Human Rights* (Westview Press, Boulder, CO, 1987)

Tomuschat, Christian, "Self-Determination in a Post-Colonial World" in Tomuschat, Christian, ed., *Modern Law of Self-Determination* (Martinus Nijhoff, Dordrecht, 1993) pp. 1–20.

Tomuschat, Christian, *Human Rights: Between Idealism and Realism* (Oxford University Press, New York, 2003)

Torres Bernárdez, Santiago, "The *Uti Possidetis Juris* Principle in Historical Perspective," in Konrad Ginther et al., *Völkerrecht zwischen Normativen Anspruch und Politischer Realität* (Berlin: Duncker & Humblot, 1994), pp. 417, 424.

Touval, Saadia, 'The Organisation of African Unity and African Borders", 21 *International Organization 1* (1967) pp. 102–127.

Touval, Saadia, *The Boundary Politics of Independent Africa*, (Harvard University Press, Cambridge, 1972)

Toynbee, Arnold J., "Self-Determination" 484 The Quarterly Review (1925) pp. 317–338.

Trifunovska, Snežana, ed., *Yugoslavia Through Documents: From its Creation to its Dissolution* (Martinus Nijhoff, Dordrecht, 1994).

Tucker, Robert W., *The Inequality of Nations* (Martin Roberston, London, 1977).

Ulam, Adam B., *Expansion and Coexistence: Soviet Foreign Policy 1917–1973, 2nd edition* (New York, 1974).

Umozurike, Oji Umozurike, *Self-Determination in International Law* (Archon Books, Hamden, Connecticut, 1972).

van Dyke, Vernon, "Self-Determination and Minority Rights", *International Studies Quarterly 13, no 3* (September 1969) 223–53.

Vale, Peter, "Engaging the World's Marginalized and Promoting Global Change: Challenges for the United Nations at Fifty", 36 *Harv. Int'L L.J.* (1995)

Vattel, Emmerich de, *The Law of Nations; or, Principles of the Law of Nature Applied to the Conduct and Affairs of Nations and Sovereigns* (Chitty, Joseph, trans.), (T. and J. W. Johnson and Co., Philadelphia, 1863).

Vedross, Alfred, 'Enstehung von Neustaaten und de Neustaaten nach dem Weltkriege' in Karl Strupp (ed), *Worstebuch des Volkerrechts und der Diplomatie vol 1* (Leipzig, De Grutyer, 1924)

Verzijl, J. H. W., *International Law in Historical Perspective* (A. W. Sijthoff, Leyden, 1968).

Victoria, Franciscus de, *De Indis et de Ivre Belli Relectiones* (Ernest Nys ed., John Pawley Bate trans (Carnegie Institution of Washington, Washington, DC, 1917)

von Bernstorff, Jochen and Philipp Dann, *The Battle for International Law: South-North Perspectives on the Decolonization Era* (Oxford: OUP, 2019)

Walker, L. 'Decolonization in the 1960s: On Legitimate and Illegitimate Nationalist Claims-making', 242:1 *Past & Present* (2019) 227–264.

Walzer, Michael, "The New Tribalism", *Dissent* (1992), 164.

Wambaugh, Sarah, *A Monograph on Plebiscites with a Collection of Official* Documents (Carnegie Endowment for International Peace, New York, 1920).

Wambaugh, Sarah, *Plebiscites Since the World War with a Collection of Official Documents* (Carnegie Endowment for International Peace, Washington, 1933).

Watson, Ian. (ed.), *Indigenous Peoples as Subjects of International Law* (Oxford: Routledge, 2018)

Watt, Donald C. *How War Came: The Immediate Origins of the Second World War, 1938–1939*, (Pantheon Books, 1989).

Watt, Donald C. *Documents on International Affairs 1962*. (Oxford University Press, London, 1971).

Weitz, Eric, "From the Vienna to the Paris System: International Politics and the Entangled Histories of Human Rights, Forced Deportations, and Civilizing Missions." *The American Historical Review* 113, no. 5 (2008): 1313–43.

Weller, Marc, "The International Response to the Dissolution of the Socialist Federal Republic of Yugoslavia", 86 *American Journal of International Law* (1992) pp. 568–607.

Weller, Marc, *Escaping the Self-Determination Trap*, (Martinus Nijhoff Publishers, Leiden, 2009).

Welsh, Jennifer (ed.), *Humanitarian Intervention and International Relations* (Oxford University Press, Oxford, 2004).

Westlake, John, *International Law* (Cambridge University Press, Cambridge, 1910).

Westad, Odd Arne, *The Global Cold War: Third World Interventions and the Making of Our Times*, (Cambridge University Press, Cambridge, 2007)

Wheeler, NJ., *Saving Strangers: Humanitarian Intervention in International Society*, (Oxford University Press, Oxford, 2000)

Whelan, Anthony, "Self-Determination and Decolonization: Foundations for the Future" 3:4 *Irish Studies in International Affairs* (1992) pp. 25–52.

Whelan, Anthony, "Wilsonian Self-Determination and the Versailles Settlement", 43 *International and Comparative Law Quarterly* (1994) pp. 99–115.

White, Robin C. A., "Self-Determination: Time for a Re-Assessment?" 28 *Netherlands Journal of International Law* (1981) pp. 147–170.

Whitehall, Deborah 'A Rival History of Self-Determination', European Journal of International 27(3) (2016) 719–743.

Whiteman, MM., *Digest of International Law, vol* 5 (US Government Printing Office, Washington, DC., 1965).

Wildhaber, Luzius, "Territorial Modifications and Breakups in Federal States", 33 *Canadian Yearbook of International Law* (1995) pp. 41–74.

Wight, M., "The Power Struggle in the United Nations", *Proceedings of the Institute of World Affairs, 33rd session* (Los Angeles, 1956), 248.

Wight, M., "Brutus in Foreign Policy: The Memoirs of Sir Anthony Eden", *International Affairs*, xxxvi, 3 (1960), 308.

Wilde, Ralph, *International Territorial Administration: How Trusteeship and the Civilizing Mission Never Went Away* (Oxford University Press, Oxford, 2008)

Wilson, Heather A., *International Law and the Use of Force by National Liberation Movements* (Clarendon press, Oxford, 1988).

Wilson, Woodrow, "An Address to a Joint Session of Congress [14 Points]" in Link, Arthur S., ed., *The Papers of Woodrow Wilson* (Princeton University Press, Princeton, 1984) volume 45, pp. 534–539.

Wilson, Woodrow, "An Address to a Joint Session of Congress [4 Points]" in Link, Arthur S., ed., *The Papers of Woodrow Wilson* (Princeton University Press, Princeton, 1984) volume 46, pp. 318–324.

Wippman, David, "Introduction: Ethnic Claims and International Law" in Wippman, David, ed., *International Law and Ethnic Conflict* (Cornell University Press, Ithaca, 1998) pp. 1–21.

Woodward, Susan L., *Balkan Tragedy: Chaos and Dissolution after the Cold War* ( Brookings Institution, Washington, 1995)

Wright, Quincy, *Mandates Under the League of Nations* (University of Chicago Press, Chicago, 1930)

Wright, Quincy, "Recognition and Self-Determination", 48 *Proceedings of the American Society of International Law* (1954) pp. 23–37.

Wright, Quincy, "The Goa Incident", 56 *American Journal of International Law* (1962) pp. 617–632.

Xanthaki, Alexandra, *Indigenous Rights and United Nations Standards: Self-Determination Culture and Land* (Cambridge University Press, New York 2007)

Young, Crawford, "Nationalism and Ethnic Conflict in Africa" in Guibernau, Montserrat, and Hutchinson, John, eds., *Understanding Nationalism* (Polity Press, Cambridge, 2001) pp. 164–181.

Ziehen, U., *Vollendete Tatsachen bei Verletzungen der territorialen Unversehrtheit, Eine völkerrechtliche Untersuchung, Beihefte zum Jahrbuch der Albertus-Universität Königsberg* / Pr., xx, Würzburg, 1962, pp. 1–2.

Zimmermann, Warren, *Origins of a Catastrophe: Yugoslavia and its Destroyers* (Times Books, New York, 1996).

Zinn, Howard, *A People's History of the United States 1492-Present* (Harper Collins, New York, 1995)

Zuijdwijk, Ton, *Petitioning the United Nations*: A Study in Human Rights (Gower, Hampshire, 1982)

# Index


Aaland Islands: and Commission of Jurists 62; and Commission of Rapporteurs 63; and League Council 64
Abkhazia 154
Afghanistan 124, 125
Africa: and African Union 171, 172; and Asia Africa Conference 91–93; and Biafran crisis 105–107; colonialism in 1, 26, 34, 39, 42–43, 46, 48, 69, 72, 84, 85, 88, 90–91; and Conference of African Independent States 94; and Congo crisis 94–95; as divided between European states 46; and global colour line 46; and Haitian Revolution 34; and human rights discourse 93, 97; imperialism in 3, 20, 21, 69, 81, 82, 86; and League of Nations 51; and Lenin 48; and mandate system 70–71, 72; and Pan-African Congresses 73, 76; partition of 46; and seen as backward 69; and self-determination 75, 82, 83–92, 95–98, 102–107, 109, 112–116, 117, 122, 127, 156; and Smuts 69; struggle for independence in 80; and unequal membership in international society 43; UN peacekeeping forces in 94; white rule in 114, 115, 123, 129, 133
African Americans 38
African Union 213*n*118
alien rule 5, 34, 93, 96, 121, 124, 125, 151; absence of 177; and Berlin 76; decolonization as freedom from 108; economic dependence after 23; and empire-as- enslavement 77*n*16; freedom from 124–125; and foreign intervention 124, 125; and human rights 93, 96; and imperialism 5, 32, 34, 93, 96, 121, 124; and racist regimes 125; and self-determination 5, 77, 93, 96, 121, 124, 125
Alsace-Lorraine 37*n*52
Americas 119, 124; colonialism in 44–46
American Revolution 33, 34, 35
Anaya, James 161, 164, 168, 180
Anghie, Antony 31, 32, 70, 117
apartheid 114, 115, 123, 129, 133
Arendt, Hannah 38, 60
Armitage, David 44*n*94
Arusha 177*n*44
Asia: and Asia Africa Conference 91–93; colonialism in 1, 17*n*56, 42–43, 76, 88, 90–91, 92–93, 99; and Goa Crisis 98–103; imperialism in 3, 20, 21, 69, 81, 82, 86; and independence movements 72, 73; and Lenin 48; and seen as backward 69; and self-determination 75, 82, 83–92, 95–98, 102–107, 109, 112–116, 117, 122, 127, 156; and unequal membership in international society 43
Atlantic Charter 26, 74, 74*n*5, 78, 79
Australia 93*n*91, 96, 117*n*47, 127, 136, 166
Axis powers 68, 71

Badinter Commission 144–146
Balfour, Arthur 51
Bandung Conference (Afro-Asian conference, Bandung 1955) 91–94, 96, 98
Bangladesh 107, 141
Belgian Congo 2, 94
Belgium 2, 46, 94–95, 96
Berlin Conference 46, 46*n*102, 70
Berman, Nathaniel 12, 50, 55, 58, 64
Biafra 105–7
Bodin, Jean 32
Bolsheviks: and self-determination 48, 51, 52, 57
Bolshevik Revolution 52
borders: and readjustment of 54, 59; and OAU 103–105
and postcolonial 102, 103–105, 106; and uti possedetis juris 45, 144, 145; and Yugoslavia 144, 145, 146, 147
Brest-Litovsk, Treaty of (1918) 53
Bretton Woods system 129

British Empire 34, 35, 35*n*40, 36, 36*n*46, 46, 72, 83, 84, 106; and Atlantic Charter 78; and British Foreign Office 51; Churchill 78–79, 79*n*26, and Lloyd George 56, 57
British India 53, 73, 84, 99
Bull, Hedley 6*n*16
burdened societies 136
Burke, Edmund 37, 37*n*54
Burke, Roland 8*n*25, 76*n*13, 91*n*85, 109*n*7, 126*n*100

Cabral, Amilcar 109
Cambodia 124, 160
Canada 150–153, 157
capital 24, 31, 32, 49, 82
capitalism 51, 52
Caribbean 1, 34
Caribbean Community (CARICOM) 213*n*118
Cassin, René 82
Central powers 50, 51
Chagos Islands 4*n*11, 120, 169–174
Chechnya 154
China 53, 101, 152
Churchill, Winston 77, 78, 81*n*35
citizenship 35, 17, 115, 155–56; and Declaration of Rights of Man and Citizens 35, 36, 45*n*95, and human rights 155; and Wilson 55
civilization 18, 32, 43, 56; and Ethiopia 67; European claims to superior 39; and Lenin 47; and Mandates 70; standard of 18, 32, 43, 44, 44*n*90, 45, 46, 49, 70
Cold War: and human rights 132, 137, and end of 138, 141, 155, 156, 157, 160, 160, 163; and intervention 118, 123, 125
colonialism: in Africa 1, 26, 34, 39, 42–43, 46, 48, 69, 72, 84, 85, 88, 90–91; in Americas 44–46; in Asia 1, 17*n*56, 42–43, 76, 88, 90–91, 92–93, 99, 98–103; for benefit of colonized subjects 71; boundaries inherited from 102, 103–105, 106; and civilizing mission 42, 44, 44*n*90, 114; and dispossession 170; and Emerson 5, 26, 81, 97, 102, 133; and human rights 93, 97; and international hierarchy 3, 9, 10, 11, 13, 15, 17, 43, 47, 108; and international law 2, 12, 13, 15, 17, 22, 29, 30, 31–32, 42–46, 47, 50, 57–59, 62–66, 70, 74–107; and international treaties and conferences 46; and League of Nations 49, 54–56, 67–73; justifications of 5, 38, 43, 44, 97; Marx 41; and organization of African states 105–107; Pan-African Congress 73, 76; and political domination 111, 112; and racial hierarchy 67, 85; and rights of citizenship and personhood 35, 17, 115, 155–56; and self-determination 47, 50, 57–59, 62–66, 70, 74–107; settler 36; as slavery 73, 88; and sovereignty 50, 67–74, 75, 76, 86, 87, 88; and UDHR 82; and UN resolution 1514 26, 75, 97, 101, 127
colonial subjects 3, 69
colonies: and Atlantic Charter 74, 74*n*5, 78, 79; and British
colonies in America 34–36, 39; and burdened societies 136; as excluded from international order 31, 32, 58, 79; independence for 1, 3, 83–87; as non-self-Governing territories 80; obligations and limited or conditional rights of 18, 58, 67, 69; political and civil rights for 88; social and economic reforms for 88; and UN Charter 80; as unequal and subordinated members 31, 32
colonized peoples: and rights of citizenship 35, 17, 115, 155–56
colonialism for benefit of 71; and civilizing mission 42, 44, 44*n*90, 114; and Western profit 73
corporations 4, 129
Covenant on Political and Civil Rights 14*n*47, 133, 166
Covenant on Economic, Social and Cultural Rights 14*n*47, 133, 166

Danzig 59
debt 34
decolonization: and American independence 33–36; and Biafra 105; and Congo crisis 94–96, 102; and economic and political

transformations 126–133; as expansion of existing international society 1, 3, 83–87; as freedom from alien rule 5, 34, 93, 96, 121, 124, 125, 151; and global economy 126–133; and globalization of nation-state 27, 76–80; and League of Nations 41, 72, 73; as nation-building 2; and self-determination 74, 75, 76, 83–91, 91–98, 100, 109; in South Africa 95–96, 118, 120, 122; and sovereignty 74, 98–99; and struggles for emancipation 72–73, 122–126; and UN 74, 178; and UN Charter 74–78; and UN resolution 1514 26, 75, 96–98; and use of force 122–126

defence 174, and decolonisation as self-defence 89, 100, 120

democracy 35, 125, 154 and human rights 132, 133, 134, 154 right to democratic governance 134; demand for statehood 133, 142, 146, 147, 148

De Vattel, Emer 29*n*11

Du Bois, W. E. B. 10, 46, 73, 188

Eastern Europe 40, 50, 56, 89, 134, 146, 156, 158, 203, 205–206

East Indies 17, 43, 179

East Timor 12, 137, 160, 186, 188–189

economic development, and mandates 77, 80, and self-determination 86, 87, 89, 90, 98, 109, and post-colonial development 92, 94 and NIEO 109, 110, 117, 118, 119, 123

Egypt 53, 73, 83–84, 113

Emerson, Rupert 5–7, 26, 81, 84, 96–97, 102, 104, 108, 133, 189–190

empire/imperialism: in Africa 1, 26, 34, 39, 42–43, 46, 48, 69, 72, 84, 85, 88, 90–91; as alien rule 34, 93, 96, 121, 124, 125; for benefit of 71; blue water or saltwater 164; as civilizing mission 42, 44, 44*n*90, 114; end of 5, 34, 93, 96, 121, 124, 125, 151; and ethics of force 122–126; and Europe 3, 18; and global economy 73; and interests of colonized subjects 35, 17, 115, 155–56; and international hierarchy 3, 9, 10, 11, 13, 15, 17, 43, 47, 108; and international law 42; and Latin America 45–46; and Lenin 47, 52–54; and morality 74; and neocolonialism 95, 118, 129; and NIEO 19, 109, 126, 129, 131; and self-determination 26, 82, 92, 97, 82, 83–92, 95–98;102–107, 109, 112–116, 117, 122, 127, 156; and sovereign inequality and hierarchy 76; as structuring international society 42; UN resolution 1514 26, 75, 97, 101, 127; and war 8*n*25, 9, 18, 27, 47

Estonia 60–61, 142, 152, 198, 200, 207

Ethiopia 32, 49, 67, 96, 103, 105, 113, 182, 186

Eurocentricism 24, 173

Europe: Africa as divided between 46; assimilation to ideals of 17, 19, 21–33, 43, 44; claims of to superiority 31, 32; conflicts and competition in 84–85; economy of 82, 126; and imperialism 3, 18; and mandates system 67–73; overseas colonies of 31, 32, 42; racially superior claims of 19; rise of nationalism 38–42, 50; and revolution 38–42; and rise of democratic nation-state 3; and slavery 59; statelessness in 60

France 17, 32, 37, 44, 59, 69, 79, 81, 83, 90, 95–96, 101, 142, 170, 184, 206–207

Franck, Thomas 6, 16, 49, 59, 134, 137, 139, 143, 150, 155–156, 186, 191, 198

freedom: individual 92; from domination 9, 10, 27; movement from slavery to 36; as non-interference 23; and self-determination 26, 82, 92, 97, 114; as Western ideal 5, 33, 34; and Wilson 57

Failed states 140

Falk, Richard 112*n*18, 152

French Africa 84, 90, 91

French Empire 72, 79, 83, 84, 85*n*48, 90, 91

French Revolution 36–37, 194, 198

General Act of the Berlin Conference 46

Geneva convention 125

genocide 106–107, 137, 164, 168, 189, 212

George, Lloyd 51

Germany 40, 53, 59–61, 67, 81, 106, 134, 142, 152, 181, 211
Getachew, Adom 9, 68, 88
Ghana 26, 94, 96, 105, 115, 205
global color line 66, 199
global south 4, 109, 118, 161
Great Britain 35, 45, 69, 80, 142, 169, 170, 174
Grenada 124–125
Grotius, Hugo 31, 102, 113, 184–185, 187, 193–194, 197, 208
Group of 77 (G77), 117, 210
Guinea 69, 105, 109, 122, 185, 197
Guinea-Bissau 109

Habermas, Jürgen 15
Haiti 49, 106, 140, 156, 160
Haitian Revolution 34
Hammarskjöld, Dag 94
Henkin, Louis 6, 185, 194, 198
hierarchical world order 31
human rights, Arendt 38, 60; breakthrough of 132; and colonialism 26, 75, 76–77; and Covenants 133, 166; emerging language of 19, 82; fora as a site of decolonisation 19, 27, 76, 77; postcolonial independence 94; and postcolonial sovereignty 16, 104, 105; and postcolonial states 21; and self-determination 20, 75; and UDHR 82
humanitarian crises 160

independence, declarations of independence 1, 34, 43–45; decolonization 2, 10, 75, 76, 84, 86, 94, 95–98; and League of Nations 56; and nationalist 40, 48–49, 51, 53, 54; and NIEO 126–129; political, economic, and legal impediments to 106; political vs. economic 112; readiness for 87, 88; and self-determination as right 2, 8, 9; of United States 34–36; and UN Charter 75; and UN resolution 1514, 87–90; and Westphalian regime 30, 30*n*16; and Wilson 49. *See also* freedom
India 4, 43, 53, 73, 84, 94, 99–102, 105, 112, 205
Indigenous Peoples 21, 31, 44, 46, 70, 117, 141, 158, 161–168, 171, 174, 176, 179–181, 183
Indonesia 1, 84, 91, 96, 102, 105, 137, 169, 212
interdependence 89, 135
international law, and custom 126; and decolonisation 84, 89–90, 91; decolonisation as disruption to 99, 100, 101, 128, 129; as European ideal 101–102, 111–116, 117; and indigenous people 141; and NIEO 127–130; and secession 156; sovereign equality in 108; and the use of force 122–126
International Court of Justice 4–5, 113, 125, 152, 169, 173, 183, 185, 187, 197
Iraq 60–61, 71, 83, 89, 154
Ireland 136, 152
Israel 118, 139, 183, 207
Italo-Ethiopian war 67
Italy 40, 42, 51, 54, 66–67, 133

Jackson, Robert 133
Japan 31, 57, 69, 166, 197

Katanga, secession of 94–95, 102–103, 117, 127, 187
Kenya 94, 103, 105, 125, 204
Knop, Karen 11, 15, 113, 145, 165, 199
Koskenniemi, Martti 4, 6, 14–15, 18–19, 21–24, 32, 39, 44, 64, 140, 161, 186, 199
Korea 53, 73, 81, 89
Kosovo: independence of 144, 147–149, 160 Advisory Opinion 152–154

labour 26, 79, 165

land 31, 36, 44, 73, 164, 166–167, 169, 173, 182, 210, 216
Lansing, Robert 53, 55
Latin America 45, 119
Latvia 60–61, 142, 148
law of nations 17, 29*n*11, 31. *See also* international law
League of Nations, and Aaland Islands dispute 63; and Ethiopia 67; and colonial exploitation 52; and Council of 54; and Covenant 49, 55; and decolonization; and eastern European states 66; and expansion

of international law 58–60; and former German and Ottoman colonies 67; founding of 58; and mandates system 69, 70; and minority protection 59, 61, 61*n*70; and self-determination 56, 57, 58; and Smuts 69
Lenin, V. I. 47–48, 54, 73, 176
Imperialism 47–48, 51–52
liberal democracy 139, 159, 191
liberalism 7, 33, 34, 77, 82, 136, 147, 159 and Wilson 48, 53, 55
liberal states 7, 19, 136, 137
Liberia 49, 96, 113, 119
Lithuania 51, 53
Locke, John 28, 33, 200
Lorca, Arnulf Becker 7, 17, 49, 181
Lumumba, Patrice 2, 94–95, 192
Luxembourg, Rosa 41

Mali 96, 104, 115
mandates 22, 40, 55, 86; and Iraq 71; and League of Nations 70–72; and presumed backward peoples 68; and Smuts 59, 54*n*35, 69, 72; as trustees 67, 72
Manela, Erez 8*n*24, 18*n*59, 72
Martinez Cobo Report 163–164
Marx, Karl 38, 41
Mazzini, Giuseppe 40, 42
Moyn, Samuel 19, 87, 110, 131–132
Moynihan, Daniel Patrick 132
Mozambique 105, 122
Mussolini, Benito 66–67

Namibia 10–11, 13, 105, 112–115, 122, 129

nationalism, and anti-colonialism 5, 8*n*24, 103, 141; and ethno-nationalism 149; liberal nationalism 7; as problematic 58–59, 141, 143; and Habermas 15; and Lenin; and liberalism; as linked to national independence 28, 37, 39, 40; and self-determination 141
Native Americans 36
natural resources, and permanent sovereignty over 118, 123, 127, 128, and self-determination 129, 166
Nazis 67
Neocolonialism 95, 118, 129
New International Economic Order (NIEO) 19, 109, 126, 129, 131
Nigeria 104–105, 107, 187
Nkrumah, Kwame 10, 95, 103, 170
Non-aligned Movement 91, 128–129
nondomination: and postimperial international order 19; and self-determination 19, 27, 75
Non-interference 20, 110, 118, 123
non-intervention; as defence against decolonization 81; and decolonization 118; and postcolonial states 119, 125; redefinition of 19, 86, 109, 119; and self-determination 86, 109, 110, 118; and UN resolution 2131 119
non-self-governing territories 2, 75, 84, 85, 86, 87, 90, 98, 99, 170
Nyerere, Julius 10, 106–107, 117

Organization of African Unity (OAU) 104, 105–107, 118, 189, 197
Ottoman Empire 31, 67, 70
outlaw states 136, 140*n*11

Pacific region 43, 48, 69, 79, 169
Padmore, George 10, 73–74
Pan-Africanism 73, 118
Palestine 51, 81, 89
Pan-African Congress 73, 74*n*2
Paris Peace Conference (1919) 61, 68–69, 176, 181
Philippines 54, 89, 105, 152
Plamenatz, John 5*n*13, 97
plebiscites 37, 50, 58, 59
Poland 41, 53, 59–61, 66, 96, 119, 127–128, 152
Population transfer 12*n*37, 81
Portugal 85, 96, 99–101, 112, 120–122, 186, 191
protectorates 140

Quaison-Sackey, Alex 26–27
quasisovereigns 9, 20*n*64, 67, 68, 133
Quebec 21, 150–152, 181, 184, 187

racial hierarchy 54
racism 73, 117
Rawls, John 136–137
Reagan, Ronald, 198
republicanism 34

Responsibility to Protect 160
Rhodesia 36, 95, 117, 120, 122, 125, 129
Roosevelt, Eleanor 74, 77
Rousseau, Jean-Jacques 28, 33, 37
Russia 48, 52, 62, 149, 183. *See also* Soviet Union
Russian Revolution 53

Saar Region 59
Schmitt, Carl 31
secession 15, 21*n*65, 52, 78; and Aaland Islands 63, 65; and Bangladesh 107; and Biafra 105–107; and Katanga 94, 95; as excluded from self-determination 78; and Sudan 104; and Somalia; 104; and Yugoslavia 141, 145, 149–154
self-determination, and Atlantic Charter 71, 79; after World War II 74, 77; and alien rule 96, 97; and anticolonial protests 73, 91, 94; and Biafra 104–106; and Bolshevism 47, 51, 52, 53; capacity for; and collective vs. individual rights; and Cold War 21; and colonialism 5, 9, 18, 19, 73, 84, 91; and consent of governed 35, 36, 53, 55, 56; and decolonization 5, 73, 74, 77, 84, 85; and defining 7, 93; and development; and economic sovereignty; and Emerson; and foreign domination 89; and historical accounts of 1, 3, 4, 6, 7, 8, 12, 33; and human rights 3, 8, 19, 76, 82, 86, 87, 93, 94; and imperialism 5, 18; and International Court of Justice 10; institutionalization of right to 27; and international hierarchies; and international order; and Katanga secession 94, 95; and language of 1, 2, 11, 76, 77, 86; and League of Nations 49, 55, 56, 58; and Lenin 47, 48; and liberalism 7, 9, 39; and mandates system 68, 69, 70, 73; and Marx 41; and minorities 62–65, 66; and national self-determination 52; and nationalism 50; and Nazism 67; and NIEO 19; and nondomination 19, 27, 75; and the people 14, 18, 52; as permanent aggression 99; and permanent sovereignty over natural resources 86; and plebiscites 50, 58; and political and legal vs. economic concerns 86; political conditions of 111; and political legitimacy 47, 79; and political vs. legal realms; and postimperial world order 3, 20, 86; and popular sovereignty 28; and preparation for self-rule 68, 69, 70, 73; revolutionary principle of 29–31; right to 1, 3, 27; and Selbstbestimmung 13, 38; and Smuts 49; and sovereign equality 28, 78; and sovereign hierarchies 17, 29; and sovereignty 12, 13, 19, 27, 47, 49, 75; and statehood 12, 15, 16; and territorial integrity 98–106; and Third World identity 92, 93, and UDHR 82; and UN 2, 74, 75, 83; and UN Charter 9, 11, 27, 75, 78, 83, 85; and UN resolution 1514 26, 89, 90, 95, 96; and war-time rhetoric 51; and Wilson 48, 49, 53, 55, 56; and rights of women 40; and worldmaking 5, 10, 18
self-government, and Atlantic Charter 71, 79
Senegal 105, 130, 141
Sinha, S. Prakash 17*n*56, 100*n*12, 109*n*8
slave trade 45, 70
Smuts, Jan 2, 49, 54, 69, 80, 212
Somalia 103, 105, 140, 160
South Africa 95–96, 118, 120, 122
southern Africa 86, 87, 103, 151, 212*n*93
South-West Africa Cases 10*n*30, 46*n*102, 69*n*112, 70, 85, 112*n*18, 122
sovereign equality, and decolonisation 8, 26; economic redistribution 126–131; and human rights 96; and imperialism 1, 3, 9, 26, 27; and international economic law 123; and international change 15, 87; and League of Nations Covenant; and NIEO 123; and non-intervention 118, 125, 157; and self-determination 16, 21, 27, 76, 77; and UN Charter 109
sovereignty: and Aaland Islands 62–65; and American independence;

and Atlantic Charter 78; and Arendt 38; and Bandung 92, 93, 95; and colonialism 14, 15, 72–74, 75–76; and decolonization 8, 9, 26, 27; and human rights 38, 110–111; and imperialism 1, 3, 43; and international hierarchy 31, 34, 50, 87; and League of Nations 50, 58; and negative sovereignty 20, 136–37, 139–140; and NIEO 126–129; and OAU 104; over natural resources 89; and pre-colonial sovereignty 10, 11; and post-colonial sovereignty 86, 109; popular 32–24; and self-determination 12, 13, 14, 17, 18, 20, 72–76, 86–87; and state failure or misrule 111; and UN resolution 1514 86, 87; Vitoria 31, 32; Westphalian 28, 29, 30; and Wilson 48

Soviet Union 77, 117, 119, 138, 141–144, 146, 155, 158, 175 *See also* Russia

Spain 32, 44, 85, 96, 123, 153

Stalin, Joseph 188

state: and creation 15, 16, 45; democratic 131–137, 155–157; export of European statehood 21–33, 43, 44; human rights as subsumed within 20, 131–137; and inequality 31–33, 42, 44; level of development of 20; violation of rights of citizens by, states 62: failed 140; as liberal 14, 48, 49, 131; limits on power of 14, 33, 50, 58, 59, 62, 63, 131–135; nation state 7, 8, 33, 38, 40; right to independence 76, 89–91; rogue 140; and people 15, 16, 18, 40, 42; and sovereignty 42; and sovereign equality 28; and state building 1, 16; and Westphalia 19, 23, 28, 29–31

Switzerland 44, 123

Syria 83, 89

Tanzania 105–106, 117

territorial integrity 15, 164, 166, 170, 173; and League of Nations Covenant 55–56; and OAU 104–106; and self-determination 101, 104–106; and sovereignty 29, 71, 118–119, 124–125, 138, 141; and Yugoslavia 144, 150, 154

Third World, and self-determination 86; and Bandung 91–92, 98; criticism of the ICJ 113, and post-colonial worldmaking 116–121, 124, 176; and the NIEO 126; and human rights 131, 133

trade, and Berlin Conference 46; and Wilsonian liberalism 55, 144; and postcolonial states 109; and UN Committee on Trade and Development 128

trusteeship 44–45

trust territories 90, 91, 99

United Kingdom 4, 96, 135, 142, 152, 170, 201 *See also* Great Britain

United Nations 78, 87, 133; and Africa 14, 73, 99, 100; anticolonial politics at 75; and Azikiwe 72; Azikiwe's vision of miniature 135–36, 137, 138, 141; collective security institutions in 63; and colonialism 71, 73–74, 90, 99; Commission on Human Rights 88, 89; and decolonization 73, 74, 98–99, 107, 178; demand for equal decision-making power in 107; and Du Bois 72, 79; Economic and Social Council 88; and egalitarian international society 169; and equality 71, 99, 107, 163; and hierarchical international order 32; hierarchies embedded in 169; and human rights 14, 71, 73–74, 78, 92, 93; and imperialism 97, 107; internationalism based in 118; and Italo-Ethiopian war 63; and League of Nations 71, 75; and Moynihan 176, 178; as new deal for world 75; and NIEO 161, 162, 163, 166, 169, 170, 171, 173, 176; and Nkrumah 101, 102; peacekeeping forces of 100; and Republic of Congo 100; and self-determination 2, 8, 10, 73–74, 75, 88–91, 92, 101, 135, 169; and

sovereign equality 91, 99, 163; and sovereignty 90, 102; and unequal membership 107, 178; United States abandonment of 178
UN Committee on Trade and Development 128
United Nations Charter 2, 99, 112, and colonial rule as trusteeship 2, 75, 80, 116; and Friendly Relations Declaration (1970) 116; and self-determination 2, 9, 11, 27, 28, 75, 76, 77, 78, 80, 81, 85, 86, 88, 98, 99; and UN resolution 1514 26, 90
United Nations General Assembly 26, 75, 83, 85; anticolonial efforts 85, 90, 91, 120, 122, 123; anticolonial majority in 83, 178; Covenant on Economic, Social and Cultural Rights 111; Covenant on Political and Civil Rights 111; Declaration on the Establishment of a New International Economic Order (1974) 128, 129; Declaration on the Granting of Independence to Colonial Countries and Peoples (resolution 1514) 26, 75, 96–98; and resolutions and self-determination 26, 75, 96–98, 111, 118, and South Africa 113, 123; Universal Declaration of Human Rights (UDHR)
United Nations Security Council 83*n*41, 84, 99, 100, 112, 120, 121, 122, 125, 140
United States 2, 36; and African Americans 38; and Chagos Islands 169; Declaration of Independence 34, 73; and Europe 69, 83; and global dominance 120; and human rights 131; and imperialism 81, 84, 88; imperialism of 13, 44–45, 117–19, 179; and Moynihan 132; and Native Americans 36; as neocolonial power 125–126; and race 20, 21, 121; Revolution 34, 35; and self-determination 131, 132, 133, 137; and UN 178; and UN resolution 1514 98; and Wilson 39, 44–45, 53
Upper Silesia 59

Versailles, Treaty of (1919) 60, 67
Versailles Conference (1919) 56
Vienna Declaration 155, 163
Vietnam 81, 129
Vitoria, Francisco de 31

West 26, 149, 158, 164
West Africa 10*n*30, 46*n*102, 69*n*112, 70, 85, 112*n*18, 122
Westphalia, Treaty of (1648) 29, 30, 30*n*14, 30*n*15, 30*n*16
white supremacy 10
Wilson, Woodrow 7, 18*n*59, 48, 76, 80, 121, 177; and Fourteen Points 48, 49; ideals of 48–49, 53, 54; and imperialism 54; and League of Nations 55; and self-determination 7, 8*n*24, 18*n*59; and self-government 132; and trusteeship 81
worldmaking 10, 77*n*16
world order 8, 10, 27, 57, 77, 86, 88, 174
World War I: end of 22; European overseas colonies after 49, 54, 67–73; and Europe's perceived moral bankruptcy 8*n*25; and imperialism 47, 51–53; and Lenin 47, 52; and war-time negotiation 47, 50–52 and Wilson 39
World War II 5, 9, 70, 84; and causes of war 67; extension of self-determination after 21, 47, 74–76; period after 8*n*22, 9, 21, 74–76

Yugoslavia, Badinter Commission 144–146, creation of 49, 60*n*67; commission on the dissolution of 87; dissolution of 140–141, 144–148, 163, 187; EC Conference on 145, 146; Jewish minority in 66; uti possedetis 144, 145

www.ingramcontent.com/pod-product-compliance
Lightning Source LLC
LaVergne TN
LVHW021725021026
849161LV00004BA/720
*9789004478589*